GLIMPSES OF WAR
Volume 1

by
British Modern Military History Society

Editors: Andy Cockeram, Jerry Cockeram,
Dr Linda Parker and Nigel Parker

Glimpses of War by   British Modern Military History
                         Society (BMMHS)

Copyright © 2021 British Modern Military History Society

ISBN: 979-87-37745-93-6

Cover art by Simon Atak
Cover production by Richard Macauley

Edited by:
Andy Cockeram, Jerry Cockeram,
Dr Linda Parker & Nigel Parker

Dedication

*'To all those who have
experienced war and conflict'*

Introduction

The concept of *Glimpses of War* arose shortly after the announcement of the first lockdown in the United Kingdom during the COVID pandemic in March 2020. Along with nearly every other organisation, business, society and sporting club, the lockdown put an abrupt and disappointing end to their activities. The British Modern Military History Society (BMMHS) was one such organisation and with under a year of talks to sell-out audiences in South Oxfordshire everything came suddenly to a halt. As a result, the monthly contributions to military charities made from the takings from each talk also stopped.

BMMHS was keen to maintain the momentum and enjoyment built up amongst its supporters and from there arose *Glimpses of War*. The Society wanted to keep making charitable contributions, and selected the charity Blind Veterans UK – formerly St Dunstan's, to receive the proceeds of the book. Requesting our supporters to send in their own or family memories of warfare – any war, any role civilian or military, any time period. Coupled with contacts with writers, historians and former military personnel, the response was remarkable – sufficient not for one but three volumes.

Articles, memories and contributions came in from across the globe. Many told of their own or their family's military experiences and others of life on the Home Front, relaying graphic details of their lives in a war time situation. Historians and writers provided more analytical articles describing specific events. For some of our contributors, it

I

gave the opportunity to put pen to paper about events that had lived in their minds, in boxes of papers and diaries in the loft or garage. For others it took some soul searching to decide whether to write of unpleasant experiences, not least one about his father as a POW under the Japanese.

Through the review and editing process, one constant feature stood out. The contributions were mainly stories of ordinary people in the extraordinary times of warfare doing ordinary and in other cases extraordinary things. Stories of great valour, such as Tasmanian Percy Statton awarded the Victoria Cross in 1915, of remarkable escapes from sinking ships or POW camps, to Gerhard Biss escaping to England on the *Kindertransport*. Others tell of people doing their bit, in letters from the Western Front in the Great War or patrolling the streets of Belfast during the '*Troubles*' or being bombed during the Falklands conflict.

Glimpses of War is not intended to be an historical study, but it does both recall and touch on numerous events and experiences in military history of the last one hundred and fifty years. Finding an appropriate and balanced structure for the book proved difficult, as quite naturally articles about the Second World War far exceeded all others. Bear with us on this as we could only work with what we received. We have printed, with minimal editing, the words our contributors submitted. There has been no attempt to validate the historical facts, as that would be a mammoth task, nor have we tried to alter the words of decades ago to suit today's political correctness. For those contributors whose articles do not appear in this volume, you can expect to find them in the subsequent two volumes already planned.

We thank everyone who has taken the time to submit articles, to all those who have assisted in the editing and production process. Bear in mind this book and the subsequent volumes is all about raising money for BVUK, a worthy charity that needs every penny especially as charity fund raising has proved difficult during the current pandemic.

If you enjoyed this book, do tell your friends, and do buy the next two volumes. It is all for an extremely good cause.

The BMMHS Team

8th May 2021

Foreword

Standing outside the main entrance to Manchester Piccadilly Station are eight blind veterans, with hands on the shoulders of the man in front, leading each other away from the station and towards their new life. This statue, commissioned by Blind Veterans UK, inspired by the iconic John Singer Sargent painting 'Gassed' and created by Johanna Domke-Guyot, captures some of the tragedy of war together with the hope of rehabilitation. Its positioning had been carefully thought through. Manchester was in the heart of the recruiting grounds for the Great War, and rail was a key mode of transport to the Front. It was also a means by which casualties were brought home: on just one day in July 1916, 132 ambulance trains made the journey from the south coast to Manchester. These eight men can be imagined returning from Flanders without their sight and starting their journey to their new life as blind veterans. Appropriately these bronze blind veterans are known as Victory over Blindness.

Blind Veterans UK, formerly St Dunstan's, was born in 1915 in response to the tragedies of the trenches in that Great War. An inspiration of the incomparable Sir Arthur Pearson, the charity was created to provide support to those who had lost their sight due to shot, shell or gas. The country was ill prepared to meet this challenge, but Sir Arthur had other ideas. His plan, which he set out as Victory over Blindness, was to rebuild the lives for the young war blind who still had decades of life ahead, and to help them to put bread on the table. At the beginning, the simplest of gestures could be the most powerful. Sir Arthur himself would visit the blind soldiers in hospital and give them a braille watch and thereby the ability to tell the time without having to ask. It was an important first step in regaining independence. Through training centres set up in Regents Park and across the country, blind soldiers were taught how to be blind. Braille was essential for those who could still feel, as was long cane training for those who could walk. The goal was to teach a trade so that the St Dunstaners as they became known could confidently step back into normal life and be both happy and successful. Many a poultry farmer, tobacconist, cobbler, telephonist and masseur was trained by the charity and a strong support network was built across the country. Over 3000 blind veterans were provided through-life support by the charity as a result of the Great War.

Over our 106-year history the charity has provided through-life support to over 40,000 veterans and their dependants, through life because the impact of sight loss on your life changes with years. Today, the charity has 4,500 beneficiaries aged 26 to 106 years. There are war blind from the Second World War and every conflict since as well as veterans who have served and lost their sight later in life due to age-related eye disease. The range of life experience is considerable, yet the beneficiaries all share these two elements: they have served; and they have lost their sight. Our purpose is unchanged from that set out by Sir Arthur in 1915, to rebuild lives. Our plan has evolved and now covers holistic rehabilitation, given that all aspects of life are impacted by sight loss. Never has this been more important than during the Covid-19 Pandemic when the blind have been hit particularly hard, and where personal worlds that had already shrunk due to sight loss have shrunk still further. We have been able to provide tailored and triaged support to beneficiaries in their homes and to find new ways to help, for example with remote rehabilitation. Through our practice and our research we are determined to make lives better, never forgetting that we are here for the blind veterans through life.

Glimpses of War brings to life the human story, that range of personal experiences. In November 2018 I was invited to take part in the Remembrance debate at the Oxford Union. Speaking alongside author Simon Jenkins and Dr Andrew Murrison MP, we spoke against the motion that 'This House believes that we have not remembered'. Although we lost the debate, it was an experience never to forget. In that rarefied atmosphere and amongst very fine minds, we considered evidence, facts and, most powerfully, personal recollections of war. It gave me a unique opportunity to reflect on the human dimension, bringing to mind the many discussions that I have been fortunate to have with blind veterans who have lived through and seen so much conflict. It is always the most humbling experience to talk to these men and women. Younger veterans who have lived through the Falklands, Northern Ireland, Bosnia, Kosovo and more recently Iraq and Afghanistan find common ground with the veterans who experienced the Second World War. If there is a common theme, it is of the futility of war and of the importance of comradeship.

In February 2021 the charity lost a cherished resident at our residential home in Brighton. Staff Sergeant Jim Hooper was a veteran of the Glider Pilot Regiment, and had taken part in Operation Market Garden, the bold plan to seize strategic bridges that would foreshorten the war. Jim and his co-pilot successfully landed 13 Platoon of the South Staffs at Wolfheze and joined elements of the South Staffs in an attempt to break through to 2 Para at the Arnhem Bridge. In fierce fighting on the outskirts of the town, Jim was taken prisoner. Over the next days and with his fellow captives, he was moved as cattle by train to Stalag Luft VII in Ober Silesia. Months later, as the Soviets advanced, the POWs were forced to march west in freezing conditions scrounging and carrying what they could. Arriving at Luckenwalde SE of Berlin, Jim with his group of Glider Pilots escaped and made contact with Soviet troops before working their way through Soviet and German troop elements to the Elbe crossing and to the safety of the US Army. Within weeks he would be back in a Horsa glider.

I first met Jim at our Care Home. By this time, he was elderly, single having lost his wife Ann, and profoundly blind. He very patiently talked me through his war experience and gave me a very personal glimpse of war, proudly clutching the maroon beret of the Glider Pilots that was rarely far from his side. I last saw Jim on a video conference with the residents during the second lockdown in 2020: I was in my house in Wiltshire, Jim was with the residents in their lounge. I talked about the challenges facing us all during this pandemic and asked the residents to be patient. At the end of my pitch, Jim stood up, put on his beret, and spoke on behalf of the residents saying how grateful they were for all that was being done and how they would do their duty and look after the staff. It was a typical statement from a remarkable man and underlined yet again the importance of the work that we do. We are privileged to help rebuild the lives of those who have served and lost their sight, and very grateful indeed to the BMMHS for their unfailing support for our mission.

Major General Nick Caplin CB, CEO Blind Veterans UK

Endorsements

'I am delighted that the BMMHS has taken this initiative to record eyewitness accounts during the Lockdowns. For historians, first-hand accounts are the building blocks of good story telling and to do so with fund-raising for BVUK in mind is doubly pleasing.'
Paul Beaver, historian, author and broadcaster

'Highly recommended... from across the different wars of the 20th century comes this unique collection of inspirational narratives of human endurance, daring exploits, fighting spirit and sheer heroism.'
Dr Helen Fry, author, historian and broadcaster

'BMMHS are to be congratulated on the timely publication of this first volume of Glimpses of War. It was a pleasure and privilege to be involved in this fascinating project, together with one of our former patients and to support the valuable work of Blind Veterans UK.'
Nicci Pugh, Senior Nursing Officer on board Her Majesty's Hospital Ship *Uganda* throughout the Falklands War

'What a marvellous time — during the many privations of 'lockdown' — to ask us all to turn out our family archives and contribute to the BMMHS's first publication. And no better charity than Blind Veterans UK to receive any profit from this great initiative.'
Major General Dair Farrar-Hockley, MC

'Those of us who study, and maybe write about, military history deal with reports, statistics, dates, strategies and outcomes. It is, however, the human story, such as those we have here in Glimpses of War, that give flesh to the bones of our research. I consider it a privilege to have contributed to this current volume. It is made all the more appropriate that proceeds will be directed to Blind Veterans UK since I too am a blind person.'
Steve Richards, historian and author, Solihull, England

'An inspired and fascinating historical collection. Powerful first-hand accounts of individuals' courage and tenacity in the face of conflict over the decades.'
Elizabeth Lockhart-Mure, author of Front Line and Fortitude, Memoirs of a Wasbie

This is a fascinating selection of material which covers many facets of war and military service - and it is published for such a good cause. Congratulations all round.
Gary Sheffield, Professor of War Studies, University of Wolverhampton

'I am deeply honoured that my great grandfather Percy Statton, who was awarded the Victoria Cross in 1915, is remembered in Glimpses of War and for such a great cause. I hope this volume and the subsequent ones raise lots of money for BVUK.'
Kerri Statton, Great Grandaughter of Percy Statton

'I felt very privileged to learn that some elements of my father's wartime career and experiences would contribute in some small way to this excellent funding initiative'.
Bill King, historian and broadcaster

Contents

Part 1 - Great War and Conflicts Pre 1939

Over hundreds of years, indeed thousands, armies big and small have crossed invisible borders or turbulent seas to fight and conquer foreign lands. Some wars were ideological, others arose through naked political ambition, and others because one party was slighted by another. Some were a grab for natural resources, and others part of religious ideologies and sometimes it has taken the form of bitter civil wars.

The wars of the last 200 years have touched on all of these and barely a decade has gone by when man has not fought man, or country attacked country.

In line with the technological and industrial developments the changing means and methods of warfare have resulted in more effective and devastating ways of waging war. The decades up to the Second World War introduced a new dimension, war in the air.

Up to the start of the 20th Century, war on land and by the sea had continued remorselessly. At the grassroots level the one common feature in every conflict of the era was the soldier on the front line – whether the grunt, the squaddie, the private. In earlier times, this was by sword, lance, cudgel sometimes on horseback wearing armour, with face-to-face bloody battles, looking their enemy in the eye within arm's length. The arrival of gunpowder saw the development of cannon, pistols, muskets which then developed into machine guns and artillery on the Western Front. Mechanisation and the arrival of the first tanks in the

First World War with huge technological advances made the industry of killing far more effective.

Supply and logistics became vital as war increasingly was more and more industrialised, with millions of tons of munitions needed to fight battles, with whole economies becoming geared up to wage war. The fighting, however, was not the only challenge facing the armies. Up to one hundred years ago, many more soldiers died from disease and illness as from battle. Medical knowledge and support, whilst well-meaning, was at best rudimentary with even the slightest wound or ailment often leading to infection and death. The First World War saw 57,000 nurses travel to the Western Front to support the troops and provide the best care they could. This coupled with a much-improved system of field hospitals and casualty clearing stations behind the lines and a myriad of hospitals, makeshift or otherwise back in *Blighty*, saw huge advances and improvements to recovery rates.

On the water, the last two centuries saw the move from the wooden ships of Nelson's day to the ironclads and dreadnoughts, and then to the great warships as seen at Jutland. Naval rivalry surrounding the dreadnought developed between Britain and Germany, while First Sea Lord, Jackie Fisher, instigated a series of naval reforms which were intended to ensure that Britain remained the pre-eminent sea power in the world.

The First World War saw the British Grand Fleet in opposition to the German High Seas Fleet. Britain maintained a blockade of Germany, but the two fleets only met in battle at Heligoland Bight (August 1914), Dogger

Bank (January 1915) and Jutland (May 1916). The Battle of Jutland took place from May 30th to June 1st 1916, and was the largest sea battle and the only full-scale clash of battleships during the war. Historians have debated the extent of the British tactical success, but the German fleet remained in port for much of the rest of the war. However, the threat of it emerging meant that Britain had to keep most of its capital ships in the North Sea.

However, a new threat evolved, the submarine. In both world wars, the threat of the 'U-boat' put supplies of food and other materials in jeopardy as losses of merchant ships mounted.

The English Channel was of vital importance to the BEF and was protected throughout the war by the Dover Patrol. The prowess of German U-boats and from 1917 their policy of unrestricted submarine warfare meant the loss of many merchant ships, but the development of the naval convoy system resulted in fewer losses of merchant shipping.

The inter war years saw the growing importance of naval airpower. The first purpose-built aircraft carrier was commissioned in 1924. Despite the Washington Naval Treaty of 1922, increasing naval rivalry developed with the USA and Japan developing aircraft carrier capacity. However, at the beginning of the Second World War the Royal Navy was still the strongest in the world.

The 20th Century saw the development and introduction of air warfare to the world. Although balloons had been used in aerial warfare from the 3rd century in China and had a part to play in the American Civil War, aircraft were not used in warfare until the Italian-Turkish war of 1911 with Italian monoplanes and dirigibles being used to bomb Turkish camps. Air dropped bombs were used in the First Balkan war 1912 and the scene was set for the role that aviation was to play in the First World War.

Balloons were employed for reconnaissance duties and artillery spotting and could communicate with artillery batteries by field telephone, but had obvious limitations in finding targets and reporting enemy activity. From early in the war, two-seater observation planes were in action on both sides of the lines gathering intelligence and directing artillery fire. They were hampered by a lack of radio equipment, relying instead, from March 1915 onwards, on transmitting Morse code or even dropping messages from the aircraft.

Actual air combat developed from the need to stop enemy planes reconnoitering, and started by throwing grenades and firing pistols at each other. Early fighter planes employing machine guns such as the FB.5 were 'pusher' aircraft, with the engine behind the pilot, and allowed a free range of machine gun fire forward, but as the pace of aerial warfare became faster, this type of plane was made obsolete, being far too slow.

Some of the first allied purpose-built fighter planes included the British Vickers FB.5 and the Morane-Saulnier L, but in July 1915 the advent of the Fokker E.1 gave the German Air Force an advantage which resulted in temporary air superiority. However, the allies were not far behind in producing fighters such as the British FE.2b, the DH.2, the Sopwith Strutter and the French with their *Nieuport 11*.

During the battle of the Somme and at Verdun, the allies developed a more offensive strategy involving close air support of troops in the trenches, resulting in allied air superiority.

In spite of new allied fighters such as the Sopwith Pup and the Sopwith Triplane, the RFC suffered heavy losses in April 1917 (known as 'Bloody April'). However, during the year with new allied fighters arriving in greater numbers, the allies regained air superiority. The German Spring Offensive was accompanied by an air assault and losses were heavy on both sides. Life expectancy of pilots could be measured in weeks. In April 1918, the British Royal Flying Corps and the Royal Naval Air Service were amalgamated to form the Royal Air Force.

The first strategic bombing occurred in the First World War with both sides developing planes whose primary purpose was bombing enemy targets.

At the beginning of the war, Liege, Antwerp and Warsaw were among the cities targeted by bombs dropped from *Zeppelin* airships. At the end of 1914, Kent was bombed by aircraft, but most of the 19 raids on Britain in 1915 were by Zeppelin, killing 181 people and injuring 455. As air defences against *Zeppelins* improved, the raids became fewer in number but were replaced by bombing raids by heavy bombers, the *Gotha* G bombers and the *Staaken* RV Giant 4 engine bombers. The RNAS and RFC planes could not fly high enough to effectively defend against the *Gothas*. One of the worst raids came on Wednesday 13th June 1917, when a bomb dropped through the roof of the Upper North Street LCC school and 18 children were killed and 34 injured. In the same raid 16 died at Liverpool Street station, and 19 at Fenchurch Street.

The aerial bombardment of London in the Great War coloured inter-war governments' attitudes to appeasement and the prospect of bombing in a future war, as Stanley Baldwin in 1932 predicted that *'The bomber will always get through.'* Practically, Londoners and the government had learned valuable lessons about the necessity for air raid precautions, the organisation of civil defence and the importance of maintaining high morale or a *'Blitz Spirit'*. The development of strategic bombers was a major preoccupation for countries in these inter war years. Despite being forbidden by the terms of the Treaty of Versailles at the end of the First World War Germany, under the guise of flying clubs and with hidden factories, secretly developed a potent air force of both fighters and bombers – the *Lufwaffe*, outstripping the development and scale of military aircraft by the western powers during this period. The first evidence of this and the use of German bombers in the Spanish Civil War, and notably the destruction of Guernica, and also by Japan in the Japanese-Sino War in the late 1930s, reinforced this attitude and foreshadowed what was to come.

Other developments were the increasing interest in navies of the use of air power and the development of aircraft carriers such as HMS *Hermes* in 1924 and the US Lexington class aircraft carriers in 1927. In the following decades, this combination of air and sea power was to transform military strategy and thinking in many arenas.

****

Steve Oliver writes about his great grandmother's brother, Samuel Owen, fighting during the Second Boer War. Only a remarkable coincidence allowed him to survive.

Samuel Owen - Saved by a Neighbour

Sam was my great grandmother's brother who was born in Bermondsey, and who at the age of 18 and one month enlisted on 4th April 1898 at Dalston, London. He served as a Private No. 5536 and at the outbreak of the Second Boer War he was sent to South Africa with the 2nd battalion of the East Kent Regiment in October 1899.

The British objective of the Second Boer War was to unite the British South African territories of Cape Colony and Natal with the Boer republics of the Orange Free State and the South African Republic (also known as the Transvaal). The Boers, Afrikaans-speaking farmers, wanted to maintain their independence. This was in part driven by the discovery of gold in 1896, which also led to many English-speaking foreigners arriving who were called *Uitlanders* (or Outlanders). Though not initially accepted by the Afrikaners, come the commencement of the Second Boer War many *Uitlanders* (even British citizens) actually served against the British Army as the political manoeuvrings and military policies had swayed many opinions.

Scroll forwards to 8th August 1901 and Sam was defending a blockhouse at Brandfort which was 20 miles north of Bloemfontein during the 'Guerilla War' period. Of the six men in the blockhouse the NCO, Sergeant Pincott, was killed and four others including Sam were wounded. What happened is detailed in the '*With The Flag To Pretoria*' publication (After Pretoria: Guerilla War, part 64 of 72 parts) priced at 6d and dating from circa June 1902.

My father noted *'my grandfather told me that the Boers were about to finish the defenders off when one of the enemy recognised Sam. Apparently, they lived in the same street in London and so they were spared'*. In his opinion the design of the blockhouses was flawed resulting in injuries and their capture. There is no mention of this event in *'With The Flag To Pretoria'* – just the detail of how they were spared and had their money taken which was 'against the laws of the war'.

Sam was discharged as being medically unfit for further service in April 1902 as a result of *'gunshot wound, left arm'* received in action in South Africa. He was entitled to the South Africa Medal with clasps for Transvaal, Driefontein, Paardeberg and the relief of Kimberley indicating he was involved in all these campaigns.

****

Historian Robin Brodhurst, ex Royal Green Jackets, has kindly provided verbatim copies of 3 letters sent from Ypres on the Western Front in 1915. Two were sent by his grandfather Harry Altham to his friend Rockley Wilson. The third was sent by another serving soldier, Max Cullinan, to his housemaster at Winchester College. All give a flavour of life on the front line and the soldiers' thoughts of home.

Letters from the Western Front

These letters were re-discovered when I was working on editing a collection of letters between my grandfather, Harry Altham, and Sir Donald Bradman, the Australian cricketer, concerning the throwing controversy of 1958-60. In researching my grandfather, I went back over his life to put him into context, and re-read the first two letters. I first came across them many years ago, before I became really interested in the First World War, read them, with interest, but put them back into a file and forgot about them. Re-reading them they shine a light onto a particular episode of 1915 that has always filled me with fascination: the German use of liquid fire at Hooge in July 1915.

The first two letters were written by H.S. Altham, my mother's father. He was born in 1888, the son of Lieutenant. General Sir Edward Altham, who in 1915 was sent out to Mudros to re-organise the Lines of Communication for the Gallipoli expedition, and did so brilliantly. Harry was educated at Repton and Oxford, making his name as an excellent cricketer. He went to teach at Winchester College in 1913, and in 1914 joined up, and was commissioned in August 1914 into the King's Royal Rifle Corps (KRRC) or 60th Rifles, whose depot was at

Winchester. Initially he was in 8KRRC, part of 41 Brigade, in 14th (Light) Division, but at some early stage he was selected to become Staff Captain in 41 Brigade. This must have been March 1915, when he was promoted Captain. 14 Division moved to France in May 1915, and 41 Brigade received a new Brigadier – Oliver Nugent[1]. They spent some time gaining front line experience and eventually the Division took over the front line at Hooge in June 1915, one of the first Kitchener New Army divisions to do so, as part of VI Corps.

The recipient of the first two letters was E.R. Wilson (ref 10 & 41). Rockley Wilson was born in 1879, educated at Rugby and Cambridge, and became a schoolmaster at Winchester in 1902. He taught (not particularly well, it has to be said) modern languages, but more importantly was involved in running the cricket. In this he was notably successful. He was a great student of the game and its history, and if Harry Altham had needed enthusing, this was where it came from. Rockley Wilson, it appears, did not volunteer in 1914, but did so in 1915.

The attack on 41 Brigade at Hooge was the first use of liquid fire on the Western Front and was brilliantly successful. There are excellent accounts of it in *The Nugent*

---

[1] Oliver Nugent had been commissioned into the KRRC in 1883, served in India and the Boer War, and commanded a battalion of his regiment (4KRRC) 1906-10. He commanded 41 Brigade 6 May – 14 September 1915, before being promoted major general and commanding 36 (Ulster) Division until May 1918. See N. Perry (Editor) *Major-General Oliver Nugent and the Ulster Division, 1915-18*, Army Records Society, 2007. Perry has recently published a biography of Nugent: *Major-General Oliver Nugent: The Irishman who led the Ulster Division in the Great War,* Ulster Historical Foundation, 2020.

Papers (ref 1) *The KRRC Chronicle 1915*[2], *The Annals of the KRRC, Volume V*[3], and *The Rifle Brigade 1914-18, Volume 1*[4]. All are mainly based on the same account supplied by Nugent to Lieutenant. General Sir Edward Hutton, the Colonel Commandant of the KRRC. There is a good account in the Official History: *France and Flanders 1915, Volume 2*[5]. Also useful is the guidebook *Sanctuary Wood and Hooge*[6], which not only gives a good account of the action, but walks any tourist through it on the ground.

The first letter gives a good account of the humdrum life of a very junior staff officer on the Q side. As he says 'My chief job is now that of universal provider of trench stores.' Nothing in his previous life could have prepared him for this, as can probably be said of all those who volunteered in 1914. The second letter is much more poignant, describing as it does the result of the Hooge action on 41 Brigade. It shows the dilemma facing so many of those moved into staff jobs: luck in being for some time out of the immediate front line, but a form of survivor's guilt at not being with their friends and contemporaries in the thick of it. The third letter was provided for me by the archivist of Winchester College, Suzanne Foster, and is written by Max Cullinan[7]

[2] *The KRRC Chronicle, 1915*, Warren and Son, Winchester, 1916.
[3] Major General Sir Steuart Hare, *The Annals of the KRRC, Volume V The Great War*, John Murray, 1932.
[4] Reginald Berkeley, *The History of the Rifle Brigade in the War of 1914 – 1918, Volume 1*, The Rifle Brigade Club, 1927.
[5] James Edmonds, *Military Operations: France and Flanders, 1915, Volume 2*, OHMS, 1928.
[6] Nigel Cave, *Sanctuary Wood and Hooge*, Pen & Sword, 1993. 2nd edition 2013.
[7] Max Cullinan was at Horris Hill and then Winchester, 1906-12 and Magdalene College Cambridge. Commissioned into 8/KRRC in 1914, MC (1916) and mentioned in despatches.

on 8th August 1915 to his old Housemaster at Winchester, the Rev. Trant Bramston. Many Old Wykehamists kept in touch with their old housemasters throughout the war, as they were to do in the Second World War, when Harry was a housemaster.

Harry spent the rest of the war on the Western Front. He became Brigade Major, 41 Brigade, between October 1916 and February 1917. This must have been unusual for a New Army volunteer, as Brigade Major was (and still is today) one of the most sought-after jobs for a rising star, and, certainly this early in the war, would normally have been a job for a regular officer. In February 1917 he was posted to become DAA and QMG 9th (Scottish) Division, and awarded the MC, for his work as Brigade Major presumably. He stayed in this post, promoted Major in 1917, until December 1918, being awarded the DSO in that year. After the Armistice he was appointed DAAG Demobilisation at GHQ and promoted temporary Lieutenant. Colonel, and was demobilised on 21st February 1919. He was awarded three Mentions in Despatches.

He returned to Winchester College and his wife, whom he had married during leave in the war, and stayed there for the rest of his life. He was a much-admired housemaster from 1927, and would normally have retired after 15 years in 1942, but the Second World War meant that he stayed on as a housemaster until 1947. During those last 8 years he kept in constant touch by letter with many of his ex-pupils who were scattered across the world playing their part in that conflict. After retirement in 1948, when, as he used to say, he was 'constitutionally gaga' he became an (unpaid) cricket administrator at Lord's, initially on the MCC committee, then as Treasurer (the senior non-professional administrator there, who sits on all committees and deputises for the President if necessary) and also as President 1959-60. In this latter role he chaired the famous ICC meeting of 1960, for which he was instrumental in persuading Bradman to attend, which successfully tackled the question of throwing. He was also chairman of the England selectors in 1954, President of Hampshire CC 1946-65, chairman of ESCA from its formation and many other cricket organisations, and was also among the best after dinner speakers of his generation, likened to Norman Birkett and Walter Monkton. He died in Sheffield in March 1965 having given, the day before, three wholly different cricket talks to three wholly different audiences: the local grammar school VI Form, the city jail and the Sheffield Cricket Lovers Society. He never talked about his war experiences as far as is known.

Letter 1.

H.Q.
41st Infantry Brigade[8],
14th Division[9],
B.E.F.

10.6.1915

Dear Rockley[10],

---

[8] 41 Brigade, consisting of 7KRRC, 8KRRC, 7RB and 8RB, was commanded in 1915 by Brigadier Oliver Nugent.

[9] 14 (Light) Division was one of the first 6 divisions of Kitchener's New Army (K1). Originally due to be numbered 8 (Light) Division, and thus the senior New Army division, 8 Division was then created from the regular battalions around the world brought back to UK. Because the other divisions had already been formed and numbered, the new 8 (Light) Division was instead changed to 14 (Light) Division, the junior New Army division. It consisted of 41, 42 and 43 Brigades. Initially, it consisted entirely of rifle and light infantry battalions, e.g. KRRC, RB, OBLI, KSLI, SLI, DCLI, YLI and DLI. It was initially commanded by Major General V.A. Couper, who retained command until March 1918, one of the longest spells of divisional command in World War 1.

[10] Evelyn Rockley Wilson, born 25.3.1879, died 21.7.1957. Educated Rugby and Cambridge, cricket blue for 4 years, captain 1902. Schoolmaster (he taught modern languages) at Winchester College 1902 – 1945, master in charge of cricket 1919-28. Played cricket for Yorkshire (1899 – 1923) and England (1 Test). When he asked for permission to go on tour with the MCC to Australia in 1920-21, the headmaster asked 'Who are the MCC, and what are they doing in Australia?' Commissioned into The Rifle Brigade in 1915, he was Adjutant at the Depot in Winchester, responsible for sending out drafts to France. Studied Turkish at SOS, London, passed as Interpreter in Turkish, and posted to EEF, Cairo and then Palestine on the Intelligence staff. He was genuinely eccentric and one exasperated senior officer said of him: 'Rockley, you may be the best slow bowler in England, but you're the worst bloody subaltern I've ever had in my battalion.' See Martin Howe, *Rockley Wilson; Remarkable Cricketer, Singular Man*, ACS, 2008.

<u>Please write</u>. I've heard a certain amount of news from various sources, but I'm longing to hear something about the cricket, and you'll know just what really interests me. If you don't write soon, I'll give you away to Schof'[11], and make him do so instead. Am <u>awfully</u> busy: work seems to run pretty well straight on from 8 a.m. to 11 p.m. with the shortest conceivable break for meals, during which you never get less than four field messages brought you. Since we've taken over part of the line as a brigade, I haven't had any exercise at all except a daily ride down to the R.E. store to a place some ½ mile from here to see what I can get, borrow or steal for the battalions. Fortunately, the way lies over fields with two ditches of a comfortable size and I go *ventre à terre*[12] the whole way, which saves time and is good for the liver.

We live in a wooden hut, one room for messing, one where 5 of us sleep, the Brigade Major[13], Squire[14] the Cambridge footer player who is Brigade Machine Gun Officer, the chaplain[15] – a capital soul late of Magdalen who would do

---

[11] Schofield Haigh, born 19.3.1871, Huddersfield, died 27.2.1921 Lockwood, Yorkshire. Professional cricketer for Yorkshire and England (11 Test matches). Professional coach at Winchester College, 1914-1920.

[12] Can mean, literally, 'belly to the ground', i.e. crawling, but also hurrying, probably both are apposite here.

[13] 41 Brigade Major at this time was Captain AG Bailey, probably a wartime appointment as he does not figure in the July 1914 Army List.

[14] Possibly Samuel Gimson Squire, born 14.1.1879, died 18.9.1962. Educated Wyggeston GS, Christ's College, Cambridge University, I first class cricket match. Taught at St. Peter's York, 1902-08, and Oundle from 1908.Ralph Tyndall Squire, born 10.9.1863, died 22.8 1944. Educated Westmister and Trinity Hall College, Cambridge, soccer XI 1884 and 1886, and soccer for England 1886.

[15] Rev. TWA Jones.

the ground staff much good – the signal officer whose favourite word is 'Pardon?' but is very good at his job, and self.

I spend my whole day on the office stool receiving and writing messages: my chief job now is that of universal provider of trench stores. Today, for example, I issued 6,000 sandbags, 58 bombs (which terrify me), 1 catapult made by Mr. Gamage for throwing ditto[16], 500 empty petrol cans, 8 barrels (looted from a brewery in Ypres), 40 periscopes made here from broken mirrors looted from another place, barbed wire and planking *ad nauseam*.

I'm sure it will amuse Broomers[17] or 'Mr. Steel'[18] to think of anyone so unpractical as a classical man dealing with

[16] The Leach-Gamage catapult designed to throw a 2 lb bomb into enemy trenches. It was effectively a combined crossbow and slingshot with a range of about 200 m. It was invented by Claude Pemberton Leach and manufactured by Gamage's department store in London. They cost £6 17s 6d to make and 20 were issued to each division. By 1916 they were replaced by the French made Suaterelle grenade launcher, the 2" mortar and the Stokes mortar.

[17] AE Broomfield, (1869-1945) mathematics master at Winchester College 1904-24. Educated at St. Paul's and Trinity College, Cambridge. Good cricketer in his schooldays, taking 170 wickets for 5 runs each in 3 years in the St. Paul's 1st XI. Seriously ill at Cambridge, forcing him to give up all games, and possibly (along with his age) stopping him from enlisting in 1914. 1st House master of Chernocke House (A), of which HSA later became House master.

[18] HC Steel, (1852-1933) Trinity College, Cambridge, 36th Wrangler, taught at Wellington College, 1878-85, maths and modern languages master at Winchester College, 1885-? Founder of the Indian Civil and Army Class there, the first attempt to widen the curriculum from Classics and Maths. In the words of his obituary he showed that 'French Prose is as delicate and keen-edged an instrument as Latin and that Napoleon's fortunes might be as interesting as Caesar's and the Peninsular War as instructive as the Peloponnesian.' He remembered all of his pupils and 'his quiet study was at times a confidential clearing

these abstruse things. It's an extraordinary life: one hardly has time to look at the paper at all, and certainly none to think about the war. My horizon is bounded entirely by the dug-out in trench P5 which wants corrugated iron, or the question of whether on the 12 inst. the ration shall be all bread, or all biscuit, or mixed – and so on. Hardly romantic you see, but I hope necessary. I haven't been near the trenches for days, but hope to go tomorrow or next day: in some places they are very bad.

It's extraordinary how some Bdes. won't even try to protect themselves: when we took it over[19], there were places in which one simply lay in the open.

A German sniper bagged two men today, but I think they know where he is, and my catapult is going to deal with him at dawn tomorrow, I hope. Enough of the war: it won't end yet awhile anyway.

Sometimes when it's hot, and the sun shines, I just long for Meads[20]. It's the first time I've ever had to do without cricket, and I pray God it may be the last.

---

house for secrets of the outposts of Empire as the conversation shifted from Khartoum to K2 and from Tidworth to Tanga.'

[19] 41 Brigade had their first experience of the front line serving under 28 Division so as to gain experience. They took over the Hooge sector of the line on 23rd July from 3 Division, and were particularly upset at the state of the trenches.

[20] Meads is the original Winchester College playing field. A beautiful ground, surrounded on two sides by a flint wall, to this day it is still used for sport, mainly Winchester College football (a unique combination of football and rugby) and cricket. The 2nd XI still play their matches there. 3 ancient plane trees, originally planted in 1781, stand within the boundary.

Write and tell me how them boys are playing: scores I get from other people all right, but I want to know how good and bad individuals are. Does that Gilbert Ashton[21] still hit the leg stump ball to square leg, and does he watch it as well as he did? How about his young brother[22]? Is he still jumpy? Does Bankier[23] still bend his knees, and can't Joy[24] bat? And so on – I fear my appetite is insatiable, but then it always was.

Well, I must stop. My love to Broomers and ask him to drop me a line when he can. Letters from home are the best things that happen out here.

Yours aye,

Harry

---

[21] Gilbert Ashton, born 27.9.1896 died 6.2.1981. Second of 4 brothers, all of whom were educated at Winchester College, and all of whom played first class cricket, 3 of whom served in the Royal Artillery, all winning an M.C. He captained the Winchester 1st XI in 1915 and he won 3 cricket blues at Cambridge, captaining the side in 1921. Served in the Royal Field Artillery, winning an M.C., but losing a thumb. He went on to be headmaster of Abberley Hall prep school for 40 years, never taking a salary.

[22] Hubert Ashton, born 13.2.1898 died 17.6.1979. Captained the Winchester 1st XI in 1916. Probably the best cricketer of the 4 brothers, playing for Essex occasionally after leaving Cambridge. Served in Royal Field Artillery, winning an M.C., and then as a staff officer (Intelligence) in 18 Div.

[23] A.A. Bankier, served in Royal Field Artillery, 1916-18. Winchester Cricket XI 1915 and 1916.

[24] This is almost certainly a misprint, when the letters were originally typed up, for J.C. Clay, born 18.3.1888 died 11.8.1973. At Winchester College he bowled fast, as well as leg spin and was in the 1st XI in 1915 and 1916. Later played for Glamorgan, 1920-49 and for England (1 Test). John Arlott considered him to be the best off-spinner in cricket until the arrival of Jim Laker. Served 1917-18 in the Royal Field Artillery.

Letter 2.

H.Q.
41st Infantry Brigade,
14th Division.

8.8.1915

My dear Rockley,

Thanks ever so much for your letter written from Cambridge: as I told you before, I'm sure you don't know how much pleasure they give me.

Yes, it's been a sad time for us all this last fortnight[25], and the bitterest part of it all is that those who sit behind and command – well behind I mean – have got the idea that it was the New Army who 'couldn't stick it'. No one who hasn't been in this salient and lived in it can have any idea of what these fellows had to face, not only in actual

---

[25] 41 Brigade had been decimated at Hooge when the Germans attacked on 30 July 1915, using flamethrowers, intense shelling and machine guns. The main attack was on 8RB and 7KRRC, who were forced to retreat from the front line. The Corps Commander (Sir John Keir) insisted on an immediate counter-attack to regain the lost trenches, and overruled Nugent's objections that there was insufficient artillery support. The assault in the afternoon was disastrous. 41 Brigade lost 55 officers and 1,181 other ranks on 30/31 July. The position was retaken a week later by 6 Division, in a properly prepared attack with adequate artillery support, at the cost of only 100 casualties. Nugent was subsequently promoted to command the 36th (Ulster) Division, and Sir John Keir was sacked on 8 August 1916 by Allenby. See Nicholas Perry (Editor) *Major General Oliver Nugent and the Ulster Division 1915-1918*, Army Records Society, Volume 26, 2007. The best account is in the official history, Edmonds, *Military Operations; France and Flanders, 1915, Volume 2*, pages 102-109.

culminating attack, but in the awful daily wastage when they had to know every morning as they woke up that before night came, they would have been crumped mercilessly from both flanks as well as from their front two or even three times. The attack itself was magnificently run by the Huns and entirely unexpected: a mine, liquid fire, and marvellously accurate shelling with high explosive 6" shells. I swear to God, Rockley, no troops in the world could have stood it.

Do you know that the 9th Division, our immediate predecessors out here, have had 2 officers and about 200 men hit in 3 months fighting, while we have lost at least 90 officers and over 4,000 men[26]? Please treat these figures as strictly confidential but if you hear people sneer at the 14th Division give them the lie for the sake of the good fellows who are gone. Poor Joe![27] After having been in all the most dangerous places all that day and escaped by a miracle, he was killed by a stray bullet walking back through a wood to his headquarters. Geoff Dowling[28] too you will have

---

[26] Edmonds, op cit, gives the following figures: 41 Brigade for the 2 days 30/31 July, 55 officers and 1,181 ORs. 14 Division, for the same period, 100 officers and 2,387 ORs. HSA's 4000 men is probably the figure for casualties, i.e. killed, wounded and missing.

[27] William Mackworth Parker, born 1.9.1886, died, Hooge, 30.7.1915. Educated Winchester College, Cricket XI 1903, 1904 and 1905. Served in the Royal North Devon Imperial Yeomanry and then R.M.C. Sandhurst, Sword of Honour and both Football and Cricket XI 1906, also represented the Army in both sports. Commissioned into The Rifle Brigade. In 1914 played at Lord's in the Centenary Week, for Army v Royal Navy. Adjutant 8RB in 1914. Commemorated on the Menin Gate Memorial, Ypres, panel 46-8.

[28] Geoffrey Charles Walter Dowling, born 12.8.1891, died, Hooge, 30.7.1915. Educated Charterhouse, Cricket XI 1908, 1909 and 1910. Played 4 first-class matches for Sussex 1911-13, with little success. Commissioned into 7KRRC, promoted Captain.

known. Jack Wormold did splendidly: I hope he gets a D.S.O.[29]. I can't write you tactical details of the fight – that's forbidden – but I can tell you that what finally smashed our own poor Brigade was that the bombardment preliminary to our counter attack failed to account for the machine guns which the Huns had got up into position. It is the old story: high explosives and machine guns!

I saw little of the fight: the general wouldn't take me further than Ypres[30]. He said, quite rightly, that my place was there, and I had a great deal of work which could only have been done there – indeed I had 2 hours sleep in about 50 hours. But all the same one feels wretched at not having been out there with one's pals. One somehow feels that one ought to be gone too. But I suppose we've just got to stick at the humdrum jobs set to us, and try to last as long as we can.

Tyndale[31] got hit in the foot, but was splendidly cheery and plucky throughout; it's funny how this life alters one's opinions and how the real stuff in a fellow comes out. There's a little fellow in 8RB whom I can see having been ragged all his life at school, obviously no games player and not very interesting to talk to, but that boy went out in the most awful shell-fire and laid a telephone wire from his H.Q. to the forward fire trench, and he's now doing adjutant in poor Joe's place, and will probably get the M.C. My

---

[29] John Wormold, born 23.2.1882, died 13.11.1957, Educated Eton, played 22 matches for Middlesex 1910-22, and also for Norfolk. He was awarded an M.C. 6.9.1915.

[30] 41 Brigade's HQ was in the ramparts of Ypres, as were 14 Division's HQ.

[31] H.E.G. Tyndale, Winchester College 1900-08. Taught at Winchester College 1911-48. Lieutenant KRRC, wounded at Hooge, then served at the War Office in Intelligence.

God, I admire these fellows from the bottom of my heart. May I be fit to serve with them when I get the chance. In less than five hours from now the 6th Division[32] will have attacked Hooge again. All the evening an unending stream of ambulances has been passing us going up to Ypres preparatory to evacuating casualties involved. I think they will get the trenches they aim at, but the holding of them will be the very devil[33]. This Ypres salient – no one knows save those who have been in it – what it costs to hold. I believe we ought to put 200,000 in one big push and straighten it out for ever. But the great ones, no doubt, know best.

What a gloomy letter I've written; please forgive. It's not all gloom, for I swear the Germans must be having a godless time here too. The sound of our 9.2s floating overhead with the leisurely purr of a distant express rejoices the heart. It gives one the same sense of inevitability as seeing Barnes[34] run up to the wicket. Geoff Colman[35] (Brigade Machine

---

[32] Commanded by Major General WN Congreve V.C.

[33] Edmonds describes the 6 Division assault as 'a model of its kind, took the enemy by surprise and was entirely successful.'

[34] Sidney Francis Barnes, born 19.4.1873 died 26.12.1967. A formidable man, he was regarded by contemporaries, and many since, as the finest ever bowler. Only played 50 first-class county matches, but 27 Tests, taking 189 wickets, including 49 in 4 matches in South Africa in 1913-14. He preferred to play league and Minor Counties cricket (various clubs and Staffordshire), and was still bowling well at the age of 54 in 1928 taking 7-51 and 5-67 against the touring West Indies, and 8-41 in 1929 against the touring South Africans.

[35] Geoffrey Russell Rees Colman, born 14.3.1892 died 18.3.1935. Educated Eton and Christ Church College, Oxford University. Oxford cricket blue 1913 and 1914, also played for Norfolk. Emergency Commission in The Rifle Brigade 1914. Served in 7RB in 41 Brigade, then in Brigade HQ. Later served in the Machine Gun Corps. Badly wounded in 1916 in the chest. He had taken over as Bde. MGO from

Gun Officer) and I played cricket today – high road, cut down bat and solid rubber ball – both in very fair form. What wouldn't I give for the chance of one season's cricket? It's rather stupid, but I have always been very ambitious as a cricketer, though not in the least ambitious in life generally, and last year I kept feeling that if I could have 3 weeks systematic coaching under you, I might really become a moderately decent player. Joe and I would both have qualified for Hampshire now, and they were, I believe, going to play him regularly and give me at least an occasional game in August[36].

By the way there is one thing I'd like you to see to for me: if I'm outed, I'd like all my cricket books – not very many I'm afraid but there are a few, and there's two volumes of '50 Years of Sport'[37] – to go to Webbe Tent[38] for future 'Lords'[39]. They may serve to while away some wet hours,

---

Squire, who was probably wounded at Hooge.

[36] HSA did play for Hampshire after the war, playing in the summer holidays: 24 matches, 1919-23.

[37] *Fifty Years of Sport at Oxford, Cambridge and the Great Public Schools*, edited by Lord Desborough. Two volumes published in 1913, and a third in 1922. Large, leather-bound volumes which are occasionally still to be seen.

[38] All pavilions at Winchester College are called 'tents', probably because originally, they were tents. Webbe tent was a thatched pavilion, erected in 1887, dedicated to the memory of HR Webbe, captain of the 1st XI in 1875, and given by his more famous brother AJ Webbe. It was replaced by Hunter Tent in 1930, which still stands, a large two-story building, dedicated to four members of the Hunter family, two killed in First World War and two in Second World War.Hugh Michael Hunter (1891-1915) served in the Wiltshire Regiment, died of wounds received at Neuve Chappelle 6.4.1915 and Richard Jocelyn Hunter (1896-1918) served in the London Rifle Brigade, k.i.a. Sailly-le-Sec, 25.8.1918. The names of their nephews, Robert Arbuthnot Hunter k.i.a. Normandy, 6.6.1944, and Geoffrey Colin Devas Hunter, k.i.a. over Germany, 18.9.44, were added after 1945.

and I'd like somehow to be connected with the cricket of the place. I'll tell my mother, and I'd be ever so grateful if you'd see it through for me[40]. Will you?

Write and tell me how you progress in the O.T.C. course. I expect at the end of a month you'll know much more about a company commander's job than I do. I'm forgetting that part of soldiering terribly fast[41].

Well, I must end; goodbye, old Rockley.

Good luck. Write soon, Harry

---

[39] The 1st XI cricket side at Winchester College is always referred to as 'Lord's', in the same way that the 1st rackets pair is always called 'Prince's'. This is because the side always played Eton and Harrow at Lord's between 1825 and 1854, when some unfortunate event meant that they were no longer allowed to play there. Eton and Harrow still do.

[40] HSA's cricket library eventually came to the editor on his death in 1965.

[41] It was unlikely that Rockley Wilson did ever know more than Harry about soldiering. See footnote 3. When a staff officer on Allenby's staff in 1918 he was asked to pay some boatmen for transporting the HQ across the Sea of Galilee and when returning to the HQ in a bad temper reported 'No wonder Jesus walked!'

Letter 3.

Flanders.

Sunday 8th August 1915.

Dear Trant,

You will have heard by now the sad news that Roger Watson[42] has been killed in action – I am writing to tell you about it. He and I were great friends from Horris Hill days and I feel his loss very much. We were relieved from pretty bad trenches opposite Hooge after a long spell in them, on the night of the 29th July and – very tired – got back to our billets behind Ypres, arriving about 2-30 am. At 3.15 am the Germans attacked the trenches from which we had just been relieved. They attacked them with liquid fire and took them. The Rifle Brigade, which were in them, losing dreadfully in officers and men, and in fact there are only 3 officers left in one battalion of the Rifle Brigade, perhaps the finest battalion in the whole Army. Well, we, weary as we were, turned out of our billets and under a tremendous shell fire succeeded in getting up to Sanctuary Wood and Zouave Wood, just behind the trenches which the Germans had taken and where the Battalion Headquarters were. We stayed there all the morning getting heavily shelled and losing men, until 2.45 in the afternoon, when the II Army commander[43] said we had got to make a counter-attack and

---

[42] Roger Watson, Horris Hill, Winchester College, Trinity College Cambridge. Commissioned into 8/KRRC August 1914, promoted Lieutenant March 1915, died Hooge, 31st July 1915

[43] 2nd Army was commanded by General Herbert Plumer, who was to become probably the best army commander on the Western Front, but was still learning the ropes and had not yet acquired his outstanding

retake the trenches; it was an impossible task for a brigade decimated as we were to charge across 400 yards of difficult uphill ground to a position which as it turned out was bristling with the enemy's machine guns.

The 4 Colonels[44], the Brigadier[45], the Divisional General[46] were all against it, but higher authorities[47] who were not there, who didn't know what exactly was the state of things, decided that it was to be done. So, we tried to attack, got about 100 yards and lost from machine gun and shrapnel fire 3 officers and over two thousand men from our brigade alone. The thing of course was hopeless. I saw Roger just before the attack about 2.30 in the afternoon and he was looking his old cheery self, almost immediately afterwards he led his men off down a trench at the edge of Sanctuary Wood getting them out ready for the attack when he was hit in the head by shrapnel and became unconscious at once –

---

chief of staff, Tim Harrington. As noted below, it was the Corps commander who ordered the attack.

[44] The four Commanding Officers in 41 Brigade were all regular officers: George Rennie and 'Verdant' Green of 7 and 8 KRRC, James Heriot-Maitland and Ronnie Maclachlan of 7 and 8 RB

[45] Brigadier Oliver Nugent was soon promoted to command the 36th Ulster Division.

[46] Major General Victor Couper remained in command of 14 Division until March 1918.

[47] The general who insisted on the attack was Lieutenant. General Sir John Keir commanding VI Corps. Like the other Corps commander in 2nd Army, Allenby, Keir did not take kindly to subordinates questioning his orders. It was not until 1917/1918 that the BEF at last understood the importance of the views of 'the man on the spot' and took to reinforcing success, not failure. Keir was later sacked by Allenby in August 1916 when serving in the latter's 3rd Army. As Nick Perry points out (*Nugent*, page 74) 'The remark, famously attributed to Marshal Foch, that it took 15,000 casualties to train a major-general, seems apposite here'.

he died about 3 hours afterwards and was buried that night, 30th July, in a quiet spot beside the adjutant who was also killed.

Roger was greatly loved and respected by his men; not a single officer in his company is left and there are very few in the whole battalion. I've been made adjutant and have had a fearful lot of work because a couple of days after the bad show, before we had time to reorganise, we were put into bad trenches again for 3 days and lost 100 more men from this battalion in them. Please forgive this very gloomy letter, but these are facts which the [senior?] generals ignore.

Yours,

Max Cullinan

 *Jerry Cockeram researched the wartime story of a distant family relative in the First World War. James Willie Barker was his mother-in-law's uncle and served in the Royal Field Artillery on the Western Front. His grave is in a small, immaculately kept British cemetery in the Pas de Calais. He rests alongside his comrades, killed on 22nd March 1916.*

An ordinary man just 'doing his bit'

A few years ago, I had the opportunity to research into the life of a distant relative, a James Willie Barker. Not too much was known about him and I gleaned what little I could from my elderly mother-in-law. James Willie was her uncle and was married to her auntie Betty. They lived up in Yorkshire on Burnt Acres Farm, a smallholding in the Dales, in the village of Todmorden, a hard but simple life with cattle and sheep in the fields with the field boundaries of the dry-stone walls that the area is famous for.

From the family's perspective, we knew very little - he had joined the army and sadly was killed, or so it was believed, during the time of the Battle of the Somme. That was pretty much all we had to go on along with an old sepia photograph of him in his army uniform. At that time there were no letters, no pay book, no medals, and no communication from a government department to say that his life had ended during the King's Service.

As I started to research and delve into the archives, it became clear that there were a lot of questions to be answered, for instance did he volunteer, was he conscripted into the army, did he join up with his mates? Was it the *'Your Country Needs You'* posters that made him sign up for the King's shilling or was it simply because he wanted *'to do his bit'*?

Also being a novice at this type of research I had very little idea as to what was out there. However, it very soon became apparent that our generation has access to so much more information today than those of previous ones.

Through the on-line resources I was able to find his service record as a gunner in the Royal Field Artillery 'C' Battery 87th Brigade. 'C' Battery was equipped with 18 pounder guns and formed part of the LXXXVII (87th) Brigade. This division was part of Kitchener's New Army and by March 1915 was undergoing training near Tidworth and was inspected and addressed by the King in July before trans-shipment to France later that month. The war diaries also reveal a number of actions in which the brigade was involved along the Western Front. And then of course I was able to determine, thanks to the good services of CWGC, his final resting place at St Vaast Richebourg.

Looking into the archives threw up a load of fascinating information that I had previously not seen before... trench maps, aerial photographs, diaries from his fellow gunners, the regimental war diaries....including the personal diaries alluding to at least a glimpse of what conditions would have been like for him - the boredom, the sheer terror of gas attacks, the mud, the comradeship, the praying you will get through this, the noise, the stench of death, the piles of discarded materials all over the battlefield, the horrors of the life at the front, the relief of a letter or parcel from home, a something to take your mind off the hell you were living in. The occasional respite, what did James Willie and his mates get up to when they were pulled out of the line for some rest and recuperation?

When your artillery battery was moved into a new position, I naively thought that neighbouring infantry would welcome this additional firepower. I was wrong as this was seen as making their lives more at risk as the artillery on both sides would range shots and the subsequent counter-battery fire on each other. Hence neighbouring units would become more exposed as a result and their arrival could upset the balance of a *'quiet'* sector.

Research also threw up some interesting what ifs or what onlys - it seems that a certain A. Hitler served in close proximity on the other side of the lines. What if his gun battery had sent a salvo of shells across to good effect? How history would have been so very different. Scenarios like that can let one's imagination run riot.

In addition, it also throws up a few surprises… Rudyard Kipling's son John is believed to be buried in Richebourg as is the eldest son of Oscar Wilde.

A few months later I was on a trip with my brother, Andy, as we had not conducted a Great War tour before. We travelled around the battlefields of Belgium and France including Passchendaele, the Somme and Verdun and a host of towns like Poperinghe and Ypres in Belgium and the French cities of Albert, Peronne, and Compiègne. We soon found out we had been over enthusiastic and tried to cover too much ground in one visit.

What struck us both was the scale of the war; the shelling defies comprehension with the Germans launching two million shells during their opening bombardment at Verdun, the *Voie Sacrée* ('Sacred Way') where French trucks took men, weapons and supplies to the battlefield at the rate of one every 14 seconds. When you visit the cemeteries at Thiepval, Tyne Cot, the Menin Gate and the countless smaller cemeteries dotted across the region it dawns on you the scale of the slaughter along the Western Front.

As we headed back towards *Blighty*, we decided to visit JWB in his final resting place in what turned out to be a small but beautifully kept cemetery in amongst a large number of now sadly largely forgotten battlefields of northern France, each with their own cemeteries and memorials, the likes of Festubert, Neuve Chapelle, Aubers Ridge and Fromelles.

What surprised us both, having found his resting place, was how emotional it was. Here lies a distant member of our family, someone we never knew, who had laid down his life for the benefit of future generations. Next to him lies a fellow comrade from his battery, who also died that day. It is of some small comfort to learn that he did not die alone and he is buried next to this fellow soldier who also was possibly his friend, both in all likelihood killed by the same German artillery shell. Driver Gillon died with James Willie Barker on March 22nd 1916.

It was very fitting to see that the cemetery was surrounded by a stone wall and sitting within a farmyard with cattle, chickens & sheep grazing. I could not help but think for James Willie that this *'squared the circle'* in that here he rested surrounded by livestock and a stone wall. A sense of closure that he could relate to, albeit not in his native Yorkshire but this time in a foreign field.

Having returned home I was also able to report our findings to Betty, my mother-in-law. I had previously not told her about the research and was able to present her with my findings complete with the photographs of our trip and James Willie's grave.

For Betty, this was totally unexpected but the outcome that it gave her was a sense of peace that she had not hankered for, but was nonetheless welcome to receive. At that point we realised that we were, in all likelihood, the only members of the family to visit his grave, which I suspect is the case for most families up until relatively recently. No startling revelations about James Willie's war record, no commendations or medals for bravery; really a typical example of a man *just doing his bit'*.

One thing the research managed to achieve was that it ignited my desire to learn more about the First World War. I then attended a series of lectures by the local Western Front Association which quite by accident triggered the foundation of the British Modern Military History Society.... squaring the circle for both me & James Willie Barker.

Historian Simon Jones has provided the transcript from the Coventry Standard of 22nd October 1915 about the miners working on the Western Front in the First World War. On the Western Front there was a 'war below ground' going on for much of the war, with both sides burrowing beneath each other's trenches to lay huge amounts of explosives to destroy their enemy above ground. They played an unseen game of 'cat and mouse' to try to locate the other side's mining activity, with on occasion hand to hand fighting taking place. British miners generally were recruited from the mining communities of Britain due to their experience of such work. The dangers for the tunnellers were huge and the effect of the enormous explosions was devastating for men, fortifications and equipment.

Miners as Tunnellers at the Front

A number of Warwickshire miners are doing valuable work at the front as tunnellers.

The first corps was formed at Rouen in July, and a further contingent left recently, gathered from the Nuneaton district by Mr H Phillips of Ansley Hall Colliery. Another contingent will shortly be sent out from the local coalfield, and this is being formed by Mr William Johnson jnr. son of the M.P. for the North-eastern Division of Warwickshire, and assistant secretary of the Miner's Association.

The depths of shafts and size of tunnels vary considerably, according to the nature of the soil, and also as to whether they are required for offence or defence. The mining system at the front is really like a huge octopus, with arms stretching out in all directions, and while the tunnellers are at work they can hear the enemy busy at the same time.

A great strain is put on the officers by this work, for they have to see that operations are conducted in such a quiet manner that not only shall the enemy not be able to hear them, but also that our area shall be able to locate the enemy.

It is remarkable how the ear gets trained to detect not only how far away the Germans are, but also how many picks are at work. It is a matter of great difficulty to dispose of the soil dug out in such a way that the enemy are not made aware of the extent of the operations. The system of mining and tunnelling is identical on both sides, and although the Germans may be better equipped with scientific instruments, our miners are better workmen than the enemy.

In an interview with Lieutenant Harold Milford of the 17th (Tunnelling) Company of the Royal Engineers (who is at present invalided at Nuneaton), a newspaper representative was told that there are many difficulties from water, gas fumes, etc. and our tunnellings are provided with air compressors and electric light.

It is not an unknown experience for the Germans to break into one of the Allies' workings, leading to an attack and counterattack, the fighting being as fierce as hostilities above ground. Sometimes, too, deadly gas hangs about in 'pockets', and several miners have been rather badly gassed.

Simon Jones was for sixteen years a curator at the Royal Engineers Museum and of the King's Regiment for National Museums Liverpool. He has been a freelance battlefield tour guide, lecturer and writer since 2004 and taught courses on the First World War for Liverpool and Lancaster Universities, and was a Guest Curator for English Heritage in 2014.

For more than a decade he has been researching the tunnelling at La Boisselle on the Somme and was lead historian for the exploration of the tunnel systems and surface archaeology at La Boisselle 2011-2015. He is the author of *Underground Warfare 1914-1918* (2010) and *World War I Gas Warfare Tactics and Equipment* (2007) as well as many articles on tunnelling, gas warfare and other First World War topics.

****

 *Kerri Statton from Tasmania, has kindly allowed us to publish a speech she gave at Zeehan in Tasmania to mark the centenary of her great grandfather Percy Statton being awarded the Victoria Cross. The local school invited Kerri to unveil "The Statton Garden" in 2018. Percy Statton served on the Western Front in the Great War with the 40th Battalion, AIF - an all-Tasmanian battalion - and won both the Military Medal and Victoria Cross. Kerri describes his background and life, his service and his actions that led to him being awarded the VC by King George V at Buckingham Palace. This is certainly a story of an ordinary man doing extraordinary things, both in war time and afterwards. Kerri has spent a life time researching the story of her great grandfather and devotes much of her time working with the Returned Serviceman's League, an organisation working with veterans.*

Sergeant Percy Clyde Statton VC MM
Background on the Victoria Cross

The Victoria Cross was instituted by Queen Victoria in 1856 in recognition of acts of extreme bravery during the grim Crimean war of 1854.

The Medal is designed in the shape of a Maltese Cross and cast from the metal of guns captured from the Russians during the Crimean War.

The Victoria Cross is the highest Commonwealth award for acts of bravery during military conflicts whilst in action.

Of the 101 Victoria Crosses awarded to Australians since 1900, 15 have been awarded to Tasmanians.

Percy's Family History

The Stattons were descendants of a mining family, who migrated to Ballarat. During the gold mining boom, they moved to Beaconsfield, Tasmania, where Percy was born on 21st October 1890 to Edward Statton, a miner and his wife Maggie. He was educated at Zeehan State School, before gaining employment as a farmer in Tyenna; he gave his age as twenty-one, to marry Elsie May Pearce on the 12th September 1907. He was in fact 17 years old, the couple later had a son and two daughters.

Despite his wife's disapproval, Percy enlisted in February 1916 and was assigned to the newly raised 40th Battalion, an all-Tasmanian manned Battalion. The Battalion embarked from Hobart aboard the troop ship Berrima on the 1st of July, bound for England. The troopship disembarked a little over seven weeks later, and the 40th Battalion spent the next three months training.

On the 23rd of November 1916, Percy embarked along with the rest of the 40th Battalion for France and the Western

Front four days later. The Battalion was transferred to Flanders in Belgium. Percy was promoted to Sergeant on the 26th of April 1917. In June, the 40th Battalion took part in the Battle of Messines.

Over a three day period during the engagement at Messines from the 7th to the 9th of June, Percy was placed in charge of supervising and leading ammunition carrying parties to the front-line. Throughout this work, he was subject to heavy German artillery and machine-gun fire, and on several occasions the party was decimated by shellfire. Despite this, the parties managed to reach the front-line on every occasion.

For his actions, Percy was awarded the Military Medal.

Western Front Deployment
On the 12th October 1917, Percy was involved in operations during the First Battle of Passchendaele when he suffered a serious gunshot wound to his right shoulder. First admitted to the 22nd General Hospital, Percy was then transferred to England, as the wound required special treatment.

Returning to duty, he was attached to the Overseas Training Brigade, prior to re-embarking on the 1st May 1918 for France, where he re-joined the 40th Battalion twelve days later.

While in action around the village of Villers Bretonneux on the 10th June 1918, Percy was wounded in a gas attack on his position. Initially admitted to the 10th Australian Field Ambulance (a Tasmanian unit) he was transferred to the 40th Casualty Clearing Station six days later.

Before returning to the 40th Battalion on the 24th June, he was attached to the American 3rd Battalion, 130th Regiment, for service over a seven day period later that month. He rejoined the 40th Battalion on the 27th July. It is not well known that Tasmanian infantry had trained Americans on *Battle Front Procedures* and trench warfare during the First War.

Percy's VC Actions

On the 12th August 1918, during the Battle of Amiens, a decisive turning point of the First World War, the 40th Battalion was tasked with the objective of seizing and holding a valley to the South of Proyart. At the same time, the 37th Battalion was to move through the village of Proyart itself, and proceed to a line just beyond the railway to the north of Proyart.

The 40th Battalion began its attack and by 8.30am had successfully advanced 800 metres. It was at this point, however, that the unit came under an intense barrage from German artillery, and were prevented from moving further forward. With assistance from a Lewis gun team under Percy's command, the Battalion's A Company managed to reach the centre of Proyart village an hour later.

At 6pm, the 40th Battalion received a message that the 37th Battalion was about to attempt to advance from the village to its own objective. From his position, Percy observed a line of German machine-gunners firing on the 37th Battalion and preventing its advance. He turned his Lewis guns on the Germans in an attempt to assist, but their attack failed. Thirteen men were assembled from 37th Battalion and rushed the position soon after, but the group was wiped out before they reached the first gun.

Percy, with Corporal Upchurch, Privates Styles and Beard, worked his way along under the cover of the road embankment. Reaching within 75 metres of the machine-gunners and armed with only a revolver, Percy led the three men as they rushed across the open ground towards the German strong point. Reaching the position, the party was able to dispose of the first gun and its crew before moving onto the second, where Percy personally shot four of the five crew members and bayoneted the fifth with the German's own rifle. Seeing this, the two remaining gun teams began to retreat but were killed by Percy's Lewis gunners.

Returning to their lines, another German machine gun opened up, killing Private Styles and wounding Corporal Upchurch. With Private Beard, Percy began to crawl back to his own lines, while the inspired 37th Battalion continued its advance and cheered the pair as they went past. Later that evening, Percy while under heavy machine-gun fire, went out and retrieved the badly wounded Upchurch and the body of Styles. By 8pm, both Battalions had reached and consolidated their positions, and were relieved by the British 17th Division the following day.

At 9am on the 27th September 1918, the 40th Battalion was ordered onto parade by the unit's Commanding Officer, Lieutenant Colonel John Lord. Addressing the assembled crowd, Lord announced that same day, the name of Sergeant Percy Statton would appear in the London Gazette announcing that he had been awarded the Victoria Cross.

Described by the Battalion's historian as a *'Reluctant Hero'*, Percy was granted three cheers before he was carried shoulder high through the ranks while the Battalion band played. The full citation for Percy's Victoria Cross appeared in a supplement to the London Gazette later that day.

In the words of Mr Frank McDonald MM, the last surviving member of the 40th Battalion; he said it was the most courageous action he had witnessed during the entire war and he should have been awarded two VCs.

I had the honour to meet Frank on his 100th birthday and we had many talks about the war years over the seven years of visiting him. I called him my surrogate great grandfather as he told me many stories of what Percy was like and they were close friends. To this day I still keep in touch with his niece Phyllis who looked after him and Margaret who is Private Beard's daughter.

His Majesty King George V presented the Victoria Cross to Percy in June 1919 at Buckingham Palace.

The Citation read:

War Office, 27th September 1918.

His Majesty the King has been graciously pleased to approve of the award of the Victoria Cross to the undermentioned Officers, NCOs and Men:

No.506 Sergeant Percy Clyde Statton, MM, AIF

For most conspicuous bravery and initiative in action when in command of a platoon which reached its objective, the remainder of the battalion being held up by heavy machine-gun fire. He skilfully engaged two machine-gun posts with Lewis gun fire, enabling the remainder of his battalion to advance.

The advance of the battalion on his left had been brought to a standstill by heavy enemy machine-gun fire, and the first of our assaulting detachments to reach the machine-gun posts were put out of action in taking the first gun. Armed only with a revolver, in broad daylight, Sergeant Statton at once rushed four enemy machine-gun posts in succession, disposing of two of them, and killing five of the enemy. The remaining two posts retired and were wiped out by Lewis-gun fire.

Later in the evening, under heavy machine-gun fire, he went out again and brought in two badly wounded men.

Sergeant Station set a magnificent example of quick decision, and the success of the attacking troops was largely due to his determined gallantry.

Later Life
From 20th October 1918 to September 1919 Percy was on special duties in France and England and during this time the Armistice was signed. Finally leaving England aboard

the troop ship, Percy arrived in Hobart on the 26th November 1919 and was discharged from the Australian Imperial Force in January 1920.

Elsie May, Percy's wife, true to her word did not wait for him. In their divorce hearing, the Judge was scathing of her, and placed their children in her mother's care: this was published in the Mercury at the time.

Following his discharge, Percy settled in Fitzgerald and worked in the timber industry, during this time he met and worked with Sergeant Stanley McDougall VC MM who was originally from Recherche,

On the 21st December 1925, he married Eliza Grace and built a home / general store at Tyenna.

In 1934, a devastating bushfire occurred in the Derwent Valley, Percy took a prominent role in the rescue work aiding families cut off by the fire. His actions are recorded in the book *Unsung Heroes.* Stanley McDougall was also involved in the fire.

In the late 1930s Percy and his wife were dancing at the Community Hall, which he loved to do, a fire broke out in the store, destroying their home and killing his step-daughter! Members of the 40th Battalion's Association and the Citizen Military Force helped to rebuild their home.

Percy's wife Eliza Grace died of cancer in 1945 and is buried at the Tyenna Cemetery.

During the Second World War, Percy enlisted for service and was commissioned as a Lieutenant.

He served through the war years with the 5th Battallion until his discharge in 1946.

After the Second World War, he worked for a while for Australian News Print Mill at Maydena as a cook in the single men's quarters. Among other things, he was responsible for providing morning tea for the bosses from Boyer but not the workers. Until one clever fellow blocked the flue of the wood fire oven and smoked them all out of the Mess Hall, from then on, they all had smokos. (*Editors' note: Percy was an ardent non-smoker*)

Percy finished with ANP and became a Commercial Agent and skin buyer, working from the town of Ouse.

In late 1946, he had a vehicle accident at New Norfolk, who was right or wrong, we probably will never know. Both he and the other driver got out of their cars quite irate, until they recognised each other, the other driver was Sergeant John Dwyer VC. Percy and John Dwyer became Local Council Aldermen, and Percy served on until his death.

In December 1947, Percy married Monica Kingston, they lived at Ouse. Monica was the mistress of the Ouse School.

In 1956, Percy was selected as one of the Australian Members to attend a Parade in London, to commemorate the centenary of the award of the first Victoria Cross.

On the 5th December 1959, Percy died of cancer; he was honoured with a full military funeral and his ashes are interred at Cornelian Bay Cemetery.

Frank McDonald said; '*He was one who believed that every*

soldier deserved a Victoria Cross and there was nothing special that he did that no-one else wouldn't have done'.

Percy's original medals are on display in the Hall of Valour at the Australian War Memorial.

There are several monuments named in his honour, such as a wing at the Royal Hobart Hospital, Ouse, Beaconsfield, Zeehan and the War Memorial in Hobart, also a building called *'The Statton Building'.*

****

 ***Roger Fowkes shares the memories of his aunt Madge, then aged 11, as a school girl in Rutland, when Zeppelins bombed their village in 1916.***

A Zeppelin Raid

Zeppelins are ships of war. They were first invented by Count Zeppelin after whom they are named. They come over to England in these Zeppelins and raid us, but their principal work is scouting. There are nine balloons so that if one is hit they can still travel along. Then there are some gondolas hanging from these balloons which the men and engines are in.

On Sunday night 1st October, the Zeppelins visited us. It was about 12 o'clock when they were first heard. It seems they had lost their way, and when they saw the woods, they thought it was a town so they dropped some bombs. No one was hurt and only a few panes were blown out of the windows. Many bombs were dropped and most of them exploded. There were 42 bombs dropped. The smell of the engines was awful. When they were first heard they were over Harringworth Woods. They then came zig-zag to Dudley's Field along the Weldon Road and dropped four bombs in it. They then came across the fields to the Lodges and dropped bombs. They then went across to the tunnel and when the gun at Corby started firing, they turned back and went over Uppingham. Many people were aroused but I slept through it all.

By Madge Fowkes, aged 11
Gretton County Primary School 1916

balloons so that if one is hit they can still
travel along. There there are some gondolas
hanging from these balloons which the [...]
and [...] an ex.

On Sunday night October the first the
Zeppelins [...] as it was about 12 o'clock
when they were first heard. It seems they
had lost their way, and when they saw
the woods they thought it was a town so
they dropped some bombs. No one was hurt
and only a few panes were blown out of

By Madge Fowkes, aged 11 Gretton County Primary School
1916.

Roger Fowkes collection

An unidentified Zeppelin airship comes in to land at its base
Friedrichshafen in Southern Germany, giving an idea as to the
size of these vast leviathans of the air, along with the need for
even larger specialised hangars to protect the airships from the
elements.

Nigel Parker collection

Air Raid...Take Cover!
Nigel Parker collection

In July 1916 40th Battalion (an all-Tasmanian battalion) embarked aboard the troop ship SS Berrima, bound for England.
Statton family archive

My Grandfather

More recently, my mother's father's father, Louis François Martinat (1893-1972), who was a blacksmith in Saint-Parize-le-Chatel (department 58, Nievre), having served during the First World War, was incorporated into the 1st Artillery Regiment the 27th November 1913. He was promoted to 'Brigadier' (corporal) the 3rd September 1914, *'marechal des logis'* (sergeant) the 8th October 1915. He was released on the 6th September 1919 and came back home.

During the war, he served sometimes as observer in the first line of infantry, and while he had to stay when the infantry went to attack German lines, he came with them and was one of the first into German lines.

He was called to the Order of his regiment (Order number 489) the 17th June 1917 for this and more of his actions during 19th, 29th and 30th April 1917. He was also called to the Order of the 8th Corps (Order number 337) on the 9th August 1918 for actions the 6th, 15th and 17th July 1918.

He was injured in his leg on the 29th October 1918 when he commanded an artillery piece from the 6th Battery of the 1st Artillery regiment but refused to be evacuated. For this, he was awarded the Military Medal the 4th November 1918 with this citation:

'Ordre N° 745, le Colonel commandant provisoirement la 16th Division d'Infanterie prononce par délégation la nomination et citation suivante pour faits de guerre :

Médaille Militaire. Martinat Louis François.

Au front depuis le début de la campagne, brave et dévoué, toujours volontaire pour les missions délicates et périlleuses.

S'est maintes fois distingué précédemment comme agent de liaison près de l'infanterie et comme observateur.

Blessé pendant l'attaque du 29eme octobre d'un éclat d'obus à la cuisse, est resté à son poste de chef de pièce et a continué sa mission; ne s'est fait soigné qu'après les tirs terminés et a refusé d'être évacué.

Le 4.11.19. Le Colonel commandant provisoirement la 16eme Division d'Infanterie.

signé : Santes Cottin (je ne suis pas sûr du nom, j'ai du mal à le lire sur le document que j'ai).'

Translated as:

'Order no 745, the Colonel temporarily in command of the 16th Infantry Division pronounces, by the authority vested in him, the following nomination and citation for acts of war:

Military Medal. Martinat Louis François.

At the front since the beginning of the campaign, brave and devoted, always volunteering for delicate and perilous missions. Has previously distinguished himself numerous times as infantry liaison officer and observer. Injured *during the attack of 29th October by a shrapnel wound to the thigh, he stayed at his post as a gunner and continued his mission, only accepting medical care when firing ceased, and refusing to be evacuated.*

4.11.19. The Colonel temporarily in command of the 16th Infantry Division.

Signed: Santes Cottin'

For his actions during the First World War, Louis François MARTINAT received the Legion d'Honneur the 23rd August 1971.

****

Local historian and researcher, Trevor Hancock describes an invaluable 'invention' used in great numbers to help wounded soldiers who had lost legs in the Great War.

The Wantage Crutch

Crutches have always been used in one form or another to help injured or ill people get around. The basic design of these aids has not changed since ancient times when those who needed crutches used branches of trees and added padding for underarm support for comfort.

The first commercially produced crutches appeared in the early 20th Century and one of these was the Wantage Adjustable Crutch. This was an adjustable crutch patented in 1916 by Dr William Dunmore Loveday, a retired Wantage doctor. These crutches were produced at five

50

shillings a pair (25 pence) and were built on the principle that the bodyweight should be supported by the hands and arms and not left to press upon the armpit.

The Wantage Crutch was in use throughout the country during the Great War 1914-1918 and was also supplied to French wounded soldiers. They were made in Wantage at the Crutch Works. This was the premises of Barlow Dobbs and Barlow builders and undertakers in Church Street, Wantage. The building is presently occupied by Knapps funeral directors. Brothers Harry and Frank Barlow had contracts with the War Office and the British Red Cross Society for over 1,000 crutches. In June 1916 they were employing around seven men producing 100 pairs a week for the war effort. Other local carpenters involved in producing the crutches included Harry Capel and Frank Heybourne. The crutches I have seen are individually numbered and the largest number seen so far is 57,836. Several thousand pairs of crutches were made during the First World War but the exact number is unknown.

Dr William Loveday was practising as a surgeon/doctor in Wantage at the beginning of the 20th Century. Born at Irthlingborough, Northamptonshire in 1864, he lived at Becket House in Wallingford Street with his wife Lilian (née Wix). By the time of the Great War he was retired; however in 1916 he was Medical Superintendent of St Katharines Red Cross Hospital in Wantage with over 500 patients. He was also a member or sometime Chairman for the local Tribunal for hearing recruiting cases under Lord Derby's Recruiting Scheme.

Awarded the Order of the British Empire (OBE) as designer of the Wantage Adjustable Crutch in the June 1918 Honours List, Dr William Dunmore Loveday OBE MRCS, LRCP finally retired to Eastbourne in the 1920s. His inventive mind continued and he patented a design for spring wire clips for using newspapers in 1931. He died on 13th April 1932 in Hartley Wintney Hampshire.

Research is still ongoing into this little-known story relating to Wantage in the First World War so if anyone can add to this, researcher Trevor Hancock would like to hear from them please.

****

Historian Simon Jones describes the terrifying ordeal of his great grandfather Sergeant Walter Stamper fighting near Ypres in Belgium in 1915 with the Canadian Light Infantry. He tells of his experiences including captivity as a POW in a letter home to his wife and daughter.

'We were simply blown to pieces'

In its first major battle, Princess Patricia's Canadian Light Infantry suffered eighty percent losses during fighting at Ypres. My great grandfather, No. 29 Sergeant Walter Stamper, survived but was taken prisoner. He described in a letter to his wife and daughter his experiences of battle, captivity and deliverance to Switzerland where he was interned.

'15th August 1916 My Darling Girls,

I hardly know how to write to you, I seem to have so much to tell you. I must start at the beginning and try to tell you my experiences in Germany. First of all, there was our capture, of course you know that was on the 8th May 1915. We were simply blown to pieces. There was just ten of us left in our Company, most of us unable to help ourselves; those that were too badly wounded to walk they shot and bayoneted them. Then, they made us lay on the ground beside them whilst they dug themselves in. All the time the shells and bullets were flying around us, and I can tell you I never expected to see any of you again. To amuse themselves they threw stones at us and called us swine. One of my men could not keep still as he was suffering so from a wound in the head; he got up and was promptly shot by them through the stomach he died about two hours later in great agony.

We laid there from ten o'clock in the morning until six at night when we were fetched into the trench and robbed of everything we had. We were then taken back and threatened if we did not give information about our troops we should be shot. We were lined up three times for that purpose. At last we reached Roullers [Roulers], where we were put into the church with a lot more of the 28th Division. We had nothing to eat from Friday night until Sunday morning, when they gave us some sourbread and a drink of water. At three o'clock they gave us a slice of raw bacon and put us on the train for Germany; at Courtran [Courtrai] the Belgians gave us a good

*meal of sausage, bread, butter and coffee; after that
we got nothing only kicks and went on until we
arrived at Giessen where the whole town turned out
to insult us.*

*We arrived in Giessen about 1 o'clock Tuesday
morning and then started our starvation diet, soup
made from maize, horse beans, chestnuts. We were
supposed to be getting meat but you could not find it
in your soup and the potatoes were so bad you could
not eat them. You can guess we were pretty well
starved until our parcels started to arrive.*

*Now that has all altered here in Switzerland, we are
practically free with the best of food and beds; we
are staying in hotels, you cannot realize the
reception we received; as soon as we crossed the
border it started, and it was nothing but one
triumphant journey until we arrived here. We were
smothered in flowers, chocolates, tobacco and
cigarettes. We stopped at all the principal stations en
route. We had a splendid breakfast at Montrean
[Montreux] and another here. I am feeling better
already and hope to be myself again. I will tell you
more next time you can write as often as you like
now, fondest love and heaps of kisses.
From Dad.'*

In 1917, judged to be of no military value, he was returned
to England for medical treatment. Even though he was by
this time 47 years of age, he sailed back to Canada and re-
enlisted at the first opportunity.

Diana Martin recounts the foundation of the TOC-H Organisation by Rev Neville Talbot, in memory of his brother Gilbert who was killed on the Western Front in 1915.

Lieutenant G Talbot Founder of 'TOC H'

Bishop Edward Stuart Talbot, Bishop of Winchester, Gilbert's father, lived at Farnham Castle from 1911-1924.

It was Talbot's tragedy not only to have to minister to his diocese during the First World War but bear the loss of a beloved son in that conflict. It is fitting that this loss led to the creation of an organisation that gave great solace and comfort to many servicemen over many years.

In 1912 at a time of international tension, Bishop Talbot preached a sermon appealing for moderation. War between England and Germany, he claimed, was unthinkable. Unfortunately, it was not. Talbot had three sons and when war came, all served. The Revds Neville and Edward Talbot volunteered as army chaplains and Gilbert Lyttleton Talbot, the youngest, applied for a commission in the Rifle Brigade. The Revd Neville Talbot was awarded the Military Cross and eventually became Bishop of Pretoria.

Three years after Talbot's optimistic sermon, on 31st July 1915, his son, Gilbert was killed. He was 23. Gilbert Talbot had been educated at Winchester and Christchurch (where he became President of the Oxford Union). In local circles, he was well known and liked, since he played for the Farnham Cricket Club and loved living at the castle. His life's ambition was to become Prime Minister and Harold Macmillan, who had a similar background, expressed the view that he might well have managed it. It was not to be. As a lieutenant in charge of a platoon of the 7th Rifle Brigade, he was ordered to take and hold a shell-crater in Flanders, and the whole platoon was virtually wiped out.

His death exemplified *'the futility of war'* of which Wilfred Owen wrote. Gilbert had just handed over his post to the 8th Battalion and marched his men back from a crater after a long and sleepless shift, when he was instructed to return immediately. The Germans, with their new weapon, flamethrowers, had incinerated the 8th. Divisional Headquarters demanded that there should be an immediate counter-attack. Gilbert waited in the cover of a wood until the appointed time, checked his watch, then cried to his men *'Come on my lads, this is our day'* and led his men out of the woods into machine-gun fire. Within seconds Gilbert was dead, the attack failed and scarcely one of his platoon survived. His batman confirmed that Gilbert had told him he knew the counter-attack was suicidal.

The Revd Neville Talbot, Gilbert's brother, resolved to recover his brother's remains. Against advice, he crept out of the far end of the trench as dusk fell, crawled through the grass on hands and knees, despite shells and snipers, dropping flat on the ground as the flares shot up from the German trenches. And at last, 30 yards away in the open, he located his dead brother. A week later, Neville and a volunteer stretcher party recovered the body. This he buried in a quiet cemetery under a wooden cross.

The sequel is quite widely known – how in December 1915, Neville founded a soldiers' institute in Poperinghe and named it *'Talbot House'* in memory of his dead brother. Led by the all but legendary Revd Tubby Clayton, it became a refuge for soldiers at the front. Talbot House was abbreviated by signallers to *'Toc H'*. In 1922 a branch of Toc H was formed in Farnham. At one of their first meetings, Bishop Talbot, then still at the castle, was elected father of the group.

There is a memorial plaque to Gilbert in the Bishop Morley's Chapel at Farnham Castle, a poignant memorial to this son at the castle. Bishop Talbot was profoundly grieved and he repeatedly sought to make over Farnham Castle to the government for use as a rehabilitation hospital, but military authorities who visited the castle, decided that adapting the place would prove too expensive.

Extract taken by kind permission of the author Roy Waight 'A Convenient Place' – A History of Farnham Castle and its Bishops.

Published 2020 by the Farnham and District Museum Society.

Although many people have written extensively over the years about the fortunes and mishaps of Farnham Castle, no one, as far as can be gathered, has written a detailed account of the history of the Castle, the Bishops who stayed there, and the relationships that have developed between the Castle and the town. This year (2020) local historian and Castle guide Roy Waight has introduced a new work which is now in print and available at Waterstones and Farnham Museum.

****

Andrew Hamilton, historian and author, describes the first day of the battle of the Somme on 1st July 1916 and the fate of one of the multitude of casualties, 2nd Lieutenant. Francis Hicking.

Silent Witness

One hundred years ago at 7.30 a.m. on 1st July 1916, whistles and bugles sounded the assault by British troops on the 17 mile German front line on the Somme, signaling the start of the most catastrophic day in British military history. The massive death toll was impossible for combatants and those at home to comprehend. Nearly 19,000 officers and men were killed, 7,000 of whom were identified and were mostly buried in the 49 cemeteries on the British front line.

In May 1922, during the 'King's Pilgrimage', George V visited a number of British cemeteries in France and Belgium. He was struck by the mind-numbing, serried ranks of graves and at Terlincthun British Cemetery was moved to comment in a speech, written by Sir Fabian Ware: *'In the course of my pilgrimage, I have many times asked myself whether there can be more potent advocates of peace on earth, through the years to come than this massed multitude of silent witnesses to the desolation of war.'*

When I was researching *Where are the Boys? The First Day of the Battle of the Somme* with Alan Reed, we stumbled on one such 'silent witness' in Fricourt New Military Cemetery where, soon after the battle started on 1st July, 134 soldiers of the West Yorkshire Regiment were mown down by machine-gun fire. They were buried virtually where they fell, in four mass graves. Only later were they allocated individual graves.

As we wandered round the cemetery, our attention was caught by something unusual: a photograph of a school cricket team taken outside a small Victorian wooden pavilion, was propped up against the gravestone of 2nd Lieutenant Francis Hicking. Serious and unsmiling, the 12 and 13 year old boys looked out at us, immaculately attired in their 'uniform' of long-sleeved white shirts, trousers, boots and hooped caps. There is something rather eerie and portentous about the photograph - in a few years' time the young cricketers' white uniform would be exchanged for khaki, and cricket balls replaced by grenades.

Which boy, we wondered, was 2nd Lieutenant Francis Joseph Hicking of the 10th West Yorks - a mere 19 years old when he was killed? Which school were they representing and how many other boys caught on camera would die in the service of their country?

We found that Francis Hicking was one of six of the boys in the photograph who later died in the War. He was born on 20th May 1897 - his parents, Joseph and Kate were grocers and wine merchants, firstly at Ruddington in Nottinghamshire and later in Cheltenham. They sent Francis and his older brother George away to Bramcote Preparatory School in Scarborough where Francis loved playing cricket and football despite being cruelly castigated in one of his school reports by a critical schoolmaster: *'Kicking jolly bad: no dash: turning his back and funking.'* He left Bramcote when 13 to attend Uppingham School and within a year of leaving, had volunteered to join Lord Kitchener's New Army that was recruited in huge numbers during the autumn of 1914.

It is extraordinary to think of a such an innocent young man, with scarcely any experience of life, arriving on the Somme in charge of a platoon of about 50 men, many considerably older than himself and then at 7.30 a.m. on 1st July leading them into an unexpected hail of machine-gun fire, without, one suspects, any outward signs of 'funk' as he strove to set an example to his men.

Francis's brother George was a lieutenant in the 8th York and Lancasters. He too was killed on the same day not far from where Francis fell.

The Hickings' parents received the news of George's death fairly soon but they did not learn of Francis's fate for an agonising two weeks. It is impossible to imagine the suffering, faced for the rest of their lives, by the Hicking boys' parents and those of the other five boys in the photograph.

At least Joseph and Kate Hicking had one grave to help the grieving process, a tangible memorial to visit after the War. George's body, however, was never recovered and he is listed on the panels of the Thiepval Memorial to the *'Missing of the Somme'*, one of 72,000 British soldiers with no known grave. Of that number, there are 12,000 names of soldiers who were killed on what Major Alfred Plackett of the 12th York and Lancasters described as *'that awful day'* on 1st July 1916, an extraordinary statistic that emphasises the brutality of the fighting and the failure of the strategy employed.

From *Where are the Boys? The First Day of the Battle of the Somme* by Andrew Hamilton and Alan Reed.With thanks to Peter Wilkinson of Bramcote School, Scarborough

American, Jim Mockford describes the stories of his two English great uncles 'Jack' Mockford and Herbert Mockford in the Great War including serving on the Somme in July 1916.

Great Uncles on the Western Front

My father, Roger Julian Mockford was the first American born in 1924.

Eighty years later as I accompanied my father to Battle of the Bulge Association meetings I learned and became interested in the story of my two English great-uncles, John Benjamin (Jack) Mockford and Herbert Mockford who served in the British Army and fought in The First World War, a war they called The Great War, and a war in which one of them, Herbert Mockford, gave his life in battle at The Somme.

I remember my grandmother Frances Mockford was very much against that war and that she wrote letters to the newspaper with her strong opinions about war. I could not have known at that age that my grandmother's opinion was very much shaped by having lived through two world wars in which all three of her sons served in the United States military during the Second World War and that she and the family had grieved upon hearing of the loss of Herbert and the news of the deaths of other young men in both wars. Uncle Jack fought in both wars. It was said that he had come back from the First World War a shell-shocked and a changed man but was able to return to his career in accounting and family life. Then he returned to serve in the

Second World War that brought its horror to another generation as well as those who had survived the First World War.

On 3rd September 1914, Herbert readily enlisted in the army on his 19th birthday. Herbert was assigned to the 7th Middlesex Regiment, 3rd Platoon and by February 1915 was in Gibraltar with the regiment. Jack enlisted on 5th December, 1914 in the London Regiment (13th) and later the 15th London Regiment.

The Battle of the Somme began on 1st July, 1916 and the most significant combat experience for their cousin David Jones was the battle at Mametz Wood that took place July 7-11th when his battalion, the Royal Welch Fusiliers suffered its first casualties. The initial assault by the 38th Welsh Division was unsuccessful as the Prussian Guards continued to hold the woods but on the 10th of July the battle turned in their favor despite the loss of about 4,000 casualties for the division. Out of David's battalion of about 800 men a loss of 251 men and 12 officers were counted on 11th July 1916.[48] The toll of shell shock could not be counted as there were many like David Jones who never really recovered from the experience of war.

In 2016, I travelled to Mametz Wood where today there is a magnificent statue of a Welsh Dragon as a memorial to the men from the 38th Welsh Division who gave their lives in the battle. The area near Albert in France has numerous cemeteries with thousands of graves from The Battle of the

---

[48] Bell, Ian, 'In Parenthesis' Program by the Welsh National Opera for the performances at the Royal Opera House, London, June 29th and July 1st, 2016

Somme. Not far from Mametz Wood we found the cemetery at Combles where Herbert Mockford was buried during the third phase of the Battle of the Somme, after the bloody offensive between the villages of Flers and Courcelette that took place in September, 1916.

Herbert Mockford had travelled with the 7th Middlesex Regiment to Gibraltar and Egypt in 1915 and he finally arrived in France in May 1916. It is unknown to what extent he had information about the location of his cousin David Jones in The Somme and whether Jones had survived the mid-summer offensive. Herbert's Middlesex Regiment by September 1916 was at Ginchy, a village on a hill that overlooks the town of Combles to the southeast and sits on a strategic junction of roads that the British Army would need to take to lead north. The next objective after having taken Ginchy was to advance to Flers in the following week.

The attack that was launched on 15th September 1916 was the beginning of the third phase of the Battle of the Somme and began with nearly one million rounds of frightening artillery bombardment and like the earlier phases of the war the effect of this intense barrage resulted in '*shell shock on men in combat*'[49].

The British Army had been developing a new secret weaponized vehicle that they called the 'Land Battleship.' Among those on the 'Landship Committee' and overseeing the tank development project was a man named Winston Churchill. The vehicle was sent to be tested in war in the

---

[49] Downing, Taylor, 'Breakdown: The Crisis of Shell-Shock in The Somme' (Little, Brown 2016).

slowly moving advance in The Somme in 1916. Herbert Mockford was among those soldiers carrying a rifle who moved out with the regiment in this attack where for the first time in war tanks fought in battle. As it turned out many of the vehicles broke down, became stuck in trenches, or moved so slowly that the tank crews began to succumb to the fumes in the hot and confined space of their cockpit before they could reach their objectives. The new weapon initially confounded or frightened the Germans until they observed difficulties in the operation and planned counterattacks. The surprise weapon may have also bolstered the confidence of British infantry such as Herbert Mockford who on the following day of 16th September was killed in action.

Sometime later that autumn, his family in London was informed of his death but I did not know where his older brother John Benjamin III (Jack) Mockford was located at that time. A service document shows that the brothers may not have been too far away from each other, or if Jack was on duty with the 15th London Regiment in combat in September 1916.

In 2016 as the Centenary of The Great War was remembered in London, my wife and I attended the performance '*In Parenthesis*', the opera adapted by Ian Bell of David Jones's 1938 award winning epic poem about World War I. We met my second cousin, a granddaughter of Jack Mockford and the great niece of David Jones at Covent Garden and saw the magnificent performance at the Royal Opera House that presented a story that took David Jones twenty years to write about his experience at Mametz Wood. The following week we visited Mametz Wood and I found the grave of Herbert Mockford. As we returned home from our Centenary of the Somme tour, I felt that I had achieved my goal of learning more about my *'Great Uncles in The Great War'* and the family connection to their famous cousin. I was grateful that Sarah Williams, great niece of David Jones (my fourth cousin) welcomed us to her home to talk about our family story and encouraged us to join her at the opera.

On Herbert Mockford's memorial card it is noted that he *'fell in the Advance on The Somme (near Leuze Wood) with the date 16th September 1916,* below which is a poem (uncredited) that reads as follows:[50]

> *'One gift he had, one royal gift he gave;*
> *A gift that meant for him the summer sun;*
> *Youth's glorious hopes, the lover's ecstasy,*
> *Life's fair adventure, scarcely yet begun.*
>
> *Ever for him, Life's brilliant banners wave,*
> *Borne on the breeze of youth's courageous spell,*
> *He shall not know the weary bitterness*
> *That haunts old age. He slumbers but too well.*
> *'One gift he had, one royal gift he gave,*
> *Proud to exchange it for a soldier's grave.'*

---

[50] Mockford Family photo album and posted online at http://www.inmemories.com/Cemeteries/comblescomext.htm. Photographs from Jim Mockford Family Album and Collection.

Ray Edwards tells of his maternal grandfather, Charles Lewis, who served on the Western Front throughout the First World War, before being taken as a POW by the Germans in March 1918.

Charles Thomas Lewis 1895 - 1981

16035 Lance Corporal, A Coy 1st Battalion, King's Shropshire Light Infantry

Charles Thomas Lewis, my maternal grandfather, was born in Laugharne, Carmarthenshire, Wales. He was the youngest of four brothers who all served during the First World War, although in different branches of the armed services, but more importantly all of them survived.

The eldest, David John 'Affy' Lewis had been in the Navy since 1902. When war broke out, he was a gunner on board the dreadnought, HMS *St Vincent*, and saw action at the Battle of Jutland.

At the outbreak of war, the King's Shropshire Light Infantry (KSLI) were on duty in Tipperary, Ireland and returned via Pembroke Dock to join the 6th Division on the Western Front. The KSLI set up recruiting offices en route. Affy's duties at the time were guarding Pembroke Dock against German attack. By this time he was a sergeant and tried to persuade brother Charlie to join him. My grandfather, keen to get into action, signed up with the KSLI. The earliest picture of my grandfather in uniform has 'Pembroke Dock' stamped on the reverse. When he went up to Copthorne Barracks, Shrewsbury, for his basic training, he was asked if he could shoot. Having grown up on a farm, he answered by scoring 10 out of 10 and was designated as a *'first class shot'*.

As he was just shy of his 19th birthday, at that stage of the war he was not allowed to go and join the battalion at the front. He was offered further training as a sniper or a machine gunner. My grandfather opted for the latter as it paid an extra sixpence a day. His certificate of employment shows that he was qualified on the Maxim, Vickers and Lewis machine guns.

He was sent to France to join A Company, 1st Battalion, KSLI. He arrived on 7th July 1915, along with 22 other machine gunners on the day Lord Kitchener inspected the battalion in the square at Poperinghe. He was part of a Vickers gun team and first saw action in the battle of Hooge, on 9th August. Hooge is a small village on the Menin Road about two miles east of Ypres. The chateau and stables were a German stronghold and the target of the attack. The support positions were set up near Zouave and Sanctuary Woods. The Vickers gun teams provided covering fire. The attack was successful and Lord Plumer, the Army Commander, congratulated the battalion on their success and gallantry at Hooge.

Affy was involved in other actions in the 'Salient' during the Second Ypres. At some point during this period he received a 'chit' granting seven days leave starting immediately. Soldiers would often arrive home filthy, lousy and exhausted. Men going home on leave were to carry rifles with their kit to show that they had arrived from the front. He was the first soldier from Laugharne to return from the front. So much fuss was made of the event, as the first returning soldier, that his equipment, gun and 'boots still caked with Flanders mud' were proudly displayed on the town square for all to see.

You can see that on a family picture that wire and stiffener had been removed from his cap, which soldiers at the front would do to 'soften' the outline and be less of a target.

On his return to the battalion, he was promoted to Lance Corporal. By this time the specialist Machine-Gun Corps was formed. Although he was invited to join the corps, he declined and preferred to remain with his pals in the battalion. He duly became Corporal Lewis, A Company's Lewis gunner.

Fortunately, my grandfather was not present for the first day of The Somme battle, but by mid-August was in place to take part in the attack on Morval. According to the battalion war diary, on reaching their last objective: Morval Mill, the battalion were to push forward strong patrols backed with Lewis guns to push the retreating Germans towards the Guards at Les Boeufs. He was wounded on or about 25th September 1916, and his name appeared on the casualty lists after that date. He was treated for his wound in Rouen Military Hospital. His wound was not sufficiently serious for him to be sent back to England, and so he returned to the battalion. He did however miss the next battle where the 1st KSLI were involved – the battle of Transloy Ridge. If he had been there, he would have been fighting alongside his next eldest brother, Frank, who was a Lance Sergeant with the 17th King's Liverpool Regiment. This was one of the last battles of the Somme campaign.

In April 1917, the battalion were in the front line between Loos and Hulluch. During one of their trench raids my grandfather came back with a German prisoner and the mirror he had been holding up as a periscope. The German did not put up a fight and gave my grandfather the mirror, willingly returning with him to the British lines. He was quite chatty and told my grandfather that he was a waiter in a hotel in Liverpool before the war. His brother Frank would have probably understood the 'scouse accent' a bit better though.

By October, the battalion was preparing for the battle of Cambrai, which my grandfather insisted on pronouncing '**Cambria**' – '*well it sounded more Welsh*'. His battalion's position was on the east side of the St. Quentin Canal, east of Marcoing. As the Germans planned to stage a major counter attack, the battalion received orders to withdraw to the west bank of the canal. My grandfather's company and one other provided 4 Lewis gun crews each with rifle grenadiers to hold off the German advance, and allow the battalion's withdrawal. By now the bridges on either side of their position were all but destroyed. The battalion and brigade war diaries state: '*After fighting a desperate but gallant rear-guard action, the battalion managed to extricate itself, with many officers and men having to swim the canal to safety*'.

On 21st March 1918, the 1st Btn KSLI were holding the ridge between Noreuil and Lagnicourt. Platoons from A, B, and C companies were disposed along the front in posts consisting of 8-10 men, some 70 yards apart. German intelligence had identified the section as one of the weaker points in the line and sent their storm troop detachments to break through after the initial bombardment. The German offensive began just before 5am with an intense bombardment which lasted for five hours. The KSLI positions were overrun by the enemy, who were using the fog-filled valley as cover. A and B companies were almost annihilated in the first hour and a half and by 7am the enemy were through.

This was one event that my grandfather would not talk about. My mother told me that all his pals (i.e. his Lewis gun section) were 'blown to bits'. Indeed, my grandfather's post was hit by a gas shell and his team of seven men were killed outright. In this sector the Germans were using heavy ordnance (4 parts phosgene gas: 1 part of high explosive). My grandfather was wounded in the leg by a fragment from the gas shell casing. By some sort of miracle, he was 'swept up' by the advancing German second wave and taken to a casualty or dressing station in Lagnicourt.

The Germans had organised their rail system to link the front line with their cities in Germany, and as luck would have it, he was put on a hospital train and found himself in a military hospital in Berlin. As a result of the poison his leg had swollen to twice its normal size and a junior was planning to amputate the leg diagnosing gas gangrene. Fortunately, a senior surgeon saw the wound and said that there was no need to amputate. He had recognised the symptoms of gas poisoning and treated him accordingly, thereby saving the leg. Whilst in hospital he was befriended by a nurse from Saxony who could speak English. She was able to relate the above story. After a period of recovery, my grandfather was sent to Parchim, a prisoner of war camp in the Mecklenburg area of north Germany.

British POWs held in north Germany were repatriated via Denmark and the Baltic ports in an operation known as the 'Danish Scheme'. My grandfather said that his ship left Danzig, and they sailed through the Skagerrack and Kattegat Straits, heavily mined by the Germans, and with two Danish sharpshooters on the bows of the ship, popping off the mines one by one to the cheers of the Tommies aboard.

The ship docked at Hull, and soon after a check-up at the army camp at Ripon for liberated POWs, he returned to his beloved Wales – to the joy and relief of the whole family.

The last of the brothers to return was Frank. Having returned to England 28th June 1918, he probably thought his war was over. However, on 11th October 1918 he sailed from Glasgow for service in north Russia where his battalion was part of an allied intervention force assembled to support the 'White Forces' in their civil war against the Bolsheviks. The battalion spent the time in Archangel.

During the Second World War my grandfather worked in a steel foundry making shell casings as well as mysterious looking metal components, which turned out to be sections of the Mulberry Harbour used on D-Day.

He always used to say that his mother lived till she was 86, and he was determined to live to that age. He died of pneumonia in Llanelli hospital, at the age of 86, on Christmas day 1981.

David John Lewis had been in the Navy since 1902. When war broke out, he was a gunner on board the dreadnought, HMS *St. Vincent* and saw action at the battle of Jutland.

Edwards family archive

Alfred 'Affy' Lewis (one of four brothers to serve in the First World War) pictured in the uniform of the Royal Marines Light Infantry.

Edwards family archive

Daisy Dobbs was a remarkable lady. She signed up with the Territorial Forces Nursing Service (TFNS) in December 1914 and served throughout the First World War. She had already been awarded the Military Medal following her rescue of patients at 29th Field Hospital in Salonika in Greece after an air raid. This in spite of considerable wounds she had incurred. However, on a trip home on leave in August 1918, she was sailing from Le Havre, when her ship Warilda was torpedoed. Daisy in her own words describes her memories and experiences. By kind permission of Geoff Botting, grandson of Daisy Dobbs.

'Warilda' Torpedoed 3rd August 1918

We had come from Salonika on leave, after two years, over land through Greece, then crossing from Itea to Italy and through France, the scenery was very interesting and so refreshing after the sun scorched land of Salonika. At Le Havre we boarded the *Warilda*, an Australian boat, which was to take us to Southampton.

When we arrived onboard, we found out that two VADs (Voluntary Aid Detachment nurses) were making their way home from France, and Mrs Long, Commander of the WAACs (Woman's Auxiliary Army Corps) and her orderly. We consisted of two sisters of the TFNS and myself, making a. number of seven altogether.

After dinner we went to see the wounded officers and men to help them talk, Oh… what an interesting time we had, the thrilling adventures which made us glow with admiration and filled us with a longing to do more for these men who willingly gave their lives for us.

How time flies; we helped fix life belts until the signal for 'lights out' made us seek our cabin, up till now we had moved very slowly, because of it being light, now we were going at a good speed, although cautiously, and we retired with glorious thoughts of tomorrow when we should see England again.

We were awakened by two terrible crashes and we felt the ship vibrating violently, the sound of running feet, and someone opened our cabin door and said, '*To your boat at once sisters, we have been torpedoed*'. We were so sure that nothing would happen that we had put on our night attire, now there was no time for dressing, only our life belts fixed on, and we made our way to our boat which had been pointed out to us the previous evening. It was so dark that we could not see, only felt some hands passing us along, while the wounded men who could help themselves lined ready to get into their boats, the stretcher cases were in the hands of the Medical Officers and the orderlies under their supervision did splendid work, everyone gave us a cheery word as we passed, even in this critical moment they never forgot, there was no panic, everyone remained cool and helped by being alert.

There only being seven women, we did not delay the rescue work which went on around us as we got into our boat, but I soon lost sight of my friends as the boat became full of wounded men. I had slipped down into the bottom of the boat to make more room, but, unfortunately it being dark I was not seen and several men walked over me, not anyone's fault, but we were overcrowded.

The boat was then lowered and should have been struck

away, but no hatchet was available, and to our dismay the plugs had been forgotten and we were taking on water quickly. Being at the bottom of the boat and not being able to move I had a very unpleasant experience, but I must have lost consciousness, for a time, for the next thing I remember was feeling myself choking with the saltwater and struggling I knew there was no chance of being saved for all the boats would be filled with wounded and other survivors, so I resigned myself hoping it would not be long.

I felt myself coming to the top, yet being drawn towards something which I found out to be the small boat upside down, the waves were very strong and dashed me against the sides unmercifully, this, with the terrible cries of the men and women in the water was horrifying, then I sank once more, not to a great depth but far enough to become exhausted with the choking of salt water and the continuous struggle. A ghastly scene was ever before me of persons floating about, and if you came too near they would clutch at you for help, this as well helped to rob you of your strength. Once more I came to the top and received the same treatment as before; how I longed to die and escape those terrible cries, as I went down again, I was sure that it would be the last time as my strength was nearly gone and everything was so hazy. Yet again I came to the top and soon I realised that I was a long way off from the boat which I could faintly see as I floated towards her, but to my horror I saw another small boat making its way towards me, and remembering *my* previous treatment I was terrified, and put out my hand to ward it off, I did not realise that the boat was the right way up and there might be a chance of being saved. There was somebody in the boat that saw me, they caught hold of my hand and tried to pull me in for I could not do much, and to make matters worse somebody caught hold of my foot, it seemed impossible to me, but my rescuer spoke cheerfully to me and after a short time my foot was released and I was lifted into the boat.

They looked but could find no trace of any other victim. When they discovered that I was a woman by my attire they hunted among the other survivors for some extra clothing, but everyone was so scantily clothed so we made the best of it. Beside myself, there was a VAD and a WAAC, about ten wounded men and two sailors in charge of the boat, the other women we thought were drowned, but we heard later that they were picked up in another smaller boat. As we put off several cries followed us and our sailors did much rescue work, they never ignored a cry for help, and if the waves took them away again the rescuers always gave them a cheery word. It took much time and hard work to get the boat away from the suction. Many of the wounded offered to help them but they always refused with a smile and said they were doing fine. We had been in the boat some time when the oarsmen recognised a cry for help. They made towards the sound and after many difficulties rescued one of their officers, and you could tell he was a favourite. After a short recovery he took another oar and we began to feel less doubtful.

Several depth charges were set off which made us feel very uncomfortable. We had a lantern and some matches but we dared not show it because of the submarine, this meant, although we had sighted several destroyers, we had lost them owing to not being able to show a light.

We had been in the boat about two hours, the waves were so strong that at times it seemed that we should be capsized, and we were all feeling very depressed and there was no sign of being rescued, when one boy in the boat tried to cheer us by singing, he did not fail entirely, soon we were all joining in. We stopped as suddenly as we had started for someone had sighted a destroyer, our only chance was to show a light and hope that we should be seen. The light was shone and we discovered that she was making straight for us and if something wonderful did not happen we should be cut into for we could not escape her. We knew what our fate would be so we waited, and to our great joy she just turned in time and the oarsmen heard a voice calling to us to catch the rope, unfortunately we missed it owing to the dashing of the waves, then we made off for the starboard side and very soon our boat was tied. The destroyer was informed that there were women on board and we were given the first chance although we would have liked to have taken our turn. The waves were so strong that they lifted our small boat up level with the destroyer and we were helped over, and each one had to wait till the waves gave him his chance of boarding.

Here we were served with cocoa and brandy to revive us, then we were taken to the Captain's cabin where we found a Tommy with a fractured femur, already reposing on the bed were a number of orderlies who told us the news. Every article of clothing that could be collected was given us although some of the Tommies had very little, some only possessed the blanket that was given them when they boarded the destroyer. We were pleased to hear that the destroyers came almost immediately the signal for help was given and within half an hour six hundred cases were saved. A sad fate awaited the boys on the lower deck; the torpedoes, (for we were struck twice) had blown away the gangways so that no help could reach them, ladders could not reach down and every effort failed, a number of engineers volunteered to stay behind although they knew that it meant death. About one hundred were lost. These men who were trapped were convalescent, and although eye cases were able to help themselves the water rushed in and they were drowned. We were warned that a number of depth charges were to be sounded, the shock was severe, but we consoled ourselves thinking that we had sunk the Hun. We stopped again to take on board some more survivors, and to our delight we found our friends and listened to their terrible experiences. We were sorry to hear that our friend Mrs Long had been drowned trying to jump from the *Warilda* into the small boat and falling between, became entangled in the ropes; every effort was made to release her but when the ropes tightened, she must have collapsed and was drawn under by the suction. The *Warilda* remained afloat for two hours, and two destroyers did try and tow her along but eventually she exploded and took the destroyers with her. We did not hear of the Captain's rescue till several days afterwards, but as far as we know all the engineers went down.

The cabin became very hot as there were so many of us in it, and the sailors were exceedingly attentive to all our wants, every wish of the Tommy was gratified as far as possible. We were glad when the port holes could be opened and the first glimpse of land was such a joy. Southampton was reached about 8.30 a.m. and we received a warm welcome from some soldiers who were waiting to embark and partly understood what had occurred by our attire. To Netley Hospital we were taken and received every attention. After a medical examination we were given permission to travel.

Here arose a difficulty which had to be faced, we had lost everything we possessed, the sisters understood and we were soon dressed for travelling. Although much bruised and stiff we enjoyed our short leave, and now the past is being forgotten and we start again.

Yours obediently,

DE Dobbs

As a foot note to this story, her future husband George Botting whilst serving on the Western Front in 1915 was also awarded the Military Medal – perhaps the only occasion in the First World War when a husband and wife couple both received such an honour, albeit not married at the time of the awards.

****

Carole Sach spent many years researching her paternal grandfather, William Pritchard, and his involvement in the First World War. Meeting considerable reticence from her parents while they were alive, Carole was able to increase her pursuit of the truth with the arrival of the internet. With little information to go by, Carole with dogged determination, was able to discover the sad details of her grandfather through Australian service and pension records. Many Australians died alongside William Pritchard at Gallipoli in 1915. Almost exactly 100 years later, Carole was able to visit the battlefield where her grandfather fell.

My Journey to Gallipoli

When I was growing up I always knew that my paternal grandfather had died in the First World War; my father was completely unapproachable about the subject so it was down to my mother to tell me that '*Your grandfather was killed at the Battle of the Somme, he joined the Australian Army, and dad and my grandmother received a pension from the Australian Government after he was killed. He has no grave as he was blown to pieces.*' '*Oh*' I would say, '*... perhaps one day we could visit the Somme and see grandad's memorial plaque*'. She would shake her head '*... no, it is out of the question, your father would not want to go*'. As I was growing up, the retort from my mother, when I misbehaved would be '*Well I don't know where you get your ideas from, certainly not my side of the family; you must get them from your father's side*'. I used to wonder who was my father's side of the family, so once again questions were asked, and my mother would reply '*oh there was a family row between your nanny and your great* *grandparents, and your father never saw his father's family again. Your dad was very small at the time and was very scared so went and hid' and that was that!'*

All I knew was that he had to have lived in the East End of London, as nanny came from that area. She did tell me once that when my father was small, he said that he used to think that perhaps his father had suffered from *'shell shock'* and in error gone back to live in Australia, and one day he would remember them and come back and find them and everything would be all right.

The years went by, my father died in 1983; my life continued as lives do, but sometimes I would ask myself, who was my grandfather? I knew his name, William Pritchard – the same name as my father but that was it, just a name.

Then along came the Internet and with it the ability to search the First World War records, so off I started my research. First, I tried the Commonwealth War Graves Commission 'Debt of Honour' web site. There were lots of Pritchards, but none killed on the Somme. There was one killed at Gallipoli, but the next of kin was wrong, I was looking for my grandmother Ada Pritchard. Many long nights followed, coffee made by my husband Steve left to go cold, and then I would give up for a few months. When I looked at my father's family tree, it was just my father and my grandmother and his half-sisters. His mother (my grandmother) had remarried in the 1930s but there was no father for my father, and then I would start searching again. I would sit down at my computer and say, '... right grandad tonight I am going to find you' then nothing.

The search went on in this way for five years. I emailed the Australian authorities but they said they had no record of the pension. I even started to wonder did this man ever exist, but he had to have existed. Talking to the family, no one knew anything, my three aunts in Australia knew nothing. However, I never gave up hope of finding him. I tried birth records, but there was the problem of trying to find someone with the name of William Pritchard when you are not quite sure when or where they were born, and there were a great many people with the same name. I also looked for the record of his marriage to my grandmother, but found nothing. I was actually starting to feel quite down, but always in the back of my head was the War Pension from Australia, so they had to be married.

Then one night I was sitting there staring at the census records yet again, and I realised that I was looking at things the wrong way round. I should be looking for my grandmother marrying my grandfather, and 'bingo' the first search up came the record of their marriage. Overjoyed, I immediately sent away for the marriage certificate and waited - it seemed to take ages to arrive!

The marriage certificate arrived and I found out that my great grandfather was called James and that my grandfather lived before his marriage at Quins Buildings, Russia Lane, Bethnal Green, London. If I said it once I must have said it a hundred times that night to my husband '... *did you know that my great grandfather was called James?*' - he would just smile and nod.

I was getting so frustrated I emailed everyone on a web site who had a William Pritchard born in London, hoping that I may not have the full story, but perhaps they might have any information. Most people responded, but of course it was all negative, so when I had the wedding certificate and knew who my great grandfather was, I started emailing everyone again, and that is when I got the reply back from one lady and she explained that I needed my grandfather's birth certificate as I now had my great grandfather's name, I could send for this birth certificate.

There were four William Pritchards born around the time of my grandfather, so I was able to fill in *'fathers name'*, emails came back saying not this one and then finally an email to say your certificate is on its way. It finally arrived and gave my great grandmother's name as Ellen Bret and that my grandfather was born in Brick Lane, London. I emailed back this lady and within about half an hour she came back and said *'hello cousin'*. I was over the moon, she said she had wondered because my father's full name was William Joseph Pritchard and she was descended from grandad's youngest brother Joseph. I then explained to her about my grandfather but she did not have any information either but she said she would try and help me as I had made her curious. So in the space of 2-3 weeks I knew the names of my great grandfather and my great grandmother, I knew where my grandparents had married, I knew where they both lived before they were married, and from this relationship I found all of the names of my grandfathers, brothers and sister, James Pritchard, Lilly Pritchard, then my grandad William Pritchard, Joseph Pritchard and finally Rose Pritchard (there were also recorded several deaths of babies who did not make it). My father's side of the tree was now getting full, but there was still the question of grandfather's death in the First World War.

Later that day the family member that I had found emailed with a link to the Australian Service records and said when she did she found the next of kin 'James Pritchard' crossed out and in red ink *'Ada Pritchard'* added. I then went through the documents that she had found on line for me and on page 25, there it was, Widow Ada Pritchard, dependent William Joseph Pritchard (my father). It even told me how much pension they received, which was £1 every other week for my father and £2 every other week for my grandmother, so why did she tell my mother that my grandfather was killed at the Somme 1916, *'that is family business'* and was the subject of a very awkward conversation between myself and my aunts in Australia (they are in fact my half aunts but as far as I am concerned they are my aunts). I just sat looking at the screen it had been there all the time, but of course how was I to know, I must be honest I cried, really cried tears of joy, I had done it, I had found him, but I knew very little about Gallipoli. But before I go any further I would like to introduce you to my grandfather.

He was 5ft 4in tall (not very tall, but one must remember that a lot of people were malnourished in those days), he weighed 10 stone 6lbs, he had a dark complexion, his hair was dark, his eyes were brown and he had tattoos on both forearms and right upper arm as well (oh dear, sorry but tattoos, how could you grandad!)

He was born in Brick Lane London in 1890. He was 25 years old when he joined the 4th Battalion, AIF (yes, this was the Battalion that went on the rampage in Cairo!) and served in 'D' Company. He enlisted at Liverpool Camp, New South Wales on 6th November 1914 and left Sydney on the HMAT *Seang Bee* for Egypt, as a 2nd Reinforcement, on 11th February 1915. This was the day before my father's 1st birthday. He left Alexandria on 5th April 1915 on T.S.S. Lake Michigan for Gallipoli. He was killed between 6th-9th August 1915 during the attack on Lone Pine, and is commemorated on the Lone Pine Memorial. There was a Court of Enquiry at a place called Fleurbaix, France, which confirmed his death in action but when I asked the Australian Government if they had the papers, they said unfortunately they have no other papers on my grandfather.

I have no pictures of him at all, no diaries nothing as I said above all I had was a name.

The Attestation Papers give his occupation as a farm labourer, but on the Marriage Certificate to my grandmother he is what we today would call a french polisher. In fact according to my relative, all the men in that family worked with wood and still do today.

It is unclear whether my grandfather travelled to Australia to enlist – certainly I was told this by my mother '... he joined the Australian Army because they paid better than the British Army, and if he was killed, then my grandmother also got a better pension' - and one must remember that £6 a month in 1915/16 was a lot of money in those days. However, he could have gone to Australia in 1914 to seek a new life and employment on the land, but war upset his plans. My feeling is that he intended that my grandmother and my father would settle in Australia with him, I suppose the thought of a bright new future in Australia was very appealing. The family row, oh well that was because his father, James Pritchard wanted some of the pension money! It is unclear why my grandfather put his father, James, down as next of kin on the Attestation Form. Perhaps he did so in case the Australian Army would not take married men from England. But that is something else for me to look up.

My grandfather's death in the period 6th–9th August occurred when the 4th Bn. of the 1st Australian Division were engaged in bitter fighting at Lone Pine. An action in which seven VCs were awarded. The attack is well chronicled – CEW Bean devotes no less than 40 pages to it in The Official History of Australia in the War of 1914-1918. He records that the attack began at 5.30pm on 6th August, on a narrow front with the first troops filing into tunnels, which extended some fifty yards beyond the front line. The attacking troops reached the Turkish front line but found it roofed over with heavy logs, which the Australians tried to remove while others went further forward and then worked their way back along the communication trenches. Much of the fighting took place in semi-darkness with attacks and counter-attacks that lasted until 9th August.

Another author, Alan Moorhead, comments in his book Gallipoli *'... it is really not possible to comprehend what happened. All dissolves into a confused impression of a riot, of a vicious street fight in the back alleys of a city, and the metaphor of the stirred-up ant heap persists ...'*

What we do know is that 1st Australian Division lost over 2,000 men during the battle. The 4th Battalion, in which my grandfather served, went in with 20 officers and 722 other ranks and suffered the loss of 15 officers and 459 other ranks killed wounded or missing (63% of those engaged).

After years of wondering and searching I now have my answers to my questions, but sometimes, I can't believe that

I found him, and now several 2nd cousins into the bargain and loads more as well, but unfortunately, I have never been able to track down the descendants of Lilly or Rose Pritchard. I must be honest it is all so overwhelming not only to have found my grandfather, but some of his family as well. So I have now arrived at Gallipoli, a different journey to my grandfather, but we both arrived at the same place.

Just a footnote, my grandmother emigrated to Sydney, Australia in 1973. I wonder, as she walked down those roads/streets, did she think of her first husband, my grandfather.

To bring this story up to date I was able to travel to Gallipoli and was there on the 25th April 2015, (although not allowed to visit him until the next day) the same day my grandad had landed there albeit 100 years later.

William Pritchard
4th Battalion, 2nd Reinforcement
Regiment No 1422
Killed Gallipoli 6th-9th August 1915

Grandad, you have lain forgotten for many years,
but not by me.
Now I have found you and you are forgotten no more.
Your Grandaughter.

****

Part 2 - Second World War

The 'war to end all wars' with slaughter and carnage that horrified the world ended in 1918. However, it ended with a German nation in social and economic turmoil on the home front and a feeling amongst many that it had not been defeated on the battlefield. And with the allies determined to exact punishment on the losers at Versailles, harsh penalties were put into place requiring sizeable reparations as well as restriction on military strength in all areas and great bitterness.

The Great Depression threw Germany into an economically disastrous position with mass unemployment, hyper-inflation and great hunger and hardship. These factors provided the fertile recruiting ground for Hitler's Nazi party. At the same time, the western powers, determined to avoid a further catastrophic war when its young men were annihilated by the million, adopted a policy of disarmament. Subsequently with futile appeasement at Munich, the western powers chose to look the other way when Austria and the Sudetenland were occupied.

When the unprovoked invasion of Poland took place in September 1939, the era of a new form of warfare took place. War from land and air poured terror on military targets and civilians alike. Home populations were no longer safe as they may have been in earlier times while their men were away at war. Mass bombing by both sides brought war to the home front, even for those not occupied. Ethnic cleansing on an unbelievable scale by the Axis Powers saw the extermination of millions of Jews, Romanies, communists and other so-called *'undesirables'*.

Science brought the development of rocket technologies, the V1 and V2, the first jet engine planes and ultimately the dropping of the first atomic bombs on Japan. Approaching 80 million people were killed during the Second World War, numbers unthinkable even after the Great War.

This section provides an insight into various elements of the 1939 to 1945 conflict. People's own experiences from the *kindertransport* to being bombed out in the *blitz*. Life under occupation and in POW camps. The heroes are represented alongside the ordinary people doing their bit to fight the common foe. This war was the defining period of the 20th century, and led to the creation of the United Nations, providing a level of peace, albeit shaky on some occasions, to much of the world for the next 75 years.

****

Chapter 1 - By Air

In the Second World War, airpower was employed in all theatres, becoming a major offensive element of the combat plans of all participating nations.

When German forces crossed the border into Poland on 1st September 1939, the world saw the first real use of *Blitzkrieg 'lightning war'* tactics by the German land and air forces against military and civilian populations. This demonstrated the devastating power of aggressive, and ruthless military action inflicting terror and panic amongst a brave yet much weaker country's forces. This tactic was repeated in western Europe in May 1940 as the Netherlands, Belgium and France fell in quick succession.

As anticipated, strategic bombing was important and in Britain the early medium range bombers such as the Hampden, Whitley and Fairey Battle were replaced in time with the Lancaster and the Halifax. The British bombing campaign was the longest battle of the war and started against Germany in 1940 and lasted until 1945. Its aim was to destroy both German industrial assets and civilian morale by area bombing.

In the early stages of the war, whilst Britain and its allies were reeling from defeat after defeat, Churchill saw the bombing campaign as the only way of hitting back, and while unsophisticated initially, the development of improved aircraft, enhanced tactics and radar technology, driven by the single-minded and controversial Air Chief Marshal Arthur 'Bomber' Harris, the scale of the war waged by Bomber Command and latterly the USAAF was vast. The devastation inflicted on many German cities was immense with raids of a thousand bombers hitting single city in a one night, the RAF bombing by night and the USAAF by day. Casualties from this bombing were huge too. Over 58,000 RAF bomber crew members were killed while civilian deaths in German cities from the bombing are estimated between 400,000 and 500,000.

The British public had expected bombs to start falling from the first day of the war. Civil defence measures were widely in place in September 1939 with air raid sirens and shelters, anti-aircraft guns, barrage balloons, the *'blackout'*, along the issue of gas masks, and mass evacuations of children away from town and cities. However, it was nearly twelve months later that the strategic and concentrated German bombing of British towns and cities, the *Blitz,* started. On 7th September 1940 and for much of the rest of the war, bombs fell on civilian populations and industrial and military targets. This was followed in 1944 and 1945 by attacks from V1 *'doodlebugs'* and V2 ballistic missiles, the *Vergeltungswaffe 'revenge'* weapons. It is estimated about 60,000 British civilians were killed by bombing and the VI and V2 programme.

The attempt by the German Air Force to obtain air superiority prior to an invasion was defeated in the Battle of Britain in which fighter pilots in Hurricanes and Spitfires as well as other types of aircraft fought German bombers such as the Heinkel He111 and their accompanying fighter escorts. The bravery and heroics of *'The Few'* is well recorded and appropriate tributes paid, but the Battle of

Britain was won by a combination of factors. The tactical and organisational skills of Dowding and Park, the WAAFs deploying fighters to where they needed to be from the control room bunkers at RAF Uxbridge and Bentley Priory, the development of radar and the home chain early warning system and the often under credited roles of the ground crews who worked tirelessly to keep the planes repaired and flying.

Air power was important in many theatres of war. From the sinking of the Italian fleet at harbour in Taranto in 1940 by Fairey Swordfish of the Fleet Air Arm based on the carrier HMS *Illustrious* to aircraft such as the Short Sunderland which hunted submarines in the Atlantic, to the handful of fighters defending Malta. The war in the desert saw the development of air support in land battles, which was utilised in the Battle for Normandy. Dakotas were heavily used in transport of material and troops, for example in Operation Market Garden and Operation Husky.

Naval aviation grew in importance with the increasing ability to target enemy fleets with air launched bombs as in the Battle of Midway. The re-supply of Slim's '*Forgotten Army*' in Burma and the supply of starving Dutch civilians in 1945 in Operations Manna (RAF) and Chowhound (USAAF), saving many lives, are further examples of the increasing dependency, on air transportation in warfare.

In August 1945, two Atomic bombs were dropped by the Allies on Hiroshima and Nagasaki using Boeing B29 Super Fortresses and ended the war against Japan.

Dutch historian, Wilco Vermeer, describes a major bombing raid by the Luftwaffe on Rotterdam following the surprise attack on the Netherlands in May 1940. Over 800 civilians were killed and thousands more lost their homes during this raid, which precipitated the Dutch surrender after just five days of fighting.

This article was translated by Cor Korpel. By kind permission of TracesOfWar.com

Bombardment of Rotterdam
Introduction

After the German invasion of the Netherlands on the early morning of 10th May, the situation for the Dutch army had deteriorated fast. On the Friesian side of the *Afsluitdijk*, (enclosing dyke, that separated the former Zuiderzee from the North Sea) they managed to hold their positions. On the Grebbelinie too, attack after attack by the Germans was pushed back with much effort. The greater part of the German airborne troops were either destroyed or surrounded. A more serious danger was that German parachutists gained control over the Moerdijk bridges and that the *9e Panzerdivision* (9th Armoured Division) proceeded in that direction by way of Noord Brabant. Eventually the struggle in Holland would be settled by a bombardment of Rotterdam.

Previous history

To open up the fortress of Holland for a rapid transit of the 9th Armoured Division, the Germans devised a plan in which the *7e Fliegerdivision* (7th airborne division) of Lieutenant General Kurt Student should gain control of the undamaged bridges of Rotterdam, Dordrecht and Moerdijk, which gave access to the heart of the Dutch defence. At

Moerdijk and Dordrecht, the Germans succeeded in remaining in control of the bridges until the advancing 9th Armoured Division, and in their wake, the XXXIX Army Corps brought the necessary relief. Quite different was the situation in Rotterdam. In spite of the fact that German airborne troops controlled almost the entire southern side of Rotterdam, including the strategically situated Noordereiland (the island in the middle of the Maas river that divides the two city parts), the Dutch managed, mostly by the efforts of three sections of marines under the command of Captain Schuiling, to keep the Maas bridge effectively under fire, so that a German crossing would likely result in considerable punishment.

14th May 1940
On the 14th May, tanks of the German 9th Armoured Divison (Major General Alfred Ritter von Hubicky) and units of the *SS-Leibstandarte Adolf Hitler* (Hitler's lifeguard) under Dietrich had already advanced into the southern part of Rotterdam. The commander of the XXXIX Army Corps, General Schmidt, had set up his headquarters in Rijsoord. These units stood under the direct orders of General GKFW von Küchler of the 18th army. On 13th May at 17:05 hours, this commander received an order from high command to break the Dutch resistance in Rotterdam with all means available and if necessary by threatening to carry out the destruction of the city. For Schmidt, one matter was obvious: a possible artillery or air bombardment had to be as limited as possible, as the German tanks needed room to manoeuvre in case fighting would break out in the city.

Negotiations had been started in Rotterdam after the presentation of the first ultimatum by the Germans. This first ultimatum had been received by the Dutch commander of Rotterdam, Colonel Scharroo. Therein he was threatened with the destruction of the city if no surrender followed. The impression had been given that an artillery bombardment would take place, followed by an air bombardment. Meanwhile in Germany the bombers were already allowed to take off.

Scharroo, supported by General Henry Winkelman (commander in chief of the Dutch forces) did not see any reason for surrender. They considered the ultimatum; an untidy, handwritten slip of paper, as well as being unsigned (the note was closed with, *the Commander of the German forces*). The German negotiator was sent back with the request to return with an official document. Since 11ᵗʰ May, Scharroo had received reinforcements of no less than five battalions. In spite of the numerical superiority he did not succeed in driving the German forces back. Winkelman then ordered Colonel Wilson and two other staff officers to Rotterdam with the command to - if necessary - relieve Colonel Scharroo and take over command.

Once he arrived, Colonel Wilson could not but conclude that Scharroo could not have acted differently than he had done. Too many Dutch troops had to be deployed to guard the city against possible attacks from northern, eastern and western directions due to the many scattered parachutist troops at large in the area and operations against the alleged actions of the Fifth Column.

And on the German side the impression was raised that the Dutch commander was prepared to negotiate, Schmidt had sent a radio message to postpone the planned bombardment.

He was informed, however, that the bombers were already underway and radio communications were no longer possible. The bombers could only be stopped by means of red flares. Colonel Scharroo sent Captain Backer to the demarcation line to receive the new ultimatum. This newly drafted ultimatum was handed over to him at 13:20 hours, after which he returned to Scharroo's Headquarters. Schmidt allowed the Dutch three hours to answer. It reached Schmidt at 16:20 hours. Backer was accompanied by two German officers. At this very moment the Heinkels approached the city. Even the German commander did not expect them so soon and was duly surprised. Immediately he had red flares fired to stop the bombers from dropping their load.

Air fleet under way

At the *Luftwaffe* headquarters they were not aware of the negotiations. As *Oberbefehlshaber der Luftwaffe* (commander in chief of the air force), Hermann Göring was very anxious about the position of his *22e Luftlandedivision* (22nd airborne division). He was convinced that the situation in Rotterdam could only be solved by an air bombardment. Adolf Hitler, as *Oberster Befehlshaber der Wehrmacht* (supreme commander of the armed forces), had also announced that Dutch resistance had to be broken at any price.

Eventually the high command gave the order to *Kampfgeschwader* (battle squadron) 54 to take off. At 11:45 hrs. 90 Heinkel He 111 bombers took off from Delmenhorst, Münster and Quackenbrück, with destination Rotterdam. The unit was divided in two groups: *Oberst* (colonel) Wilhelm Lackner commanded a group of 54

Heinkels, whereas *Oberstleutnant* (lieutenant colonel) Otto Höhne commanded the remaining 36. The plan was that the aircraft would arrive over Rotterdam at 13:20 hrs.

The aircraft commanders knew that if the bombardment was postponed, red flares would be fired. The message of Schmidt reached General Kesselring at 12:35 hrs. The squadron of Oberstleutnant Otto Höhne saw the flares and broke off the attack. The group of Oberst Wilhelm Lackner, approaching from the east, continued and dropped their bombs on the city.

The Bombardment

In Rotterdam the air raid warning was given. A great number of people fled into shelters, laid down on the street or pressed themselves against the facades of large buildings. In a quarter of an hour, 158 x 250 kg bombs and 1,150 x 50 kg bombs fell down on the city. The damage was enormous. power was cut off, houses caught fire. The fire spread so fast that the entire heart of the city was reduced to rubble. When the smoke cleared on 15th May, one could take stock. About 800 people were killed. Over 80,000 people lost their homes and 24,000 houses were destroyed.

At 15:00hrs. Colonel Scharroo ordered his sub commanders to cease fire. At 15:50hrs he offered the surrender of Rotterdam to General Schmidt, with the approval of the representative of General Winkelman, Lieutenant Colonel Wilson. At 15:30hrs. Wilson arrived at the General Headquarters of General Winkelman at The Hague. *'I'm coming from hell'*, he said. Having been told that Rotterdam had been bombed, was on fire and had surrendered. Winkelman was shocked, but not prepared to issue immediate orders for total capitulation.

Meanwhile Scharroo was on his way to inform his troops of the intended surrender. Due to the bombardment, so many roads were blocked that he was not able to reach his headquarters until 18:30hrs. In the meantime, Göring lost patience and ordered a new a bombardment on Rotterdam. A second wave of bombers took off around 15:30hrs and would reach Rotterdam somewhere around 17:30hrs and 18:30hrs. German General Schmidt considered this totally unnecessary and reported immediately that his troops controlled the northern part of the city, which was definitely not true at that time.

Meanwhile the news had arrived that the Germans had demanded the surrender of Utrecht under the threat of the destruction of the city. This was enough for Winkelman. Obviously the Germans were determined to destroy all the big cities in case he would continue fighting.

Aftermath
Up to the present day, a debate is going on about the question whether the bombardment should be considered a tactical bombardment, a strategic bombardment or simply an act of terrorism. The target in itself, the inhabited centre, did not have any military significance. Rotterdam however was a defended city, in the middle of a frontline. In spite of the criticism, one might take Hitler and Göring's view of such bombings, that the city was a legitimate strategic target. After all, the intention was to force the Dutch into capitulation. However, by bombing the inhabited centre of Rotterdam, instead of the positions held by the Dutch, it

could not be considered a tactical bombardment but took the character of terror bombing. In particular the subsequent threat to lay the entire city of Utrecht in ashes underlines this.

Since the Second World War, there have been many discussions in various articles about this issue. Often it has been said that it must be considered an '*accident*'. The German planes were supposed to be sent back by firing red flares and owing to circumstances these flares were not noticed by some of the planes.

Under international law, however, one thing is clear. Back in 1938, the 19th assembly of the League of Nations unanimously accepted principles that forbade the bombing of civilian targets, no matter the circumstances. Even on 1st September, this principle was endorsed by Hitler himself. The order, given to the crews of the bombers, was also clear, deliberately dropping bombs on civilian targets, without distinguishing between civilian and defended military targets. On this basis, one can certainly speak of terrorist bombing. It goes too far, however, to list this bombardment in the scale of, for instance, London, Coventry and cities like Berlin, since the bombing of Rotterdam happened to a defended city. It was after all the Dutch supreme command that wished to defend Rotterdam to the utmost. Where international law is concerned, one can certainly speak of an act of terrorism, the debate on this issue however will always have supporters and opponents.

Dr. Stephen Bungay, historian and a Director of the Ashridge Strategic Management Centre, assesses the strengths and weaknesses of both sides in the Battle of Britain – a decisive period not only in the Second World War but in British history. Dr. Bungay explores those factors that allowed the RAF to defeat a larger and more experienced Luftwaffe and those who were the key figures behind the strategy and its implementation.

A Perspective on the Battle of Britain
'The Battle to the Strong - The Making of a Victory'.

The Battle of Britain has been presented as a David and Goliath conflict, but who was really strong, and was it the weak or the strong who won?

The Battle of Britain pilots, most of whom were the age of students, were perhaps the most attractive group of warriors in all history. Throughout most of time, civilians have generally feared soldiers as people who would steal their chickens and rape their daughters, whereas the Battle of Britain pilots upheld civilised values on behalf of western civilisation. Churchill decided to turn them into heroes as 'knights of the air', referring to them as *these splendid men, this brilliant youth'*. There were only about 3,000 pilots with about 600 to 650 aircraft against the most experienced, powerful and at the time most capable air force in the world. Their image as glamorous, brave and nonchalant is not undeserved – but perhaps it has seduced us into thinking that they alone are responsible for the victory in the air.

In fact, the foundations of British success were laid back in the 1930s by a large number of people led by a few older men who developed the world's first fully integrated air defence system, which was in effect an analogue intranet, which could process and distribute vast amounts of information very rapidly.

It was a bit like a fisherman's net. If a hole was cut in it, information flows always had an alternative path. In the First World War, information was carried along temporary phone lines which if damaged, knocked out all information. By contrast, the only thing that would really affect the command and control effectiveness of the air defence system was a big hole, but the system was also self-sealing, as the damage done to it each day was repaired overnight.

Each level of the system had a clear role. HQ Fighter Command at Bentley Priory in Stanmore contained the Filter Room that turned the raw data into information for the Groups, the largest of which was 11 Group located in the bunker at RAF Uxbridge which covered south east England. It was the Groups that made the operational decisions about which forces to use against which raids. They passed their orders to the Sectors which actually scrambled the squadrons and talked to the pilots.

Where did all the information come from?

Some of it came from radar but it could only detect out to sea and not low down. Later the original Chain Home was supplemented by Chain Home Low, but it was still possible to fly under it. The Observer Corps provided valuable information about numbers, altitude and what was happening inland, but they could not do anything at night or in bad weather. What radar did was to give 20 minutes warning although if raiders came from Calais, it would be less, as it was only 20 miles away, and real raids were hard to detect as there was always aerial activity of some sort in that area. However, in general radar meant that the RAF did not have to rely on 'standing patrols' over the sea and it thus functioned as a force-multiplier by directing defending aircraft to just where they were needed, so that the defences could be conducted effectively by just 52 Squadrons. Fighter Command still flew standing patrols, but fewer than they would otherwise have needed. The work of the fighters was co-ordinated with balloon barrages and anti-aircraft guns under the control of army personnel based in the Group Control Rooms.

It has often been said that we were saved by the British invention, radar, but in fact the first working radar was developed by the German Navy in 1934. A mobile German Navy radar unit which had been developed for use at sea was set up outside the headquarters of Airfleet II at Cap Blanc Nez for convoy spotting near Cap Blanc Nez, but the *Luftwaffe* itself showed little interest in radar until British bombers began making regular incursions into German airspace. It was the German Navy that warned the *Luftwaffe* that Wellingtons were making the ill-fated daylight raid on Wilhelmshaven in the very early days of the war.

The architect of the British defence system was Major General Edward Ashmore, who had flown in the First World War in the RFC and became head of London Air Defence during the First World War. It was not very effective. Shooting down the Zeppelins that began bombing Britain was so rare and considered so dangerous that the first pilot to do so was awarded the VC. The anti-aircraft guns defending the capital against the Gotha bombers which replaced the Zeppelins were killing more civilians through falling shrapnel than they were killing German airmen, so they were told to fire blanks to appear to be doing something.

However, although the means at his disposal were ineffective, Ashmore had grasped the principles of what was needed to defend the capital. He created the observation posts which in 1925 became the Observer Corps (which became 'Royal' in 1941 in recognition of its work in the Battle of Britain) and he appreciated that a proper control system was needed on the ground.

The builder of that system was Hugh ('Stuffy') Dowding, whom General Pile, head of AA Command, described as strange and difficult, but nevertheless the most impressive airman he met during the war. Dowding combined great imagination, vision and attention to detail. During the Battle of Britain, he did not run the battle, leaving that to his Group Commanders, but worked on building up Fighter Command's capabilities. His most pressing problem was night interception, but it was only in 1941, due largely to his efforts, that the twin engined, radar equipped night fighter was available. He was ousted not by the big wing controversy but by the lack of night capability. However, the most important operator of the system was Air Vice-Marshal Keith Park who ran 11 Group, with about half of Fighter Command's strength, during the 4 months of the battle.

In truth, because of the tireless work done before the war began, the margin of victory was not narrow. Although the RAF was outnumbered, its fighter strength was close to that planned; the attempted airfield destruction by the *Luftwaffe* was ineffective; the RAF never came close to running out of aircraft and despite short dips, the number of pilots available rose steadily during the battle; and the *Luftwaffe's* switch to bombing London changed nothing. The battle was won by superior strategy and leadership rather than simply by the heroism of the 'few'.

Let us look at numbers. Here is a comparison of front-line aircraft of both sides at the beginning of July:

Aircraft Availability	Germany	Britain
Single seat fighters (est)	1,107	754
Twin seat fighters	357	149
Bombers	1,380	560
Dive bombers	428	0
Reconnaissance aircraft	569	N/A
Coastal command	233	500
TOTALS	**4,074**	**1,963**

The critical figure in the defensive daylight air battles is the number of single-seater fighters. In these, the other *Luftwaffe* aircraft were largely targets, and the RAF bombers, where the largest discrepancy in numbers lies, were not engaged. About 75% of the fighters were operational, so the fighter command started with about 560 fighters to oppose about 820 German ones. As a rule of thumb, the attacker needs about three times the strength of the defender, so the German advantage of 1.5 to 1.0 is not large. Moreover, the British fighters were operating from their home bases with supply, repair and maintenance facilities to hand whilst the *Luftwaffe* were using improvised or captured airfields. Most importantly, the *Luftwaffe* was producing about 200 fighters a month, and assumed the RAF's replacement rate was the same. This was confirmed by a German spy, code named '*Ostro*', but *Ostro* had been turned into a double agent by MI5. By July 1940, Britain was in fact producing about 450 fighters a month. The RAF also had a very effective Civilian Repair Organisation which refurbished about 30% of the damaged aircraft returned to operations. So as time went on, the *Luftwaffe's* initial advantage eroded and by the end of the battle Fighter Command had got stronger.

The German objective was never very clear, but most agreed that they had to gain air superiority over the potential invasion area. Theo Osterkamp, the head of the fighter arm of Airfleet II calculated early on that to achieve this and have sufficient strength to protect the invasion fleet from British bombers and the Royal Navy, they could only afford to lose 10% of their number. To do so and weaken Fighter Command sufficiently to control the airspace they needed a kill ratio of 5 to 1, which meant selecting only the best opportunities. But to inflict damage on a sufficient scale they also needed a big air battle. He realised the *Luftwaffe* could not have both.

The alternative was the destroy Fighter Command on the ground, but the Dowding system made surprise very difficult. In the course of the battle only about 20 aircraft were destroyed on the ground. British pilots wrote off far more than that in accidents. Airfield damage was quickly repaired as gravel, bulldozers and shovels had been provided. The only vital targets at airfields were the Ops Rooms at Sector Stations. Kenley was down for 2 hours on 18th August and Biggin Hill for several hours on 1st September. Both recovered rapidly as second and third lines of defence were in place in shops in Biggin Hill & Caterham villages. The only airfield to be abandoned was Manston due to buried unexploded bombs, which in reality were more of a problem than the ones that actually went off as intended.

Biggin Hill was the most heavily attacked airfield - 11 times in 7 days. On 4th September the Station Commander, Group Captain Grice, went up to take a look at his station from the air. There was one hangar left standing. At 6pm that evening it was blown up on his orders. The German reconnaissance aircraft sent over the following morning reported that no buildings were left and so after the small raid already planned for that day, the *Luftwaffe* left Biggin Hill alone. Grice was put on a charge for *'willful damage to the King's property'*, but was quickly let off and joined his pilots to celebrate in the nearby White Hart.

The Kenley Ops Room was moved down to a butcher's shop in Caterham and the telephone line which ran through trees up Caterham Hill to the airfield was checked every day by someone armed with a shot gun, to guard against squirrel attack! The Biggin Hill Ops room moved to the village. Both stations were preparing a third, permanent location well away from the airfields. All of these were small targets, which would have been hard to hit even if the *Luftwaffe* had known of their existence, which they didn't.

The critical factor in Fighter Commands ability to continue was the availability of pilots. There was a gap between pilot availability and the number required, known as the 'establishment' strength. The reason was that Dowding decided to increase the number of pilots per squadron from 18 to 24 in order to give the pilots more opportunity to rest. The number of replacement pilots steadily rose, but at the end of August and beginning of September, losses outstripped replacements. The main reason for this was that inexperienced squadrons were being sent to 11 Group. These nine units suffered 40% of losses but only made 25% of claims. On 7th September, Dowding changed the replacement system so that rather than replacing complete squadrons, individual pilots were sent to the squadrons so that the experienced ones could show them the ropes. After this, losses stabilised.

Changing the target from the airfields to London was a relief, but made no real difference in military terms. The airfields could have withstood further attacks. The Ops Rooms were unknown to the enemy and were hard to hit and two crucial ones were no longer on the airfields; equally the repair organisations had been strengthened and the *Luftwaffe* was failing to catch fighters on the ground.

The choice of targets had no impact on the air fighting. London's docklands were closer to Calais than airfields such as North Weald, which had already been attacked, and three of the five days on which the *Luftwaffe* gained a favourable kill ratio came after they targeted London. Those days made little difference because, as Osterkamp had predicted, the numbers involved were small. The

RAF's overall favourable kill ratio of about 1.9:1 hardly changed.

Failures in the German strategy included poor use of intelligence, not making a clear choice between the aim of siege versus decision, poor target selection, poor use of bombing methods and of use of fighters along with naïve assumptions about air fighting.

The strengths of the British defences were:

- Dowding's system which made best use of the limited forces

- Good resourcing in terms of supply, repair and maintenance

- It was planned with a low potential for major failure

- Flexible tactics

- Focus on destroying the bombers

- Park's operational brilliance

Success in the Battle of Britain was vital because it allowed Britain and its Empire to continue to oppose Hitler long before the US entered the war. Indeed, it was a precondition of the subsequent invasion and liberation of Europe, which could not have been done by US forces without Britain as a base and an active ally. It was to remain Britain's only clear victory for two years, but it was in 1940 that Britain came closest to capitulation or defeat. Coming to terms with Germany was then on the political agenda, and Churchill's position was far from secure. After the Battle of Britain, making peace was never contemplated and Churchill's authority never seriously questioned. It was British belligerence that meant that Germany was eventually defeated not just by the Soviet Union, but by western democracies, which saved Europe from total domination by either Hitler or Stalin resulting in a world today which is far richer and safer.

In the way that they actually behaved in Britain's *'finest hour'* the two protagonists swapped the national characteristics they usually ascribe to each other:

The British	**The Germans**
Highly professional leaders	An amateur leader
Determined & ruthless	Romantic & chivalrous
Well prepared plan	Improvised plan
Exploited latest technology	Poor use of technology
Disciplined teams	Heroic individuals

The winning values included people taking a realistic view of their own role, making modesty a virtue, hard work, good personal relationships governed by mutual respect, and great teamwork. The pilots did not flout authority but equally did not take it too seriously, bolstering each other's morale through their infectious humour. In contrast with the *Luftwaffe* 'Experten' who were concerned to maximise their personal score, RAF aces like 'Sailor' Malan would allow new pilots to gain confidence by allowing them to make an easy kill. The issues involved were very simple: Bob Doe took the attitude *'they came here without being asked and they might hurt my mum'*. The ethos which lay behind the victory is as valuable in war as it is in peace. Perhaps we should seek to re-invigorate them today.

Biographical notes – Stephen Bungay, Director, Ashridge Strategic Management Centre. www.stephenbungay.com

After graduating from Oxford and the University of Tübingen, West Germany, Stephen worked for The Boston Consulting Group for a total of seventeen years before subsequently joining the Ashridge Strategic Management Centre in 2001. He teaches on executive programmes at several business schools, including Ashridge, and is a regular guest speaker at the Royal College of Defence Studies in London. He also works as an independent consultant and conference speaker.

In 2004 he appeared as principle historian in the Channel 4 series 'Spitfire Ace' and has continued to contribute to a range of television programmes since then. His current work is focused on the most effective ways of developing strategy in an environment of high uncertainty.

****

Chris Leworthy, tour guide at the Battle of Britain Bunker at RAF Uxbridge, describes the role of the bunker during the Battle of Britain and how important it was to Britain's air defences. The bunker was central to the co-ordination of fighter squadrons put to the air to thwart the Luftwaffe as they tried to get air supremacy in advance of the proposed invasion of Britain in mid-1940. 'The Few' may have won the battle in the air but the Bunker and all those connected with it, in whatever capacity, made sure the squadrons were in the air at the right place and at the right time.

The Battle of Britain Bunker

The Battle of Britain Bunker is an underground control room, located in Uxbridge, Middlesex. It played a pivotal role in the successful defence of Britain during 1940 when it acted as Headquarters of No. 11 Group Fighter Command. In addition to this, it played a vital part in many other campaigns, most notably in support of Operation Overlord in June 1944.

The bunker was constructed in seven months, completed in August 1939, a matter of days before the declaration of war and was a key part of what became known as the *'Dowding System'*, the world's first integrated defence and interception system, named after Air Chief Marshal Sir Hugh Dowding, Commander-in-Chief of Fighter Command during the Battle. This system linked together RDF (Radar), the visual tracking activities of the Observer Corps, Fighter Command headquarters at Bentley Priory, the four groups of fighter command, sector airfields and squadrons. As well as this, it controlled and integrated the activities of barrage balloon defence, air raid warnings and anti-aircraft fire.

The bunker is accessed by 76 steps and is 60 feet underground. It is air-conditioned, bombproof and gas proof and all utilities are supplied to the facility by pipes which run down the length of the staircases.

No. 11 Group assumed responsibility for the defence of southeast England and London, and was responsible for operational command of the RAF's response to incoming hostile raids in 1940. It was the bunker at Uxbridge, at that time under the command of Air Vice-Marshal Keith Park, which decided the appropriate response to incoming hostile raids as soon as the direction and size of each raid became apparent. Orders for response in terms of the squadrons to be utilised, as well as the height and location to which they were to be dispatched, were passed to seven sector airfields, which then assumed responsibility for bringing those aircraft into contact with the enemy and returning them to a home airfield. The sectors operated from main, satellite and forward airfields, utilising the most appropriate, depending upon the direction and progress of incoming raids.

The bunker was visited by King George Vl and most notably by Winston Churchill on 16th August 1940 when having witnessed a ferocious day in the battle he spoke the famous words: *'Never in the field of human conflict was so much owed, by so many, to so few'*. He visited again on 15th September 1940 and observed Parks' masterly defensive strategy together with the supremely effective working of the Dowding System which inflicted major losses on the incoming hostile raiders and changed the course of the Battle. This key day has now become known as Battle of Britain Day, because of its importance to the outcome of the Second World War. It is no exaggeration to say that without this visionary system and the response from each of its components, the Battle of Britain would not have been won.

The bunker is best known for its vital role in the Battle of Britain but also played a major role in support of Operation Overlord, the June 1944 Allied landings in Normandy, when, under joint RAF and US command, it controlled 171 fighter and fighter-bomber squadrons. It carried out a phased plan to deliver air supremacy over northern France and to prepare the way for the beach landings by attacking German infrastructure, including radar and gun placements, as well as providing total beach cover on D-Day itself. So successful were the plans executed that almost no enemy aircraft was reported as attacking the landing beaches on June 6th.

The bunker continued in operation until the departure of No.11 Group in 1958, when it was put into storage. It was reopened as a Museum in 1985, before passing to London Borough of Hillingdon, which opened a Visitors' Centre in 2018, and had the vision to make this historic building more accessible to visitors of all ages.

Today, visits and tours of the Bunker are available each day, with full details on the Bunker's website. The visitor is able to see the Operations Room, with its original Plotting Table and Squadron Status Board, set out as they were on the morning of 15th September 1940. They will listen to a vivid description of the Bunker's role and vital importance, and will visit the Controller's Cabin, from which key decisions were made during the Second World War

As well as these areas there is a new Visitors' Centre, which gives fascinating detail on the components making up the Dowding System, as well as useful background on the Battle itself.

For anyone with an interest in those key events, in which 544 young Fighter Command Pilots lost their lives in order to change the course of history, this is a unique, historic and important site to visit.

Note: the views expressed in this article are those of Chris Leworthy and do not necessarily represent the views of Hillingdon Borough Council or the Battle of Britain Bunker

****

Geoff Simpson, historian and author, describes the sad but not untypical story of Geoffrey Gledhill during the Battle of Britain. Only 19 years old, his Hurricane was shot down and Geoffrey was killed. He is buried in a small churchyard in Normandy.

Geoffrey Gledhill - One of 'The Few'

Sergeant Geoffrey Gledhill arrived at No 238 Squadron to fly Hurricanes on 4th August 1940. A week later the boyish looking 19-year-old flew his first sortie. He and the rest of his section did not return.

Sadly, death on a first sortie was not a unique occurrence in the Battle of Britain. Perhaps Geoff Gledhill was unfortunate in a sense. He was part of a day of bitter fighting over the Dorset coast in which Fighter Command suffered heavy casualties. Sometimes it is referred to as the Battle of Portland. This was a time when the Germans were very keen to eliminate the Portland naval base as a threat to invasion of Britain.

Geoff Gledhill had been born in Cardiff in 1921 but the family settled in Harpenden, Hertfordshire. Gledhill joined the 3rd Harpenden troop of the Boy Scouts and seems to have thrived in that environment. Writing in 2017, Colin Gaskin, a younger member of the troop recalled, *'I first came to know Geoff when, I as a cub scout and Geoff as leader of the Peewit Patrol of the Troop, regularly took part in the parents' evenings which the scoutmasters organised to demonstrate to parents what their children got up to during the weekly meetings and at camp and other occasions. It was traditional at the parents' evenings to finish with an indoor version of a typical camp fire when stories would be told and songs sung. One of these songs, a roundelay [short and simple song with a refrain] Green Grow the Rushes-O, was usually sung with Geoff responding as number two – 'Two, two the lily-white boys clothed all in green ho ho' I can still remember his firm countertenor voice on the many occasions he sang.'* There was also a story about a camp where a boy became stuck up a tree and it was Geoff Gledhill who worked out how to rescue him and then performed that feat. He was clearly looked up to by the younger scouts.

At the beginning of 1939 Geoff Gledhill joined the RAFVR. He was called up on 1st September. From

February to June 1940 he was at 5 Flying Training School, Sealand, in north east Wales. He went on to Lincolnshire to convert to Hurricanes at 6 Operational Training Unit, Sutton Bridge.

Then it was off to Middle Wallop in Hampshire, and a part of Fighter Command's No 10 Group, to join 238. On Thursday 8th August, with Geoff Gledhill awaiting his first operational experience, 238 was engaged in the defence of Convoy Peewit, as it made its way westwards in the English Channel.

During that day the squadron lost a high proportion of its senior pilots. Flight Lieutenant Donald Turner, 'A' Flight commander, was shot down into the sea and killed, as was Flying Officer Derek MacCaw. The CO, Squadron Leader *'Jimmy'* Fenton, had been detained both by the adjutant and paperwork and Flight Lieutenant Stuart Walch from Hobart, Tasmania, led the sortie. Later Fenton took off on a solo search of the Channel. He did not find missing aircrew, but did discover a Heinkel He 59 on the water. He attacked, but was hit by return fire, ditched, injured, and was picked up by a Royal Navy vessel. He would not return to the squadron until 13th September.

On 11th August, with major German formations approaching the English coast, 238 was ordered off and split in two. Flight Lieutenant David Hughes (who would be killed on 11th September) led 'A' Flight east of Weymouth while Stuart Walch and 'B' Flight were vectored south of Swanage.

Having crossed the coast, Walch and those following him ran into the enemy. Kristen Alexander, in her book, Australia's Few, recorded that 'B' Flight was caught between two waves of enemy aircraft and therefore heavily outnumbered. Flying Officer Michal Steborowski, from Poland and Sergeant Gledhill got into trouble and it appears that Stuart Walch tried to rescue his colleagues. Facing overwhelming odds all three Hurricanes were shot down into the sea. Blue Section was gone.

The squadron diary noted that Geoff Gledhill hardly had time to get to know his new comrades or they him, but described him as, *'A gentle boy, ruddy of countenance.'* His body crossed the Channel and he is buried in the churchyard of the farming village of Criquebeuf-en-Caux, Normandy.

At the end of his life in the 1990s Air Commodore *'Jimmy'* Fenton could still name all the pilots of 238 killed under his command in the Battle of Britain and was still concerned that, with more operational experience before taking command, he might have been better equipped to save some of them.

****

Geoff Botting tells of his father, Jesse Botting, who joined the RAF in 1940. Flying various planes in various roles, he went on to a newly formed Air Sea Rescue squadron flying the amphibious plane Walrus, rescuing allied and German airman from the sea. A dangerous role but greatly appreciated by those rescued.

Jesse Victor Botting

In September 1940 Jesse Botting was working as an 18-year-old machinist making shell caps in the Woolwich Arsenal when it was bombed by the *Luftwaffe* in the first big raid on London. He immediately volunteered for the RAF.

After training as a wireless operator and then a period at various RAF ground stations sending course directions to pilots he was sent to Air Gunnery School before being posted, in November 1941, to 23 Squadron, part of Fighter Commands No. 11 Group.

With 23, then with 418 and 605 squadrons, he spent 15 months flying in Bostons, a twin-engine fighter/light bomber, on night intruder operations. The task of these intruder squadrons was to destroy enemy bombers over their home aerodromes in the Occupied Territories. They would linger over enemy airfields to catch German planes, with their guard down, returning from night-time operations or, when a big raid was scheduled, to divert the German night fighters from attacking RAF bombers and, ideally, keep the enemy's night fighters on the ground altogether. A small bomb would then often be dropped as a parting gift.

Mosquitoes replaced the Bostons which removed the need for wireless operator/air gunners, and Jesse was posted to

118

277 squadron for RAF Air Sea Rescue training and then to Algiers in April 1943 as part of the initial complement of the newly formed 283 ASR. Aircrew of all nations were rescued. Jesse's first rescue, just four days after the squadron became operational, was three downed Germans.

Rescue work was dangerous. Norman Franks in his book on ASR in the Mediterranean writes that 'it took extraordinary courage to land this comparatively small, single-engined amphibian aeroplane [the Walrus] on the sea, often under the eyes of the enemy and attempt to take off with the extra load of rescued personnel. On one occasion a rescued German pilot pulled a gun on Jesse. On another occasion his Walrus had rescued a German pilot off the island of Pantelleria when it was hit by enemy gunfire from the island as it attempted to take off and had to taxi to land from where the gunfire had come. They eventually made it to harbour and, fortunately, found themselves greeted by a small group of allied troops that had just taken possession of the island.

In August 1943 the squadron moved to Palermo to support the campaign in southern Italy and Jesse's rescues included USAAF fighter and bomber personnel. Two rescues of pilots from the 52nd USAAF Fighter Group in three days produced two highly appreciative letters to Jesse's CO.

Major Samborn of the 2nd Fighter Squadron writes, '*it was through precision and accurate coordination that the concerned pilot was located while deep in enemy waters, and it was through W/O Botting's intrepid efforts that this pilot is safe and flying with this squadron again*'.

Lieutenant Colonel Robert Levine USAAF writes, *'you are to be congratulated on having such men as W/O Botting in your squadron. His extraordinary achievement in helping the pilot land deep in enemy waters, thus endangering his own life to rescue a pilot of this group, is an achievement that the officers of this group will never forget'*.

Jesse's later comment on the rescue was that *'the guy never even bought me a drink. He bought me the whole bar!'*

He returned to England in June 1944 to an offer of a position as a gunnery instructor at RAF Training School, which he took. Then a spell with the ATA's programme of flying important European personnel back to their countries after fleeing to England when the Germans invaded.

After some 18 months with the ATA, he was recalled to the RAF and, shortly afterwards, demobbed.

****

RAF Bradwell Bay in 1941/2 with the Canadians of 23 and 418 Squadron Photos taken as publicity shots in support of the RAF's Intruder operations.
Geoff Botting collection

RAF Bradwell Bay in 1941/2 with the Canadians of 23 and 418 Sqadron Photos taken as publicity shots in support of the RAF's Intruder operations.

Geoff Botting collection

Witold `Lanny' Lanowski was a Polish fighter pilot whose remarkable career spanned four air forces during his flying career. His son Krys Lanowski tells of how his father flew with 4 different air forces in the Second World War. While a highly successful fighter pilot with several kills, and numerous decorations and honours, his rather 'difficult' relationship with higher authority prevented him achieving higher rank and recognition.

Witold `Lanny' Lanowski
Early Life

Witold was born in Lwow Poland 1915 (Lwow eventually became part of the Ukraine following Poland's occupation by the USSR), to a Polish father and German mother. His father was a Doctor of Law and held several directorships and his mother was a carpet and kilim rug designer. He was a gifted sportsman competing in swimming, water polo, cross country skiing and shooting when he represented his country against Czechoslovakia in a shooting competition.

His flying career started when he was invited to attend a gliding course in 1934 and the bug bit! He qualified as top student and decided that this was what he wanted to be, a pilot.

In 1935, Witold entered Deblin officer cadet school and graduated as first pilot in 1938, but whilst in the cadet school he continued with his sports including pentathlon and became overall Polish ski champion in downhill, slalom and cross country and also won the Polish shooting championships.

He graduated from Deblin in 1938 with some of the notable Polish pilots of the time including Miroslaw Feric (303 Squadron), Tadeusz Sawicki, Stanislaw Skalski (CO 317 Squadron) and Jan Zumbach (303 Squadron). Witold's first posting as a pilot was to 121 Fighter Squadron in Krakow and whilst there he continued his training for the world ski championships. In February 1939 he won the inter-services championships.

1939 saw him posted back to Deblin flight school as an instructor where he was to teach some of the pilots who would be influential in his later career, namely Zbigniew Janicki, Tadeusz Andersz and Boleslaw Gladych.

Second World War
Following hostilities breaking out with the Germans, on the 13th September 1939 Witold received orders to lead the remaining cadets out of the school south to Romania to escape internment. On the 19th September, he was captured by the Czech militia and handed over to Ukrainian soldiers but managed to escape from the convoy. Following a gruelling journey through Czechoslovakia, Romania and Hungary they eventually landed by boat at Marseille on the 12th November 1939 where he was posted with other pilots to 145 Squadron at Villa Coublay flying in defence of Lyon and Paris.

It was here that Witold's reputation as a rebel escalated, when the Polish pilots were displeased with the Polish authorities regarding the leadership of the air force, and Witold aired his and the other pilots' views. He was arrested by the Polish high command and imprisoned for *'gross insubordination'* for court martial and possible execution.

With the capitulation of France and his escape from prison, he boarded a boat at Marseille docking at Liverpool on the 12th July 1940. Between August 1940 and September 1941, he was unable to be picked by the commanding officers of the Polish fighter squadrons who were frustrated with the fact that a skilled and seasoned pilot was being blocked to them by the Polish high command due to his views and previous arrest.

Witold was posted to 55 OTU as an instructor and was finally picked as a fighter pilot by 308 squadron flying Hurricanes and on the 30th December 1941 was transferred across the airfield to 317 squadron flying Spitfires with the equivalent rank of flying officer.

October 1942 saw him decorated with his second *Cross of Valour* on the insistence of Skalski his squadron commander. In April 1943, he attended fighter leader school where he graduated and was immediately posted to 302 Polish Squadron as `A' flight commander (at the same time Boleslaw Gladych was transferred from 303 squadron to 302 squadron as `B' flight commander). His C.O. at 302 Wacław Król forwarded him on several occasions for the *Virtuti Militari'* but was rejected by the Polish High Command yet again as was his promotion to squadron leader, even though as `A' flight commander he had often led 302 Squadron into battle. By 23rd February 1944, he had completed 97 operations and 220 combat flying hours.

In March 1944, the Polish high command wanted to give Witold a desk job but he refused, and with the help of the Polish Chief of Staff Brzezina, who was a friend and fan of Witold's, he was posted to the 354th Fighter Group of the

USAAF 9th Air Force flying Mustangs from Boxted air base as an intelligence officer. Witold was furious that he had been blocked from operational flying by the high command and it was here with the 354th that he got his famous nickname `*Lanny*' due to the difficulty the Americans had with his surname.

Following several visits with Gladych from Northolt in his Spitfire whilst with 302 Squadron to Halesworth, he went for discussions with Francis Gabreski and `Hub' Zemke. Lanny was subsequently transferred to the 61st Fighter Squadron of the famous 56th Fighter Group, Zemke's *Wolfpack*.

This had come to fruition due to the fact that Gabby Gabreski being of Polish extraction had flown with 315 Polish squadron at Northolt in January 1943, where he met Lanny and Gladych whilst being tutored in combat flying by Andersz.

On return to the USAAF and given command of the 61st Fighter squadron, Gabby petitioned for the transfer to the 56th of seasoned, skilled Polish fighter pilots. This would boost the pilot numbers as the 56th was very short of combat pilots at the time. Several Polish pilots who were transferred to the 61st Fighter Squadron as operational combat pilots including Janicki were lost in combat with the 61st. Those transferred included Gladych, Sawicz, Rutkowski, Andersz and Lanny.

This attachment effectively ended in August 1944. At the request of 'Hub' Zemke and Dave Schilling, Lanny and Gladych stayed on with the suggestion by Zemke, that they apply for a US commission and he was temporarily given the rank of 'Captain' during their stay with the 56th. The commission was never granted due to the Polish high command blocking his promotion yet again. This despite letters being written most notably by General Kepner, who said that Lanny flew wing, element leader, flight leader and 61st squadron leader on missions. However, this was to no avail. On 15th May 1944 he flew the P-47 Thunderbolt for the first time with his first combat mission on the 21st May.

It was with the 56th that Lanny was able to excel at being such a skilled combat pilot that he was accordingly decorated by the Americans with the Air Medal with 2 silver clusters and 4 oak leaf clusters. He was also decorated with the American Distinguished Flying Cross by General Jesse Auton on 25th November 1944 and was granted permission to wear *'Senior Pilots wings'* on his uniform. It was during this time that Lanny was able to display his iconic nose art on the cowling of his P-47 which became one of the most well-known nose art decorations for a US fighter of the war. He created this nose art in 1941 but due to the stuffiness of the RAF rules and regulations was unable to display it on any of his previous fighter planes.

Both Zemke and Gabreski had the greatest respect for Lanny and requested him to fly as their wingman on several occasions, competing with each other for Lanny's 'affections' which often meant Lanny handing over his 'Polish flight' to Gladych to lead whilst he flew as wingman.

The *'Polish flight'* had been set up to allow Gabreski to rotate his new additions to the 61st Squadron to gain combat experience with the Polish veterans through their tutorage. Lanny often didn't claim kills if these rookie pilots had fired on the enemy as well, giving the kill claims to them to boost their confidence.

Whilst with the 56th he was credited with a further 4 kills (2 previous kills with the Polish Air Force):

- FW 190 on 22nd May 1944 (2nd day of combat flying with the 56th)

- Bf 109 on 27th June 1944

- Bf 109 on 5th July 1944

- FW 190 on 18th November 1944 which was the strafing mission to Hanau with all three squadrons of the 56th taking part. Lanny engaged a total of three FW 190s that day but only claimed one as he was unsure of hits for the kill on the other two. This kill whilst flying *Silver Lady*

- He also destroyed a Bf 109 on 27th June 1944 whilst flying HV-M (P47-D) but did not claim the kill. Lanny gave full credit to his wingman, Patterson, after he had initially fired on the 109 on his first pass only scoring a few hits with the 109 turning away trailing white smoke. Lanny then chased and destroyed the 109.

- He also didn't claim a He 111 destroyed on 28th August.

Lanny didn't claim 'ground' kills, as to him, it was just like shooting trains, tanks or trucks…but, he has been credited with 4.6 ground kills by the USAAF in their official records:

- 4 x Bf 110s destroyed 5th August 1944 whilst on a Ramrod mission to Bremen / Osnabruck (source USAF records via Peter Randall)

- 0.6 Ju 88 destroyed 16th August 1944 whilst on a Ramrod mission to Hannover (source USAF records via Peter Randall)

Lanny was given the first production P-47 mark `M' rolling off the production line (44-21108) which was designated HV-Z (bar) in honour of *Silver Lady'* which was retired and transferred to the 9th AF December 1944.

Witold `Lanny' Lanowski's decorations for the Second World War were:

- General Service medal
- War medal 1939 – 45
- Air Crew Europe star
- 1939 – 45 star
- French 1939 – 45 war commemorative medal
- Polish 'Cross of Valour' & bar
- American Air Medal with 2 silver and 4 oak leaf clusters
- American DFC

****

Witold *'Lanny'* Lanowski (on right) Polish fighter pilot served in four air forces during his flying career. The pilots are standing in front of P-47 Thunderbolt called '*Silver Lady'*

Lanowski family archive

Stephen Billyeald writes about his father's service in the RAF in the Second World War. Peter Billyeald was awarded the DFC and the MBE.

Squadron Leader Peter Billyeald

Peter joined the RAFVR in 1938 at the age of 20 *'to learn to fly at somebody else's expense'* as he put it. He learned to fly at Tollerton Aerodrome, near his home town of Nottingham.

At the outbreak of war he was sent to Flying Training School at Peterborough where he flew the Hawker Hart & Hawker Hind – biplanes developed in the 1920s & 1930s.

In July 1940, Peter was posted as a Pilot Officer to 40 Squadron at Wyton, Cambridgeshire, which had been operating Blenheim bombers in France and had suffered heavy losses. Peter flew his first operational sortie in a daylight attack on Caen aerodrome in September. More daylight raids followed but these soon turned to night raids after further losses became unsustainable.

In early 1941, the squadron welcomed the conversion to Wellington bombers – the Blenheim was unsuited to night flying as well as being slow, cold & outdated. The extended range of the Wellington led to raids into Germany and on his 39th operational sortie Peter's aircraft was hit by flak over Berlin damaging the hydraulic system. On his return to base he had to land without flaps and without brakes, he ran out of runway and was only able to stop the aircraft by hitting the back of the gunnery range. The Wellington was destroyed and it was fortunate that no one was killed – two of the crew were injured.

Having completed his first tour – and having destroyed one of its aircraft – the RAF sent Peter to Moreton-in-Marsh (21 OTU) as an instructor! He spent the next 18 months training pilots to fly Wellingtons and he also met his future wife, Paddy Barr, who was a WAAF serving as Assistant Adjutant at Moreton. Peter was recommended for an AFC which was downgraded to a Mention in Dispatches.

In November 1942, Peter was posted to 464 Squadron at Feltwell, Norfolk as a Squadron Leader for his second operational tour. 464 was an Australian squadron operating Lockheed Venturas on escorted daylight raids on northern France and the Low Countries. It was during this time that the squadron took part in Exercise Spartan in March 1943. The prime purpose of the exercise was to develop Army / RAF co-operation in readiness for the invasion of northern Europe. Peter led several of the raids during the exercise including the high-level raid on Pangbourne on 7th March, as well as others on Sonning, Goring, Didcot and Wallingford.

Peter completed his second operational tour of 19 sorties in May 1943 for which he was awarded the DFC. He was posted to Staff College and then to HQ of 2nd Tactical Air Force, where he remained until the end of the war. Peter received a second Mention in Despatches and was appointed MBE in the 1946 New Year Honours list.

Peter died in April 2004 and his ashes were scattered over Tollerton Aerodrome and thus the final entry in his log-book has a similarity to the first!

Peter's two log-books recording every flight that he made between 1938 and 1953 have been kept. There is also a file containing full details of his RAF career including contemporary photographs and extracts from Squadron Operations Record Books copied from the National Archive.

BILLYEALD, Peter, A/S/L (77779, RAFVR) – No.21 Operational Training Unit - **Mention in Despatches** - Awarded as per **London Gazette** dated 1ˢᵗ January 1943. Originally recommended for an Air Force Cross for New Year Honours List, downgraded to this award; text in Public Record Office Air 2/8871.

'For over a year Squadron Leader Billyeald has performed flying instruction duties, during which period he has turned out some excellently trained crews; in addition, he has completed 210 instructional flying hours while serving as flight commander. Both as a flying instructor and flight commander this officer's work has been of the highest order. By his keenness, energy and drive he has set an outstanding example to instructors and pupils alike.'

BILLYEALD, Peter, A/S/L (77779, Royal Air Force Volunteer Reserve) - No.464 Squadron, Royal Australian Air Force - **Distinguished Flying Cross** - awarded as per **London Gazette** dated 11ᵗʰ June 1943. No citation in that publication; following text from Air Ministry Bulletin 10475, drafted when he had flown 38 sorties (137 operational hours).

'Squadron Leader Billyeald is an outstanding officer who has completed numerous operational missions, most of them as flight commander. He has invariably displayed keenness,

determination and leadership of an exceptional nature. His earlier operational experience, which extended over a long period, has contributed much to the efficiency and spirit of his present squadron. His example both on the ground and in the air has been most praiseworthy.'

****

 **Jim Wright recounts to Nigel Parker, his story as a navigator in Lancaster bombers, and the raid as part of 97 Squadron Pathfinder Force on Konigsberg in April 1944. He and his crew went on 42 operational missions, with all surviving the war, a remarkable feat considering the Bomber Command losses. After the war, Jim fought tirelessly until his 97th year to get recognition for the Bomber Command flight and ground crews, culminating in the unveiling of the Bomber Command memorial in Green Park, in London and a Bomber Command Clasp to the 1939-1945 Star.**

Bomber Command's longest operation

Königsberg was the ancient and beautiful capital of East Prussia, on the edge of the Baltic Sea. It was built on a series of four islands, and was known for the mathematical puzzle of how to cross its seven bridges only once and its spectacularly high sand dunes. Until 1944, it had been largely unaffected by the war with its population, unless having joined the armed forces, largely continuing with subsistence farming and minor industries. Being so far up, on the Baltic coast it was too far away from Britain for aircraft of Bomber Command to reach without taking a very perilous journey past some of the heaviest defended areas of occupied Europe.

On the 9th April 1944 Anthony James Wright, Jim to his colleagues, was a navigator of a Lancaster with 630 Squadron operating out of East Kirkby, Lincolnshire and they had been assigned to carry out a mining operation of the Konigsberg Canal, near Pillau; this being their twenty-fourth operation; the round trip taking nine and a half hours and was completed without incident.

By the 26th August 1944, Jim and the rest of his crew, the pilot being P/O Ken Ames, had been transferred to 97 Squadron, Pathfinder Force operating out of RAF Coningsby. It had been assigned to lead Bomber Command's furthest operation of the war and to light up the city of Königsberg with marker flares for the follow-up force of 174 Lancasters to destroy the port facilities. The round flight took over ten hours, flying over 950 miles, the eastern part of the city being largely destroyed and all the Lancasters returned safely, although five Lancasters that had been assigned as part of a diversion force to lay mines off Danzig and Kiel were lost. On a follow-up operation two days later a force of 189 Lancasters attacked the city, a large proportion of the city being destroyed. Due to a twenty-minute delay in opening the bombing due to low cloud, the German night fighter force was fully alerted and fifteen Lancasters failed to return.

To be able to go out night after night on bombing operations took a remarkable amount of courage. Jim and his crew stayed together through forty-two operations, serving with three squadrons, although on their fifth operation to Kässel with 61 Squadron, Syreston their Lancaster was shot up by a Focke Wulf FW 190. Jim, having his oxygen supply cut by a cannon shell which sliced through his Gosport tube, passed out, only being discovered barely alive on the return trip. The aircraft made a crash landing at Coltishall and Jim spent two months in hospital recovering from his injuries, and his pilot, Ken Ames, receiving an immediate DFC for getting his aircraft and crew back.

On the plus side the Lancaster gunners claimed the Focke Wulf as destroyed. Ken Ames and the rest of the crew carried out one operation without Jim when they were posted to the newly formed 420 Squadron. The crew had their fair share of incidents when on their eighth operation to Berlin they were attacked by a Messerschmitt Bf 110 which they claimed as destroyed, along with damaging a Messerschmitt Bf 109 and a Junkers Ju 88; this was along with avoiding all the heavy flak that was fired up at them. On other occasions they were shot up by Junkers Ju 88 night-fighters and a Messerschmitt Bf 109 that they claimed as destroyed over Frankfurt.

After completing forty two operations and numerous other flights, the crew were stood down for a rest and assigned to training duties; they were never called upon to carry out any further operations during the war. They deemed themselves to be very lucky as many of their friends and colleagues, in fact over fifty-five percent of Bomber Command aircrew, failed to return.

At the end of the war Jim, having been awarded the Distinguished Flying Cross for his service, stayed in the RAF with Training Command rising to the rank of Wing Commander before transferring to become a civilian Navigation Officer with the air traffic control department at the new Heathrow airport.

Jim and his crew remained in contact throughout their lives, being one of the few full crews to make it through to the end. Jim recorded in his log book the names of a few close contacts who were lost during operations; aircrew tended to avoid getting to know other crews too closely as it was easier to cope with when they died.

Jim was always very conscious of his luck having survived, while so many had not and was very troubled that Bomber Command aircrew never got the recognition that they duly deserved post war, with neither a campaign medal or a memorial. This despite the fact that they operated from the first day of war to the last and took the war to the enemy when there was no other means. They also suffered the highest casualty rate of any of the services; only the German U-Boat crews had a higher percentage loss.

In 2001, due to his involvement in the bombing of Königsberg, Jim became involved in a push to find where the airmen who were lost on the second Königsberg raid were buried; most were listed as missing, although it was known that their bodies had been buried by the Germans. However, their graves were lost in 1945 when the Soviet army captured Königsberg and annexed it into the Soviet Union, renaming it Kaliningrad; all the German cemeteries were erased. The Russian Government made an offer to allow a memorial to be erected in the centre of Kaliningrad honouring the Bomber Command aircrews and that if the positions of the lost graves of the airmen could be identified from records, headstones could be erected by the Commonwealth War Graves Commission but these offers were vetoed by the British Government.

This prompted Jim to question once more why there was no proper recognition of those who had served in Bomber Command unlike the other services and he set out to rectify matters. In this quest, he gained support from across the world, through politicians from the Commonwealth and allied nations, as well as many notable historians. In the end, a memorial was erected in Green Park, London. At its centre are bronze statues displaying seven bomber crew who had just returned from an operation. Following an even longer campaign for the government to approve the award of a campaign star, a clasp to be worn on the 1939 - 1945 Star was approved to be awarded to all Bomber Command aircrew, although recognition was sought for all who served in Bomber Command on the basis that no aircraft would have taken to the air without the support of the many ground crew.

After eighteen years of campaigning at the age of ninety-seven, Jim had to give up his battle due to his failing eyesight but he certainly made the world sit up and acknowledge that the aircrew who volunteered to serve with Bomber Command deserved far more than just to be forgotten and they were still a formidable force to be reckoned with.

****

Group Captain David Drew describes an RAF operation in the Second World War to bomb a specific target in Copenhagen in March 1945. Operation Carthage was a plan to bomb the Gestapo Headquarters in the centre of the city, where leaders of the Danish resistance were being held and interrogated. Under extreme duress and torture, there was every possibility that the resistance fighters might be coerced into revealing secrets vital to the allies war effort including details of all the resistance movements in the city. It was vital this did not happen.

Operation *Carthage*

On the afternoon of 20th March 1945, some 80 men gathered in the main briefing room at RAF Fersfield, 16 miles south-west of Norwich. Most of them were in their early 20s and were already veterans of air combat; they had flown in from Rosieres-en-Santerre in France and RAF Bentwaters, UK.

The men listened attentively to briefings that afternoon and evening; they also took time to examine a scale model of the centre of the city of Copenhagen. They were now ready for a bombing mission the following day.

In March 1995 I was honoured to be invited, along with other members of my family, to the 50th anniversary commemoration of that mission in Copenhagen. Indeed, all remaining survivors of the raid, with their close relatives and the families of those who were killed, had been invited. I hasten to say that I fell into the third category, although I was, by then, a Wing Commander (Wg Cdr) in the RAF. I felt privileged to meet so many of the surviving aircrew who very readily gave their personal accounts of the raid and other missions. We were all treated royally, given hotel accommodation for two nights, and treated to several receptions and a dinner hosted by their Minister of Foreign Affairs. Danish TV channels carried documentaries about the mission and the anniversary was commemorated in all the main Danish media. But why was Operation Carthage, as the raid was called, so important to the Danes?

Following the almost bloodless German invasion of Denmark on 9th April 1940, the Danes formally accepted that there would be no resistance to Nazi operations. In fact, quite a few Danes became active collaborators with the Germans. But covert resistance did eventually start with ex-military, university students and the press taking the lead[51]. In early 1942 the British Special Operations Executive (SOE) parachuted agents into Denmark with the aim of setting up a secret army and carrying out acts of sabotage. As the war progressed, they became bolder in their actions and some were captured, often given away by other Danes.

A resistance cell was established in the city of Aarhus in 1943, led by Pastor Harald Sandbæk. Unfortunately, Sandbæk was later betrayed and, with two other senior members of his cell, imprisoned and interrogated in the

---

[51] For a full account of the Danish Resistance Movement 1940/5 see 'The Giant-Killers' by John Oram Thomas, published in UK by Michael Joseph Ltd, 1975. ISBN 0 7181 1340 3. p139

Gestapo headquarters for Jutland which had been established in the city's university. Because of the importance of these men and the information they might give away under interrogation, a request was passed to the RAF to bomb the commandeered buildings of the university, accepting that the resistance men would probably be killed. The raid took several days to plan, during which time Sandbæk and the others were tortured regularly, but it went ahead on 31st October 1944. Twenty-six Mosquito light bombers accompanied by 8 Mustang fighters took part in the raid, which happened to hit the commandeered buildings at the same time as Sandbæk was undergoing another interrogation and while a conference of some 240 Gestapo from all over Jutland was taking place. Miraculously, Sandbæk survived, as did one of his friends, but his interrogator and torturer were killed, along with 55 other Gestapo, German army personnel and Danish collaborators[52].

Meanwhile the Gestapo in Copenhagen had been busy. Danish *stikkere* (informants) were found in all areas and regularly betrayed the resistance men and women. By early 1945 up to 26 resistance men were imprisoned on the top floor of the *Shellhus* in the centre of the city, a building which, before the war, had been the Danish headquarters of the Royal Dutch Shell oil company. Taken over by the Gestapo, it had been repainted, but stood out because it was the only building in the area that was camouflaged.

---

[52] For further details, see 'Mission Completed' by ACM Sir Basil Embry, published by Methuen and Co Ltd in 1959, Catalogue No 5885/U, Pages 273-276. Embry's assertion that all 240 Gestapo were killed arose from early reports after the raid; theses have since been corrected.

Major Svend Truelsen was the Danish liaison officer working in the Danish Section of the Special Operations Executive (SOE) in London in 1945. He received a message from the leaders of the Copenhagen resistance cell who had not been captured, that with so many resistance fighters held by the Gestapo, there was a danger that details of the whole Danish resistance movement would be extracted. He immediately contacted Air Vice-Marshal (AVM) Basil Embry, the Air Officer Commanding No 2 Group RAF, with whom he had established a good rapport before the Aarhus raid. He asked for a similar mission to be carried out against the *Shellhus*. Embry accepted the importance of the situation but, in early 1945 the weather was generally pretty atrocious, and he also had to cover other priority targets in France and the Netherlands. However, from postcards, photographs and possibly aerial reconnaissance he had an accurate model made of the centre of Copenhagen and eventually received clearance from the Air Ministry to plan an attack. Nevertheless, he wanted confirmation that the Danish resistance was in as parlous a state as it appeared, and that they were prepared for many deaths among those held prisoner in the building. Furthermore, Embry was concerned that, because the *Shellhus* was surrounded by many residential buildings, there might be collateral damage. Consequently, he arranged for Ole Lippmann, a 21-year old Danish resistance leader, who had to flee to England in July 1944, to return to Copenhagen to ascertain the situation. Fifty years later I heard Lippman recount how he spent some hours walking in the Jægersborg Gardens, working out the best course of action and weighing up the pros and cons. He signalled Truelsen in England, asking Embry to mount the raid, saying that his friends would sooner die from the bombing than at the hands of the Germans. He also passed on up-to-date information on anti-aircraft defences and the news that the German cruiser *Nuremburg* was moored in Copenhagen Harbour. Embry scheduled the raid for 21ˢᵗ March.

Eighteen Mosquito bombers in three waves, drawn from 21 Squadron (Sqn) RAF, 464 Sqn RAAF and 487 Sqn RNZAF, would carry out the raid. Two Mosquitos from the RAF's Film Production Unit (FPU) would photograph the results. For fighter escort and flak suppression they would be accompanied by 28 Mustang Mk3 fighters from 64 and 126 Sqns and 1 Mk3 and 2 Mk4 Mustangs[53] of 234 Sqn based at RAF Bentwaters under the command of Wing Commander Michel Donnet. A Belgian Air Force pilot, 'Mike' Donnet had escaped from Belgium following the invasion of his country in 1940, by repairing and then flying a Stampe biplane to England with his friend Leon Divoy. They had then both joined the RAF[54].

Following a final briefing, the first wave of aircraft took off at 0835. The local time over the target was to be 1115 as that was when most Germans would be in the *Shellhus* and

---

[53] I met OC 234 Squadron, Jas Storer, in 1995. He told me that his unit wasn't originally earmarked for Operation Carthage, but as they had received 4 brand new aircraft on 19 March, he persuaded Mike Donnet that they should be allowed 'to come along for the ride'. They were given the task of preventing any German aircraft taking off from Copenhagen's military airfield at Vaerlose and then covering the withdrawal of the force.

[54] For a full account of Michel Donnet's escape from Belgium and subsequent service with the RAF, see 'Flight to Freedom' by Michael Donnet, 2ⁿᵈ edition published by Wingham Press Ltd in 1991, ISBN 1 873454 07 4. I was lucky enough to meet this charming and affable man after he had retired as a Lieutenant General in the Belgian Air Force. He spoke very highly of my uncle, David Drew.

many of the incriminating files and dossiers would be out of the safes and in use. Group Captain Bob Bateson, with his navigator Squadron Leader (Sqn Ldr) Ted Sismore, led the raid, as they had led several other successful Mosquito attacks. His No 2 was Sqadron Leader Tony Carlisle and No 3 was 'Wing Commander Smith' (aka Air Vice-Marshal Embry, who should not, because of his rank, have been flying on operations, but actually did so regularly).

With 50 knot winds and in stormy conditions, all aircraft were to fly at about 270 knots and were to remain at or below 50 feet for the whole flight except to pull up over obstacles such as electrical cables or chimneys. Embry had declared that if he saw any aircraft above him, he would shoot it down – a rather unnecessary threat as most of the attacking force was behind him. He describes the ride as being 'rough and boisterous'[55] and most pilots had difficulties with visibility because of the salt spray that caked their windscreens. Once over Denmark, many of the people they passed saluted, if they didn't dive for cover. Three Mustangs had to return to UK following bird strikes.

The first six Mosquito bombers and one FPU Mosquito approached the *Shellhus* from the south, increasing speed to 320 knots. Five of them released their bombs, which successfully hit the West Wing of the building. The air raid warning was only given when the first bombs hit the *Shellhus*.

Sadly, Wing Commander Peter Kleboe's aircraft clipped a 30-metre high railway lighting mast; his bombs released and one destroyed a house, killing 11 civilians; the other

---

[55] See 'Mission Completed' pages 277-278.

bomb failed to explode and was later defused. His aircraft's port wing then caught the roof of a nearby building; it sheared off and he and his navigator were killed when his aircraft crashed near the Jeanne d'Arc School.

The second wave was now running in from the west. Seeing the smoke from the ruins of Kleboe's aircraft the leader headed for that; he realized his error at the last moment and he and one other managed to carry on to hit the *Shellhus*. Sadly, one aircraft dropped its bombs on Kleboe's Mosquito with disastrous results.

The five Mosquitos in the third wave mistakenly dropped their bombs in the Frederiksberg area around Kleboe's aircraft and the Jeanne d'Arc School. A total of three bombs hit the school. The main staircase collapsed as the children were being shepherded towards the cellar; other damage then sealed the entrance to the cellar where there were many deaths from drowning when the water pipes burst, a situation exacerbated when the fire brigade tried to extinguish the flames in the school. The official death toll shows that 86 children, 10 nuns, 4 teachers, two firemen and two rescue workers were killed. In addition, 67 children and 35 adults were injured.

As for the *Shellhus,* it is, in some ways, fortunate that no more bombs fell on the building as only eight prisoners were killed but 18 escaped with relatively minor injuries.[56] Twenty-six Gestapo and 30 Danish collaborators were killed and most of the documentation on the resistance was destroyed. Another 16 bodies were found initially, but it is

---

[56] Experiences inside the *Shellhus* during and after the raid are well-documented in 'The Giant-Killlers'.

unclear who they were; the remains of another 20 to 40 people were found later. The official police report states that 125 people died in the building, but the exact number is certainly indeterminate to this day[57].

Meanwhile some of the Mustangs had flown ahead of the bombers to draw and suppress anti-aircraft fire. One aircraft was hit by flak and the pilot, the 22-year old acting squadron commander of 64 Sqn, made a crash-landing in the *Faelled Park*. He succeeded in passing his dog tags to a Dane who tried to help him before he died in the cockpit. Three other Mosquitos and one other Mustang were shot down, either over the city or on the return flight. Pilot Officer 'Bob' Hamilton from the Mustang was taken prisoner, but the other six Mosquito aircrew were all killed or died while trying to escape to Sweden.

Some might consider Operation Carthage to be another glorious British disaster. Many Danes were killed, 87 of them children. Six aircraft and 9 aircrew were lost. But the Danes still celebrate the anniversary of the raid[58]. By destroying much of the information about the resistance and by preventing the further interrogation of the prisoners in the *Shellhus*, the raid secured most of the Danish resistance movement. This meant that the final overthrow of the

---

[57] Various accounts put the total number anywhere between 75 and 200.
[58] I am indebted to Derek Carter, who lives near Copenhagen and has made an extensive study of Operation Carthage; he hopes to publish a book about it shortly. He has conducted me and several members of my family on visits to the main sites in the city associated with the raid and attends all ceremonies of commemoration. He was instrumental in persuading the Danish Government to place a memorial on the rebuilt *Shellhus* which was unveiled on the 50th anniversary of the attack.

German regime in Denmark was completed more easily and quickly when the Allied forces arrived.

So, what is my connection to this event? The Acting Squadron Commander of 64 Sqn was my father's younger brother; he had joined the RAFVR in 1941. By the age of 22 he had flown catapulted Hurricane fighters from merchant ships in the North Atlantic convoys, retrained on Spitfires to support the D-Day landings, and had escorted transport aircraft to Arnhem. Many of his early operations over the continent involved air-to-ground firing, particularly of trains and enemy convoys, but he was also credited with shooting down a Bf109 and, with his wingman, an FW190 and a Ju88. By late 1944 he was a flight commander on 64 Sqn when it received Mustangs for long-range bomber escort. During one of these sorties his squadron commander was killed, and David Drew took command of the situation and of 64 Sqn in the air; for this he was awarded the DFC. Although it was initially thought that his aircraft was hit by anti-aircraft fire from the *Nuremburg,* subsequent investigation shows that he was killed by flak over Copenhagen and he is buried in Bispebjerg cemetery, Copenhagen, alongside Wing Commander Peter Kleboe RAFVR and his navigator Fg Off Reg Hall RCAF.

****

 *Steve Cross tells the story of his father's wartime experience flying as a navigator in a Bomber Command Lancaster Pathfinder squadron in the Second World War. Taken from hundreds of letters written during the war between he and his then girlfriend and future wife, Peg, and other documents, Steve recounts the training in England and Canada, and operations over western Europe of his father Fred Cross. Fred was just 20 years old when he flew his first operational missions.*

Flying Officer Fred Cross, DFC

Fred Cross grew up on a council estate in Bristol. He was 15 years old when the war started and he worked at the ES & A Robinson Waxed Paper Co Ltd factory in Fishponds, Bristol. On the same council estate there lived a young woman called Peg (Margaret) Cardinelli who started working at the same factory in late 1940. Fred was a shy young man, but he was attracted to Peg Cardinelli, whom he saw at work every day.

Early in 1942, when he turned 18, Fred signed up to join the RAF. Bristol had suffered heavy bombing in 1940, so he had an idea of what war entailed; but he was up for doing his bit. His call-up to the RAF provided the impetus for him to seek a date with Peg. However, he was still too shy, so he got a friend at work to tell Peg to meet him outside his home on the council estate at 6:30pm on Friday 13th February 1942, so that they could go to the cinema together. Peg arrived at the right time, but there was no sign of Fred. Being a strong young woman, and not wanting to miss the film, after waiting a few minutes she set off for the Odeon

Cinema in Kingswood (a 15 minute walk). Fred, who had been watching from a window, with a mixture of trepidation and joy, finally decided to 'man up', put his coat on, and ran after her.

Once they'd seen the film, *'Suspicion'*, starring Joan Fontaine and Bristol boy Cary Grant, Fred was more relaxed and told Peg about his call-up and how his training would start in August, later that year. That was their first date and they obviously got on because they stayed together throughout Fred's time in the RAF. To keep in touch during his RAF service, Fred and Peg wrote each other letters, almost daily, and many of these have survived, in particular the ones that Fred sent. Peg numbered each envelope. They range from No. 1 (dated 4th Aug 1942) when Fred first arrived at No 1 Aircrew Reception Centre, RAF Regent's Park, London to No. 557 (dated 13th May 1945).

In those first couple of weeks in London, Fred wrote of new experiences, including seeing London Bridge, Buckingham Palace, St Paul's, Westminster Cathedral, the Houses of Parliament and many other places for the first time. By late August Fred was in Brighton with the Air Crew Disposal Wing. As he sat writing one letter a Spitfire flew overhead and fired at an enemy plane. Fred wrote that *'This sort of thing goes on all day'* adding that *'Last night, when I arrived, I saw oil on the waves. I expect that it was from a ship that was sunk in the Dieppe raid'*. This refers to Operation Jubilee, an attempt by British Forces to seize and hold a major port and show that they could potentially open a western front. The raid was a total failure apart from the possible collection of some forms of intelligence information, and the ship that Fred referred to was a Royal Navy vessel that was sunk.

From Brighton he was transferred to Ludlow where he was *'miles away from anywhere and out in the fields'*. They were sleeping in tents and seemed to be spending their time digging trenches. He wrote that he washes *'in the middle of a field in ice cold water, stripped to the waist, at 6 o'clock in the morning'*. He wasn't impressed with the two picture houses there either, stating that *'They are about the size of our front room'*. Fred always referred to Ludlow as 'Mudlow' because of all the rain made the fields where they camped extremely muddy.

From Ludlow, Fred was transferred to the ITW (Initial Training Wing) at Newquay, in mid-October. Here he studied things like meteorology, map reading, navigation and took lots of tests; but he managed to get out of some of the more boring duties by doing *'paintings and drawing pictures for the RAF. This is OK, as it gets me well in with the Flight Sergeants and officers'*. Fred's artistic skills were so well received that the Commanding Officer asked him to do paintings for the Beachcroft Hotel in which they were staying. By late January 1943, Fred had passed his exams and he sent Peg this photo of the 43 trainees and 5 staff who attended the No. 7 ITW at Newquay.

In February 1943, still in Newquay, Fred got excited and told Peg that *'We had egg for tea today, dearest, real live egg. Not the tinned stuff, but just taken out of the shell, and it tasted lovely. It is the third egg I have had in the last six months!'*

In late March 1943, he went to Elementary Flight Training School at, RAF Shellingford, Berkshire and flew Tiger Moths. Within days he wrote to Peg *'Today I did loops, stalls, turns, dives, glides, and gliding turns, and it's ever such funny feelings you get in different manoeuvres. For instance, darling, when you do a loop, your stomach goes down in your boots, and your eyelids feel too heavy to keep open, but altogether it's pretty good up there, and sometime I'll take you up for a flip, maybe'.* This letter shows how a lad, just turned 19, was having such a great time and his confidence was growing rapidly. Fred even says in one letter that *'it's you that will keep me going right through this war, darling, because I'd meet Jerry in a Tiger Moth, with you behind me'.* That's how determined he was to help get the war won. They even started talking about getting engaged around this time.

By mid-May 1943 Fred was back in Ludlow for a few weeks then he learnt that the RAF wanted him to train as a Navigator, and he was transferred to Heaton Park, Manchester, where RAF crew were stationed before being posted overseas for final training. In a letter dated 18th July 1943, Fred wrote that he's on a ship, but for security reasons, he couldn't say where it was going. He did say *'The very first meal I had aboard was delicious, especially the sweet. It was entirely fruit - cherries, peaches, apricots, pineapple, everything, except bananas. Hope you're not too jealous, darling.'* In fact he was on an epic trip across the Atlantic and told Peg that *'I've seen a couple of things today, darling, that I've never seen before. I've seen flying fish, & turbots, and a whole school of porpoises.'*

By late July 1943, Fred was able to tell Peg he was in Canada. He would be away for 6 months. He wrote Peg some details of this amazing journey... *'Well here I am, sweetheart, safe and sound, and just getting used to oranges once again. We have just arrived here at Moncton, after travelling by train for nearly 2 days. We passed through New York on the way up, darling, and I saw the Statue of Liberty, Broadway, Grand Central etc, etc. It's a grand sight, especially as we have been used to blackouts and the like. I'll bring you to see NY sometime, dearest, if we can. It's something all should see. Well, darling, I'm feeling fit and well, except for 3 inoculations we have just had... We have grand food here, and plenty of it'*.

Many years later, with one of their sons (who worked in upstate New York in the early 1980s), Fred and Peg did visit New York, and saw all the sights he mentioned in that letter. However, his son didn't know of Fred's wish to take Peg to New York until both had passed away, and the surviving letters were found in a large box in the attic of their old house.

By mid-September, Fred was at APO No 1006, Rivers, Manitoba. The Acting Pilot Officer school was more or less the last stage of training before Fred could actively take part in operations with Bomber Command. He described the journey across Canada to Peg... *'All there was, was miles and miles of forests and lakes. It seemed nothing to travel for hours on end and not see a sign of civilisation. Anyhow, Peg, it was lovely country, and is really an experience'*. The training in Rivers was tough, and they worked long hours. Fred's aim was to become a Navigator. He flew 40 times during just over 4 months based at Rivers.

His Log Book from December 1943 shows the range and type of procedures he was learning. He finished the course in February 1944.

By July, he was part of Bomber Command, in 35 Squadron (Pathfinders), based at Graveley, near Huntingdon. He used to tell a story of how, when the trained lads all met for the first time, they got to know each other socially and this interaction was part of how they became crew members on specific planes. His first mission out of Graveley took place on the 23rd July 1944; it was a night raid on Kiel. They dropped six 2000lbs high explosive bombs, experienced flak and witnessed German night fighters.

By the end of July, in just nine days, Fred had flown five missions, including two more sorties over Germany (Stuttgart and Hamburg) and two over France (Caen and Foret de Nieppe). In no time at all this 20 year old lad had become an experienced RAF crew member. These first five missions logged up over 25 hours of flying time, of which 80% were night flights.

Fred's Log Book for this period includes his hand written notes of what the crew experienced during those early days as a Pathfinder with Bomber Command. Needless to say, as he had done throughout his training days, he continued to write to Peg. However only about a third of the letters have been found.

The earliest surviving letters from this period were from early September 1944. In one he wrote about the reality of war, something he didn't do often... '*We hit an ammunition dump, and made an explosion which spread flames up to about 1000ft, with smoke spreading up to 6 - 7000ft. Anyhow the smoke went far above us. Most of Le Havre is being bombed right out by now. I only hope the civvies are well out of the way, as they are supposed to be'.*

One of the scariest moments that Fred Cross recounted in his letters to Peg Cardinelli was of an operation that his plane was scheduled to be on, to the Urft Dam, on the 4th December 1944. Just after taking off from Graveley their *'control column jammed, and we were forced to turn back after jettisoning all our bomb load into the sea. We had a pretty stiff time of it, too, almost had to bail out, but managed to get back OK. Dave was sweating away on the stick, with both of us pulling at it, trying to get it to move. We were really tired out, when at last we got back to base, and made quite a perfect landing without the use of the ailerons'.* Dave was Squadron Leader L D Leicester, an Australian, who was one of the youngest Squadron Leaders in Bomber Command.

Less than two days later, during an operation to Soest in north Germany, they were attacked by a Messerschmitt Me 163 *'Komet'* rocket powered fighter. In his letter to Peg, Fred wrote that they suffered no damage at all, and with typical dry humour, and in 'keep calm and carry on' mode, he wrote *'they hadn't better try that too often though, because I don't like it, and will complain to someone about it!!'*

Other stories that Fred told his family include the time when their plane shook and the pilot thought that something had hit the rear turret. As they didn't need the navigator at that moment, Fred was told by the pilot to go to the rear of the plane and see what had happened. It turned out that the rear turret had been smashed off (hit by a friendly bomb) and all that was left of the rear gunner was part of his arm. However, research suggests that this happened to another plane in 35 Squadron during a raid that Fred was on, to Leunam on the 14th January 1945. Perhaps the family memory is of the actual story, but they interpreted it as relating to Fred and not to the other plane.

Four days later, on the 18th January it was Fred's 21st birthday, and the family recalled a story of the crew singing to him on a plane, after a raid. Again, the family story is different to what Fred's letter told Peg... '*Well, darling, I've spent quite a quiet birthday today, except that when I walked into the ante-room, all my pals started to yell, at the top of their voices, 'He's 21 today, he's 21 today etc etc'. Boy, did my face go red - you can bet it did, especially as the Station Commander and Squadron Commander were there. Still, the boys are really great types, and we have bags of fun together*'.

Another story that Fred told his family occurred around this time, and he also wrote about it in a letter. This episode was about navigation kit playing up on a raid. Fred struggled to figure out where they were, but then, in the small portion of the screen that was visible, he spotted a river that he recognised from the maps that he was using for this raid. From researching the letters this turned out to have happened on the 4th/5th February 1945 during a night raid on Bonn when their navigational equipment went on the blink. Then Fred spotted a certain river bend, and figured out where they were, so their aircraft, alone, carried out a bombing raid on Koblenz (40 miles south of Bonn), before Fred guided them back to base without the navigation kit!

There's even a story about a crazy Russian Roulette game at the base one night. The lads thought it was for a laugh, and the revolver wasn't loaded. Then one of the boys picked it up and fired it at a wall and a bullet made a dramatic impact! Perhaps unsurprisingly, this story wasn't related by Fred in his letters to Peg and also there doesn't appear to be any reference to it on line! So it is not clear if this one is true or not!

Squadron Leader Ken Gooch was Fred's pilot for all of the 23 operations that he flew on from the 1st January 1945 until he finished his tour, and his 61st 'op', on the 3rd April 1945.

Later that year Fred was awarded the DFC (as he told Peg in letter no. 577, dated the 15th May 1945) and in November he and Peg got married, near the council estate in Fishponds, Bristol.

****

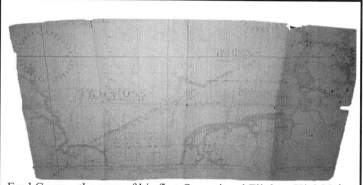

Fred Cross - His Log Book detailing his first five flights in July 1944.

Steve Cross archive

Fred Cross – the map of his first Operational Flight – Kiel 23rd July 1944.

Steve Cross Achive

Fred W T Cross with Pathfinders Crew and ground staff at RAF
Graveley, Huntingdon.

Steve Cross archive

Fred W T Cross and crews during flight training, 20th Jan 1944
(Rivers, Manitoba, Canada).

Steve Cross archive

Fred Cross was awarded the DFC as he told Peg in letter no. 577, dated the 15th May 1945. In November he and Peg got married, near the Council Estate in Fishponds, Bristol.

Steve Cross archive

John Boyes, military writer and former army officer, describes the bombing attack on Hitler's lair, set high in the Austrian Alps, near to Salzburg. The so-called 'Eagles Nest' near the small town of Berchtesgaden was symbolic of the Nazi regime. Ironically, Hitler rarely used it aside from photographic opportunities with people he wanted to impress, and never spent a night there. It is said that he was scared of heights. At the time of the raid with allied forces advancing deep into Germany from both east and west, as it turned out the war in Europe had under two weeks to run, and Hitler less than a week to live.

Destroying the Führer's mountain retreat

Since this year we celebrate the seventy-fifth anniversary of the end of the Second World War, it seems an appropriate time to reflect on the events of 25th April 1945.

The final acts of the war in Europe are taking place. The American and the Soviet forces meet each other at Torgau on the River Elbe. Soviet artillery is now within range of Berlin. For the Australian and New Zealand squadrons of the RAF, ANZAC Day commemorations are underway, but some squadrons are anxiously awaiting the return of aircraft deployed earlier that morning. With few meaningful targets left to bomb, Bomber Command's operations were being curtailed. But Hitler is not yet dead and there was to be one final show of force against the crumbling Reich.

On that day, at dawn, bombers from RAF Bomber Command squadrons and US Eighth Air Force Bomb Group units took off from their bases in eastern England. The targets for the 282 American B-24 crews on Mission 968 were the rail marshalling yards at Salzburg (44th BG),

Hallein (446th BG) and Bad Reichenhall (392d BG). They were escorted by 203 long-range P-51Ds. The RAF's targets were, however, psychologically more significant. Their main objectives, in fact not far from the American targets, were the SS Barracks and the *Berghof*, Hitler's residence in the mountainous Obersalzberg enclave where it was thought by some that the Nazi hierarchy were preparing to make their last stand in the 'Alpine Redoubt'. Some sources claim that a third target was also involved. This was the *Kehlsteinhaus* or 'Eagle's Nest', a tea house constructed for, but little used by, Hitler and perched on a rocky outcrop on the Kehlstein Mountain.

The crews had been briefed four times over the previous three days but the operation had been subsequently cancelled. On one occasion the crews had been ordered to stand down just after the engines had been started. Special charts were issued as the usual plotting charts did not cover the target area. The stations had been locked down and guarded after the first operation was cancelled in case of any security leak. But now the weather over the mountains had at last cleared. Three hundred and fifty-nine Lancasters from twenty-five squadrons in Nos 1 and 5 Groups and 8 Pathfinder Force (PFF) along with sixteen PFF Mosquitos took part in the operation. They were accompanied by a protecting fighter shield: 131 Mustangs equipped with long-range tanks from thirteen RAF Fighter Command squadrons and eighty-eight US 8AF P-51s.

The RAF fighters took off on *Operation Ramrod 1554* at around 7.00am and the operational plan was for the fighters to sweep to the north, south and rear of the bombers. The length of the bomber formation, however, made it difficult to provide totally effective cover. The 105 Squadron Mosquitos were fitted with '*Oboe*' precision bombing system to guide the bombers to their targets. With the Reich territory now being overrun by the advancing allied forces resulting in correspondingly reduced areas of air defence, passage to the target was now less hazardous until the target area itself was approached. The bombers routed via Andrews Field, Cap Gris Nez and Paris before heading for southern Germany. Flak batteries, however, were still present and although scattered, were still willing to mount a stiff if somewhat dispersed resistance to the incoming bombers.

The American aircraft appear to have suffered worst in this context as twenty B-24s were damaged although only one airman was wounded. Australian, Canadian, Polish and Southern Rhodesian crews flew alongside their British compatriots and the aircraft reached their target between 0930 and 1000hrs with the Master Bomber marking the target at 0946hrs. Protecting flak units were still present, but the smoke generators designed to cover the area in the event of an attack no longer had enough chemicals to operate. A few jet fighters reported in the area may have been scrambled, but only a lone Arado 234 reconnaissance aircraft was seen by one of the crews. Fifty-nine aircraft dropped their bombs on the SS Barracks – target for the second wave of bombers - with the remainder targeting the *Berghof* along with the Göring and Bormann residences. Of the senior Nazis, only the disgraced Göring was there at the time and he quickly took refuge in the underground tunnel system that criss-crossed the area.

Most of the bombers carried the 'PLUMDUFF' bomb load mixture of one 4,000lb (H.C.) MkII 'Cookie', three 1,000lb HE and up to six SBC incendiary bombs, although some equivalent American bombs were also used where British bombs were in short supply. Nos 9 and 617 Squadrons, which specialised in precision bombing, carried the last of Barnes Wallis's 12,000lb 'Tallboy' (M.C.) bombs to be dropped in the war, hoping that these earthquake bombs would penetrate the underground bunker system. Weather conditions in general were mixed with only a light snow cover over the target although some crews reported *'clear above - five tenths cloud cover over the target.'* Other crews reported clear conditions and good target visibility. Unfortunately, problems were experienced with the target marking Mosquitos receiving the Oboe signals in the mountainous area and this along with the cloud caused thirty-two Lancasters to abort with most dropping their bombs in the general area of the primary targets. One hit a bridge in Berchtesgaden, the only damage done in the town and a 635 Squadron Lancaster III (F2*E: PB926) from 8 PFF suffered a hung load over the target due to an unserviceable distributor. The crew subsequently dropped their bombs on a level-crossing at a railway station in Prien am Chiemsee on their homeward journey. Three aircraft did not return.

One from 300 Squadron (BH*Z: PD383) was damaged by flak and the pilot and flight engineer were wounded. The aircraft was homeward bound but such were the injuries that it diverted to the Advanced Landing Ground at A-68 Juvincourt in north-west France. This airfield ironically had been one of the main *Luftwaffe* bases during the occupation of France but after falling into allied hands had been taken over by the USAAF. The second crew were not so lucky. Lancaster III (PG*F: LM756) from 619 Squadron was hit by flak and crashed in the mountains near the Austrian village of Adnet.

The squadron's unenviable task had been to fly interference raids, circling around the target to attract flak. Four of the Canadian crew including the pilot were killed in the crash, among the last in Bomber Command to die in the war* and three crew members parachuted to safety and were taken prisoner. The crew who died are buried in the Klagenfurt War Cemetery in Austria. A third Lancaster I (AR*M: NX585) from 460 (RAAF) Squadron was hit by flak blowing away a bomb bay door and disabling the two starboard engines. Five of the crew baled out but the rear gunner's parachute had been shredded by the gunfire so he joined the pilot for the crash landing which happened at Traunstein to the north west of Berchtesgaden. Fortunately, both men, along with the other crew members, survived. Even with long-range tanks, the Mustangs were flying at the limit of their range and a number stopped at Advanced Landing Grounds on their return journey to refuel.

No bombs were dropped on the *Kehlsteinhaus*. This remains the subject of speculation. The building would have been very hard to identify in the snowy peaks and very difficult to hit. More likely perhaps is the generic use of the 'Eagle's Nest' name to refer to the Berghof as Berchtesgaden was used interchangeably with the Obersalzberg and that the tea house was too small a target to identify. Some claim that the mountain tea house was never on the target list. Realising by then that rebuilding post-war Germany, an enormously costly project, would become a priority, the house may have been seen as the basis of a developing tourist industry in an area where other rebuilding projects would have been difficult.

Although the tonnage of bombs dropped was significant, Hitler's Berghof was only damaged, as too were Göring and Bormann's houses. Other properties such as Albert Speer's studio with its panoramic window remained intact. The complex of underground tunnels which connected the main buildings, built too deep to be penetrated, was undamaged. On 4th May, the US Third Infantry Division moved into the area and took over control.

Demolition of the three main properties was to happen in the early 1950s when the area was handed back to the Germans. Although the 25th April was effectively the last day of US Eighth Air Force bombing missions, two days later USAAF P-47 Thunderbolts attacked the Berchtesgaden railway station but made no incursions into the Obersalzberg. On 29th April, the aircraft of Bomber Command and the USAAF would start Operation Manna and Operation Chowhound respectively, the dropping of humanitarian food supplies to starving Dutch civilians and once cessation of hostilities had taken place, they flew liberated POWs back home.

Perhaps surprisingly, this final act by Bomber Command has remained in relative obscurity over the years. Marshal of the Royal Air Force Sir Arthur Harris's belief in the war winning potential of unrestricted bombing was falling out of favour and Harris himself makes little reference to it in his memoirs. In the end, the awkward truth was that only ground forces could achieve victory and the spectre of Dresden, however distorted the true facts about this may have been, and indeed still are, was beginning to haunt political and public minds. The war was over and it was time to move on. The sacrifices made by Bomber Command were not referred to by Churchill in his victory speech, sowing seeds of anger amongst veterans of the Command. It was to be sixty-seven years before the bravery of these men was to be truly recognised with the dedication of the Bomber Command Memorial in London's Green Park.

In 2002 a detailed bomb survey of the target area was undertaken prior to the construction of a new luxury hotel on the hill on which once stood *Landhaus Göring*. This revealed an amount of unexploded ordnance and the revelation of a 'near miss' Tallboy crater some 150 yards from the Berghof. Today, little remains of the Nazi era, most of the remains having been systematically removed. However, the *Kehlsteinhaus* remains intact and this mountain eyrie still attracts thousands of tourists annually, maybe confirming why it was spared?

* The last Bomber Command casualties of the war occurred on the night of 2nd/3rd May when two Halifax bombers (RG375 and RG373) from 199 Squadron collided over Kiel whilst flying a Mandrel radar jamming screen. It was feared that the Germans were assembling ships to take troops to Norway. During the same night, one of the attacking force Mosquito NF Mk XIXs of 169 Squadron (MM680) was hit by flak and also crashed near Kiel. The crew of Mosquito MM637, also from 169 Squadron, was killed whilst flying a training sortie on 6th May.

** Electrical transformers at Traunstein were the target for the 458th BG, so it is possible that the Lancaster was hit by flak batteries protecting the site.

My thanks to archivist Florian Beierl for his help with interpreting the Obersalzberg's history and for his guided tour of the underground tunnel network.

****

 **James Deacon's father, Stanley, was part of the Pathfinder force in the Second World War. The Pathfinders were used to mark out bombing targets shortly before the allied air forces bombed German cities. It was a very precise and important role as errors could lead to the following bomber forces dropping their bombs on the wrong target or in the wrong locations. It was also very dangerous with the pilots facing the same perils as the main stream bomber forces, night fighters, anti-aircraft fire (FLAK) and flight across huge distances over occupied Europe. Whilst a matter of life and death at the time, airmen on both sides were just doing their job, and this brief piece shows there was no animosity amongst those involved.**

RAF Pathfinders - Post-War Reunions

The elite Pathfinder Force, part of 8 Group Bomber Command, was formed in July 1942 with the objective of improving bombing accuracy and to make use effectively of the new developments in bomb targeting and navigational aids. Commanded by the respected Air Vice-Marshal Don Bennett, the Pathfinders became a tight-knit collection of 19 squadrons. The community spirit in the face of constant danger was very strong. So much so that after the war, some key members formed the Pathfinder Association with club premises in Mayfair, to maintain their contacts and comradeship.

Like the rest of the RAF Bomber Command, the Pathfinders suffered heavy losses during 1943-44 from night fighter attacks from Germany's *Luftwaffe*. Despite this, less than 25 years after the end of the Second World War, key members of the Pathfinder Association were invited to a reunion with former *Luftwaffe* fighter pilots, some of whom they must have encountered previously in life and death struggles in the dark skies over Germany.

The delegation of seven from the Pathfinder Association flew to Germany on 4th October 1967 to a warm welcome in the Officer's Mess at *Jabo-Geschwaders* (Fighter-Bomber) Nr.42 at Sobernheim, near Mainz. The hosts included Major Herget, former Group Commander NJG4 fighter group and fighter ace with a record of 72 aircraft shot down including 1 whilst piloting a twin-jet powered Me262. Willy Herget became a great friend of the '*Britischen Comrades*'; a friendship which included a follow-up reunion and continued until his death some years later.

From Sobernheim they travelled on to Coberg on 5th October and then on to the *Luftwaffe* airbase at Furstenfeldbruck near Munich on Saturday 7th October for an air display and dinner, before returning to England on the Sunday.

During this visit the Pathfinder delegation were each presented with a specially published book listing the biographies of all the *Luftwaffe* fighter pilots with their photographs. The book is dated 7th to 8th October 1967.

The visit between the two former enemies had been a great success, and such was the friendship that a second reunion visit was made to Germany in October 1972.

The second reunion was held between Friday 12th October and Sunday 14th October 1972 with the delegation of former RAF aircrew being honoured guests once again in the Officer's Club at the Furstenfeldbruck *Luftwaffe* base. For the official dinner on the Saturday night, it is interesting to read that the dress code for dinner was tactfully stated as 'dark suits, no decorations'.

Two years later, in London, the Pathfinder Association held their annual dinner. Guest of Honour was Adolf Galland, former *Luftwaffe* fighter ace, the youngest General of the German armed forces at the age of 30, who later developed a successful post-war career in aviation.

****

A strafe a day…
Deacon family archive

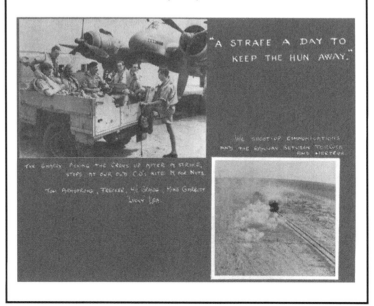

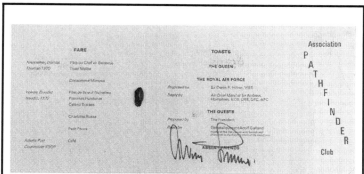

Luftwaffe fighter Ace Adolf Galland signed Deac's Menu at an RAF Pathfinder Association reunion.
Deacon family archive

Beaufighters Malta.
Deacon family archive

The Lysander typically used by SOE for dropping & collecting agents.

Peter Foote collection

A visit by King George and Queen Elizabeth to Methwold on 26th May 1943. This was a morale boosting visit following the disastrous operation by 487 squadron on a power station in Amsterdam on 3rd May in which the squadron lost ten out of eleven aircraft.

Billyhead family archive

Lancaster over a well-lit target.
Peter Foote collection

A Lancaster of Bomber Command releases its bomb load consisting of a 4,000 lb "Cookie" blast bomb and multiple containers of 4 lb incendiary bombs.
Peter Foote collection

The airborne drop – Parachutist exiting from a Dakota.
Peter Foote collection

Pre-flight briefing.
Geoff Botting collection

174

Log Book Night operations with 571 Squadron over The Reich.
Deacon family archive

Stirling aircraft towing Horsa gliders over Holland.
Peter Foote collection

Photos from Jim Wrights personal album.
Nigel Parker archive

Photos from Jim Wrights' personal album.
Nigel Parker archive

Chapter 2 - By Land

The dread of war and the appeasing attitudes during the inter-war years was to a great extent fuelled by the memory of the carnage on the Western Front, where millions of casualties on all sides were inflicted. Immense artillery bombardments and the power of defence with the machine guns slaughtered men in their thousands whilst fighting over a few yards of muddy field.

The Second World War still saw huge losses but it varied from theatre to theatre. In western Europe, with great mobility of forces with the improved development of the tank and a more open-minded tactical approach, the German '*Blitzkrieg*' prevented the allied forces digging in. The German advance lead by the *Panzer* armies supported by the *Luftwaffe* and the French and British soldiers retreat to the coast, saw movement that could barely be imagined twenty five years earlier. Caught up with this pace of attack were millions of civilians fleeing the invaders.

Four years later, the invasion of the Normandy coast saw the strength of combined operations with land, sea and air forces working closely together. Ultimately it fell on the allied soldiers to take the towns and while some proved more difficult than others with high casualties, such as Caen, but with huge resources pouring across the Channel to supply the vast armies, it took under a year from D-Day to the German surrender.

Operation Barbarossa in the summer of 1941, when a surprise attack on 'their ally' Russia was made by the German army, saw a different war from the west. Initially, using much the same '*Blitzkreig* 'tactics as in the west, this was coupled with a level of cruelty and barbarism on both sides and it seems a disregard for either casualty numbers or the 'rules of warfare'. The advance was stopped at the gates of Moscow by a combination of the Russian winter and an overstretched supply chain. Massive battles dwarfing anything seen in the west took place across the huge landscapes of the steppe. Kursk, Stalingrad, Leningrad are but a few huge bloody battles that took place. Millions perished, and soldiers surrendered at their own peril. Few who went into Russian captivity returned.

The war against Japan was in totally different conditions, and it took the allied armies over two years to get used to them. The surprise attack on Pearl Harbor by the Japanese Imperial fleet was followed hours later by a sudden attack through much of south-east Asia. The nimble and fleet footed Japanese soldiers adopted tactics alien to their opponents, coping with the jungle conditions far better, until the likes of Bill Slim and Windgate learned the art. Cruelty inflicted on allied POWs was extreme and the stories from the Burma Death Railway and elsewhere are well recorded.

The trench warfare of the Great War was largely avoided, but the soldier on the ground faced different and no less challenging situations and conditions to contend with. House to house fighting, crossing great waterways, the steamy tropics, the Russian winters, and hot fly-ridden deserts were but a few challenges facing ground troops from all nations, while the technological advancements added terrifying fire power from tanks and planes for those spending night after night in their foxholes.

 *Ben Hodges tells of how his grandfather, Frank Coslett, was a regular soldier and ended up being rescued from Dunkirk in 1940. Frank felt being in the army was a good role until the fighting started!*

Soldiering was wonderful until Hitler

When I was 10 years old, I went with my parents to stay with my nan and grandad. My mother and father had gone out for the night with my aunt and uncle, leaving me with nan and grandad. My parents returned home quite late and were somewhat surprised to see me still awake. My nan explained that grandad had been telling war stories and she hadn't had the heart to send me to bed.

Frank Edward Coslett, my grandad, like many children's grandads of my era, served in the Second World War. But what always made him more interesting to me, was that he had been a pre-war regular soldier. Having come from a comfortably middle-class family in Penarth South Wales, he enlisted in 1933 as a private soldier in the South Wales Borderers. After basic training at the depot in Brecon, he served with the 2nd Battalion in the UK for the best part of a year, before being posted to the 1st Battalion in India.

Initially he was based in Karachi, before being posted up to Rawalpindi. His time was spent either on operations on the North West Frontier or playing cricket, hockey, football and swimming. He enjoyed life in India. He developed a love of Indian food, which unfortunately, my nan did not share! In 1935 he was involved in the relief effort following the Quetta earthquake. Around this time, he also succumbed to the habit that many soldiers got into, he got tattoos. The one he had of the cartoon character, Betty Boop, always fascinated me as a kid. In 1936, he was transferred into the 1st Battalion, King's Shropshire Light Infantry. His elder brother had 'purchased' him, as was the practice at the time. Older siblings could claim their brothers and bring them into their own units.

He returned to England in 1938 and was based in Bordon in Hampshire when war was declared. He was a 24-year-old Corporal serving in the Signals Platoon. The battalion proceeded to France with the British Expeditionary Force and, from what he told me, he spent the phoney war digging trenches, going on patrols, drinking beer and singing in the Mess. He had been a chorister at Magdalen College School and his voice was in much demand!

When the war got hot, he found himself in retreat to Dunkirk. He described to me how he literally dug himself into a shell scrape in the sand to protect himself from the Stukas. The King's Shropshire Light Infantry were pretty much the last unit to be evacuated from Dunkirk. He told me that he went home on a paddle steamer and that it had reminded him of the ones he used to catch from Penarth to Weston-super-Mare when he was a child.

Perhaps the final word should be from the man himself. He told me, *'Soldiering was wonderful until Hitler came along. After that it got a bit serious.'*

****

 *Rosemary Postlethwaite kindly allowed BMMHS to publish the diary extracts of her father, George Johnson, who served in the Royal Artillery, and went ashore in Normandy on June 11th 1944, as the allied armies were consolidating their bridgehead following the D-Day landing 5 days earlier. The diary shows glimpses of what it was like for troops preparing to cross the channel.*

GE Johnson War Diary Normandy 1944
Part 1: Preparation for Normandy landing June 1944
June 3ʳᵈ

At 1915 hours, I am proud to lead the troop out of Yarmouth on the move down to our Marshalling Area. Given a good send off by a large percentage of the officers of the Regiment. The CO, the 2 i/c, the adjutant. and others. We are due to arrive at the Marshalling Area at Canning Town, East London at 0930 hours the following morning.

June 4ᵗʰ

… we are led into the Marshalling Area by MPs. What a shock! This is just a blitzed area, where no buildings are left standing, surrounded by armed guards and barbed wire. How distrustful – who would desert anyway?

June 5ᵗʰ

It is hot in the Marshalling Area and the dust from the rubble and debris of the blitzed area is unbearable.

Final steps of waterproofing carried out. 200 francs (£1) paid to each man, and any English money converted into French currency. A sealed bundle of maps of the area in which we shall land is issued. How curious I am!

June 6th

Early call. Breakfast at 0300 hours. Moved from Marshalling Area to docks in steady drizzle. Arrived at India Docks at approx. 0500 hours to be told civilian dockers would not start loading onto the ship until 0800 hours.

Carried out final stages of waterproofing. Dockers commence to arrive at 0845 hours – slowly and with languid tread – there's no hurry. The longer the war lasts, the longer they will have a steady, well paid job. We would give anything (within reason) for a cup of char!

The dockers, after many a conference on this and that, commence to 'prepare to load'. A harbinger of good tidings arrives to inform all and sundry that the 'Second Front' has started. We, the poor bloody Pongos, were anxious on receipt of this news to get on with the job as we gathered, or assumed, it might be advisable to get as much material into that bridgehead as possible in the time laid down by the schedule. Obviously, we were mistaken because the dockers considered it to be a good excuse for the return of their hands to pockets and, lo and behold, they were again in conference. I turned away in disgust, and as I did so, I saw with my red-rimmed eyes a WVS van (*for tea*) pull up a hundred yards away. There was some controversy at the front. Imagine my disgust when I was informed she was unable to serve the troops as all the tea aboard was <u>for the dockers.</u> (*they*) made their first haul at 1010 hours and loading continued until a few minutes to twelve when they knocked off for dinner with a promise to be back at two.

June 7th

This ship is a Motor Transport Ship number 96. We have aboard, lashed down, in five separate holds just over 200 vehicles and guns with six hundred men slightly over strength as the accommodation is for 290 men. So over 300 men above decks.

..cooking only consists of dishing out tins of bully and hard, dry biscuits, plus one bar of chocolate, half a dozen sweets and seven cigarettes per man per day.

June 8th

We leave the dock at last at 1200hrs and slowly steam down river. We are given a good send-off from some men and girls on the river side waving and cheering. The remainder of the troops line the starboard side and watch the Kent side. I saw many a wistful look both then and later when we got round North Foreland.

****

Christopher Chadwick recounts the interview with his father Robert Stanley 'Stan' Chadwick who was serving with the King's Own Yorkshire Light Infantry (KOYLI) in Normandy in June 1944. Stan's brother Bert was also fighting in the same regiment in Normandy at the same time. Stan tells of his experiences of those first 3 weeks of fighting to establish a foothold in Normandy before the breakout into France.

Sergeant Stanley Chadwick in Normandy 1944

Many times as I sit back and relax in my armchair, I think of my old Regiment, the 1st/4th Battalion KOYLI, landing on the beaches of Normandy, fully fit and ready for action. We lost many good Officers and men. They all put up an excellent performance. I cannot speak highly enough regarding our Commanding Officers, Company Commanders and other Officers and men of all other ranks. I have the highest respect for all of them.

I had been attached to practically all the Companies in our Regiment, and my Section never once let them down. My prayers go out to all those killed in action, and those still alive, and I thank God that I got through. Memories will stay with me until I die, I shall never forget the comradeship, dangers and experiences that I saw with the Regiment.

Looking back on the landings at Normandy, the experiences of our campaign have made me realise how men with only TA experience can be trained to become exceptional soldiers. The training I encountered was first class. The Commanding Officers and all other officers were excellent in all duties performed.

The few pages here consist of many escapades, most of which are still clear in my mind. How I would love to contact any of the men from my section. I would love to have a good chat with any of the senior officers who were on that campaign. After all these years, many places and names have been forgotten / merged, but I trust this is a reasonably true record.

I wish to give my congratulations to Captain Armitage and Sergeant Kelly, Platoon Commander and Platoon Sergeant, who had the difficult job of keeping the platoon active, especially with all the losses we suffered.

I was called up for duty with my brother Herbert (Bert), and I was very proud when he received his gallantry medal, and he certainly gained my respect the way he rose to the rank of Major. I also congratulate him on gaining the award of MBE.

On leaving the beaches the section met up against enemy artillery. The crews dismounted and ran for cover, shrapnel was bursting all about us. We were split up, running in all directions and diving for cover. I dived in the low ground following Sergeant Hudson who got shrapnel in the lower arm and a serious wound in the hand; he received treatment from the following first aid men.

As we settled down and returned to our carriers we climbed aboard and moved on. As we moved, an artillery air burst was exploding about our heads. Luckily for us slight damage on our section caused us to go for cover in the undergrowth. Our naval guns gave good support and the ack-ack guns kept the planes well above. I took command of the Carrier Section and we travelled on by the left of Bronay, being harassed by German machine gun fire hitting our carrier. Fortunately the armour took most of the hits and we carried on and joined up with 'C' Company.

After a short time in the line, we were given the next objective, which was the taking of Cristot (16th June '44). My section was allocated to 'B' Company, and positions of defence were taken whilst we awaited further orders. The company was under heavy fire from the Germans, whilst Colonel Walker our battalion commander was viewing the enemy area. He gave all the leaders information on how it was going to be dealt with. 'B' Company was positioned in line, well concealed waiting for instructions. Colonel Walker positioned himself forward in the centre of the forward line. My carrier section was to the left of him.

Our supporting artillery started firing and Colonel Walker gave the signal to move forward. As we moved forward with the Colonel German artillery started firing at us, all hell was let loose. The Colonel was great giving orders as we moved, shouting at people to keep moving. I was moving on foot to direct my carrier by the routes with cover. We had heavy losses whilst moving despite good support from our own artillery. It was a miracle to get through, due in no small measure to the encouragement given the men by the way Colonel Walker led us, without him we would have been wiped out. I passed several who had been hit by shrapnel, we couldn't stop to help them, quite a few of them died as the firing settled down. I got my carriers into safer areas and left the drivers to camouflage them.

Tessle Wood (25th June 44)

I positioned my men on the corner of Tessle Wood facing the north east side. As we positioned I noticed two light tanks on my left who were supporting us, then looking forward I saw a Tiger tank positioned behind cover. A German machine gun opened fire on us missing by a few feet. The Tiger tank opened fire at the two light tanks, two shots only hitting each tank and putting them out of action. Just one man got out of a tank and was badly shaken. I ran towards him and guided him to safe cover. He was shell shocked so we passed him on for medical attention. The Germans withdrew giving us time to settle down. We dug in (digging two men slit trenches).

The Germans quietened down but bombarded us with shells and there were airbursts. We stayed in our positions all night, then early morning I moved my section towards 'C' Company. The company was having a rough time, so I placed my carriers in good supporting positions. A couple of hours went by and a platoon commander came to me and asked me to go to 'B' Echelon and bring two large containers of tea. I decided to go with my driver, my other two carriers were well supported, so we set off toward 'B' Echelon taking a zigzag route. German machine gun bullets were rapidly hitting the rear of my carrier, we came under fire for a good twenty minutes before finally getting clear and carrying on for about a mile to 'B' Echelon. We quickly loaded the large tea containers and set off back for what we knew would be a difficult journey but despite German machine gun fire and artillery fire made it to a place to stop within a dip. I made my way toward a platoon in position, where an officer came towards me with about six men. He thanked me and they unloaded the containers, to distribute the tea that the men in positions enjoyed greatly. I took my carriers back towards the right of 'C' Company. Things got quiet for a while and it gave us time to get organised, but the Germans didn't give us much time to rest, they were continually firing air burst at us, and machine-gunned us regularly.

The rest of our carriers were attached to other companies, and we heard they were having a rough time, in fact they lost a few men. The carrier platoon training had done us a lot of good, we were expert at camouflaging and making our dug-outs quite safe, we checked our weapons and received supplies of ammunition and daily food packs.

A few days passed and night time came. A Pioneer Platoon came to our positions equipped with mines and explosives. They went to our left to a likely area where they could do some damage. About two hours passed when we heard a very loud explosion. We were informed that a German shell had exploded near them and they had dived for cover. Some of the mines had been ignited ready for laying and the word was that ten of the Pioneers had been killed by their own mines, as by diving for cover one of them had fallen onto a mine. It was terrible, we went to the area it happened and saw the grizzly remains (29th June 44).

My sections duties were to dig in on the left of 'D' Company, which was south west of the wood. An officer (Lieutenant) ordered us to dig in, in front of the trees, whilst it was dark. I protested, stating that there was some high ground in front of us. The officer replied that we would be out before day-break came. My section, about seven or eight yards apart, got what we had expected as did a platoon of 'D' Company. 'Gerry' opened up with quite a number of mortar attacks, and a creeping barrage. As the barrage came closer we hoped it wouldn't reach us, then we had a downpour of shells right amongst us. My trench was almost a direct hit. My gunner fell with shrapnel wounds to the stomach. I was also hit, with a blast to the head, and stretcher-bearers carried us away. I never got to know what happened to my other men, as I ended up in the casualty department off the line. I was lucky I suppose, that it was only a slight injury, and after recuperating I returned to my unit. I had practically a new section.

****

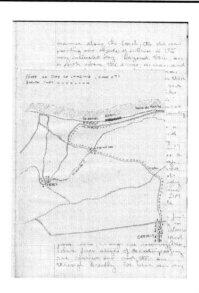

Maps from George Johnson's D-Day Diary.
Johnson family archive

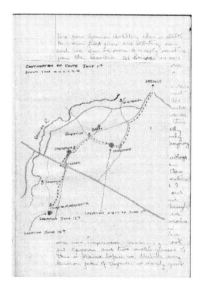

Stan (l) and Bert (r) Chadwick 'Brothers in Arms'.
Chadwick family archive

Bert Chadwick (on the ground) training in Iceland 1941/2 with
KOYLI under the watchful eye of Course Officer Richard Todd.
Chadwick family archive

In British military history, the name Arnhem is synonymous with a very brave defeat against insurmountable odds. Operation Market Garden was a bold plan in September 1944 to shorten the war by using allied airborne forces to capture key river crossings in order to cross the Rhine and advance into Germany. At Arnhem, despite bitter, dogged fighting and, having held out for nine days with dwindling supplies and growing casualties the British airborne forces were faced with surrender. About 2,500 of the men were able to evacuate across the Rhine under cover of night, but the remainder of the survivors – some 6,500 men, many wounded and injured - were taken into captivity. It took four more months to cross the Rhine in January 1945 and to enter Germany, with the war ending a further four months later.

Sandra Stamper tells the story of her father Ivor Royles. Ivor fought in North Africa, Sicily and Italy, and with 1st Airborne Parachute Regiment, 3rd Battalion B Co at Arnhem. He won the Military Medal in North Africa, and was taken prisoner at Arnhem.

Ivor Royles - A Prisoner at Arnhem

This is the story of my father, Ivor Royles, and his service in the Second World War. Born in 1919, dad enlisted with The 8th Denbighshire Royal Welch Fusiliers on 17th January 1940. He served in North Africa, Sicily Italy, and Arnhem. He was one of the first volunteers to become a Parachutist and qualified as a Parachutist on 30th November 1941.

Dad didn't talk much about the war and what he did, but I have managed to put some stories and anecdotes together from what we have gleaned over the years.

North Africa

Dad won the military medal in North African campaign

The way dad told the story of his being awarded the military medal was that he and his Sergeant were on duty checking things out when they came across German soldiers in a wadi. They decided if they didn't do something about it, the Germans could discover them first and it would be too late to warn their HQ. They took matters into their own hands and between them made the Germans think there were more than the two of them by shooting and shouting and succeeded in distracting them and in capturing approximately 30 German soldiers whom they marched back to their camp. Their CO was furious with them and told them it would be a court martial for not reporting to HQ first, or, if they were lucky, an instant promotion. It transpired they were lucky and they were promoted, my dad from a L/Cpl to Sergeant.

Dad also told us a story that made him smile. He was on guard duty when Field Marshal Montgomery (who was not liked by many of the soldiers, my father one of them) appeared at the guard post and when asked for the password to enter didn't know it, but said my father should know who he was and he didn't need it. My dad said he could not enter without the password as that was his instruction. Needless to say, my dad didn't give in. His CO called him in and dad thought the worst, but he told him Field Marshal

Montgomery had been very impressed that at least one soldier followed instructions!

Sicily and Italy

Dad often told us his story of how he was requested to join a group of officers to go on a mission to capture a high ranking German officer. There were 12 of them and they were stripped of all identity (my mother was also informed of this), given enough money to see them through their journey and given a deadline of where they were to be at the end of the mission to be picked up by a submarine.

Their mission was successful but when they got to their end destination there was no submarine. They decided not to give up and hijacked a fisherman and his boat, telling him they would pay him well if he took them on to their final destination with their prisoner.

When asked who the German officer was dad said they had only been given his Army Number, so we never knew who it was other than that their mission was successful.

Arnhem

Dad said very little about the battle at Arnhem, other than he was on the first lift on 17th September 1944. When looking at photos in a book on Arnhem with him, he was quick to point out that his platoon was responsible for the death of Major General Friedrich Kussin the head of the Feldkommandantur 642, the regional garrison command responsible for the Arnhem sector, (who was with) his colleagues in their vehicle. They had come across the vehicle as they travelled the Tiger route from their landing zone.

He only ever said the battle was horrendous, they quickly ran out of food and water and ammunition. They hid in cellars and he often mentioned Fitch and Urqhart for whom he had great respect. All we do know for certain is that the horrors of this battle stayed with him as a few weeks before he passed away he would wake up with nightmares saying they should get out of the window as the Germans were coming.

At the end of the Battle of Arnhem my mother, who was about four months pregnant with me, received notification from the MOD saying my dad was missing and if she received communication from him she should contact them. She also received a booklet from the 3rd Battalion containing copies of letters from Field Marshal Montgomery, Lieutenant General Brian Horrocks, Dwight D Eisenhower, etc. honouring all those who were missing or killed in action.

My mum did receive a postcard from dad dated 5th October 1944 telling her he was a POW and was in Stalag XIIA. She informed the MoD of this. She then received another postcard dated 9th November 1944 saying he was being moved to Stalag VIIIC.

Dad did talk a little about the long march they had to endure, moving from one camp to another which he said lasted 33 days and nights. They had almost no food, just bits of bread and unidentifiable soup and beans, a tin of which had to be shared between them. He said they couldn't safely stop for toilet purposes as if they stopped when supposed to be moving, they could get shot.

Whenever he related this story he would have tears in his eyes, so we never pushed him to say more.

Following the liberation of the POWs, he returned to the UK on 11th April 1945. He spent three months recuperating in an Army Reception Centre. The only food they could manage to eat were raw eggs which they were told would aid their recovery! When he finally arrived home on the 19th July 1945, he weighed just 6st.

He often told us about an incident on the journey home. He took a train from London to Chester then a bus from Chester to Mold, which passed through the village just outside Mold, where my mother lived with her parents and me. On the bus he overheard people talking about him and saying *'why is that tramp on the bus?'* This amused him, especially as he knew why he looked like he did. Bless him.

When the bus approached the spot where he should disembark he saw posters with his name on everywhere. The villagers had got word that he was on his way home and had formed a welcoming party for their hero. He wasn't having any of it of course and stayed on the bus, getting off a little further up the road and walking home across the fields.

At least my dad got home safely and was able to rebuild his life. He went through a great deal in the war, both in action and in captivity. It was not an easy war for him and millions of others. I am extremely proud of what he achieved in the service of his country, receiving not only the Military Medal for gallantry, but also 1939-45 Star, Africa

Star and 1st Army clasp, Italy Star, France and Germany Star, War and Defence medals.

****

Kriegsgefangenenlager   Datum: 6/10/44

I HAVE BEEN TAKEN PRISONER OF WAR
IN GERMANY I AM IN GOOD HEALTH WE
WILL BE TRANSPORTED FROM HERE TO ANOTHER
CAMP WITHIN THE NEXT FEW DAYS PLEASE
DO NOT WRITE UNTILL I SEND MY NEW
ADDRESS
          KINDEST REGARDS IVOR XXX

Kriegsgefangenenlager   Datum: 9 11 44

After Arnhem, Ivor Royles sent postcards home to explain he
was now a POW.

Ivor Royles family archive

199

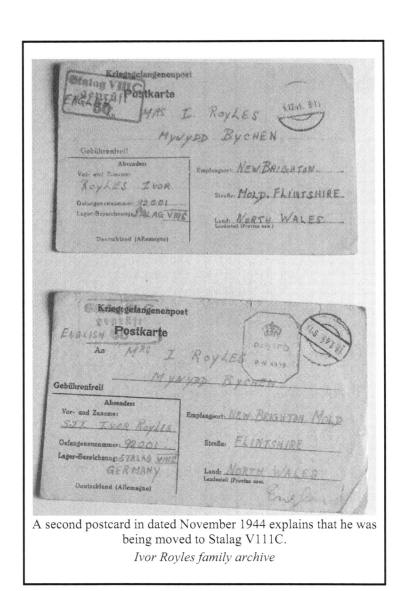

A second postcard in dated November 1944 explains that he was being moved to Stalag V111C.

Ivor Royles family archive

Paras landing.
Peter Foote collection

Paras on the ground.
Peter Foote collection

Jane Chadwick recounts the experiences of her father Herbert 'Bert' Chadwick during the Second World War. Bert joined up in 1939 with the King's Own Yorkshire Light Infantry, saw service in Norway and Iceland before joining allied forces in the battle for Normandy in 1944, where his brother Stan was also fighting. He saw service throughout Northern Europe through to the surrender of Germany, ending up in Austria in 1945 as part of the occupying forces. Bert continued as a career soldier eventually retiring in 1972 having seen service over much of the globe. Many years after the event, Bert Chadwick wrote down his memories of the action during which he won the Military Medal in Normandy.

Herbert Chadwick From Miner to Major

I was born nearly 12 years after the end of the Second World War, and lived the first few years of my life in a military family, moving round the world between military bases or locations as father's job demanded. From Berlin to Malaysia, from Shrewsbury to West Byfleet. In fact, I attended eight different schools by the age of 12, sometimes schools on the bases or local schools and for a period as a boarder in UK whilst my parents were abroad. That may account for the fact I didn't get my university degree until I was in my 40s! Sometimes father was away on active service – fighting – so not having him around too much was quite normal for me as a youngster.

My father - Bert to his friends and family - was born into a mining family in Wakefield in 1919 - one of two sons and three daughters. My grandad Albert was also a miner working down the Sharlston Colliery. It was a tough life for them all with no money and few luxuries, so it was a real bonus when Bert got a job aged about 12 as the delivery boy for the local grocer. Once he had learned how to balance on a rickety bike laden with fruit and veg, he was given 'damaged goods', over ripe bananas being his favourite.

Bert left school at 14 and started down the mines. He joined the TA as soon as he could, and when war was declared, he signed up for the King's Own Yorkshire Light Infantry (KOYLI) as his father had done before him in the First World War.

April 1940 saw him posted to Norway as part of the disastrous yet valiant attempt to stop the German invasion of that country as part of the Mauriceforce at Namsos under Major General Adrian Carton de Wiart. This preceded the invasion of most of Western Europe the following month.

The Battalion was hastily evacuated and moved to Iceland, where they became part of Alabaster force, the occupying garrison. There he served under a certain Lieutenant Richard Todd (later the well-known actor who played Guy Gibson in the famous Dambusters film, and many more roles).

His next bit of active service, after months of training, saw him with the 1/4 Battalion KOYLI land on Gold Beach on D+3, 9th June 1944. His younger brother Stan landed on Gold Beach the same day.

Bert served throughout the Battle of Normandy, including Operation Martlett, the battle for Caen and, later in 1944, the Second Battle of the Odon. He was later involved in clearing the Channel Coast in Operation Astonia, garrisoning 'The Island' during the aftermath of Operation Market Garden, where they then fought in the Battle of the Scheldt. The Battalions' last battle was during the Second Battle of Arnhem.

It was during this time in the early stages of the Normandy campaign, he was awarded the Military Medal. 42 years later, he wrote his own account of what happened and why he gained the award – *see verbatim account below.*

His battalion ended the war as part of the occupation forces in Austria, after the Russians had withdrawn to their agreed zone. The battalion was based in a railway town of Murzzuschlag, about an hour from Vienna, using the local school as their HQ. Here Bert met my mum, Helle, a young Austrian teacher who was helping the allied forces as an English translator. They married in late 1946 having gained the permission of his CO.

The Russians had left Austria in a terrible state after their short occupation, leaving a trail of physical and emotional misery. I still have elderly relatives who remember this, but that is a tale for another day.

Along with all the other volunteers, at the end of the war he was routinely discharged in late 1946. His Commanding Officer wrote as a testimonial on his Discharge Certificate:

'A young soldier who by sheer determination, courage, industry and hard work rose from the rank of Private to RSM. A fine type of man, an excellent leader, a good organiser and an untiring worker.

Awarded the Military Medal for Gallantry in action. Highly recommended for any position of trust. (signature undecipherable, Record Officer, Infantry & AEC Office, York 31st October 1946).

The following day, 1st November 1946, my father signed up at Minden as a full-time soldier in KOYLI. He was formally discharged from the KOYLI in February 1957 when he was given a commission on its amalgamation into the Light Infantry.

His Certificate of Service record in the section Final Assessment of Conduct and Character state:

Military Conduct: **Exemplary**

Testimonial: '*Chadwick has been an outstandingly successful Regimental Sergeant Major. His conduct in action earned him the Military Medal and his excellent work since then has earned him an MBE in the New Year's Honours List. He has now been commissioned as Quarter Master and so the army will continue to benefit from the services of this exceptionally loyal, intelligent and efficient man.*' Signed CO, Stensall, 2nd February 1957.

During the next 15 years he served all over the world including Malaya, Cyprus, Kenya, Aden and BAOR including as part of the battalion guarding Rudolf Hess in Spandau prison in Berlin. He eventually retired from the Army in 1972.

I recall as a 12 year old (about 1969) being allowed to visit my father at work at Copthorne Barracks in Shrewsbury. I went into the barracks and announced myself to the sentry, saying I wanted to see Captain Chadwick (he was the Quartermaster at the time). He gave me a wry smile and let me pass through. I walked across the parade ground on to my father's office, which was incredibly austere, with army issue dark wood furniture and a picture of the Queen Mother (as the Light Infantry Colonel in Chief) on the wall. Dad and I left his office, walking out of the barracks and, to the amusement of a 12 year old, people stopped and saluted him. He was clearly very important!

It seems he was quite a stickler for protocol and doing things *'right in the Army way'* and at his funeral in 2002 he was described as a *'bloody terror.'*

After the army, he worked initially as an Army Careers Officer and then tirelessly as a fund raiser for the British Heart Foundation.

He had travelled the world, gained deserved honours and huge respect from his peers through great integrity, courage and hard work. I am incredibly proud of what my dad achieved. Certainly, from very humble beginnings, he made it from miner to major, and not many have achieved this.

Major Herbert Chadwick MM, MBE - verbatim account written by Bert Chadwick in 1986 about the fighting in Normandy where he was awarded the Military Medal. *(provided courtesy of his daughter, Jane Chadwick).*
   My dad, Major Herbert Chadwick, won the Military
   Medal in Normandy in June 1944. Here are his

words about what happened, written some 42 years later. He was a Sergeant and only 24 at the time.

1/4 KOYLI BRONAY June 1944

After taking over from the Green Howards on 13th June, we were soon made aware of front line conditions. The enemy's Spandau machine guns swept our area at regular intervals, interspersed with mortar and artillery shell fire.

The day after our arrival our platoon, No 13 of 'C' Company, under command of Lieutenant Wilson was given the task of occupying a wooded area on the very edge of the enemy front line. The wood was situated just in front of a railway embankment behind which the Germans were in strength. There was no doubt, they had troops in the wood and our orders were to take it, hold it for 24 hours and if possible, take prisoners to establish the identity of the units opposite us.

The plan was to take it before dawn on the following day and with this in mind Lieutenant Wilson held an 'O' Group *(Observation group)* on the high slopes of the Bn position where we were able to survey the approaches to the wood. It was no easy task and we deliberated for some time. The whole area to the front and sides of the wood was open cornfield, almost breast high. It was possible to get within 300 yards of it under cover of a hedgerow after which we would have to go over open ground. It was decided to move the platoon to this position in the early hours where it would wait while Sergeant Chadwick (the Plt Sgt), and 22 men went forward to probe the left side of the wood to try and establish the strength of the enemy.

The platoon reached the far end of the hedgerow around 1am and after Lieutenant Wilson had decided he would not move until I returned, I set off with my 22 men. We crawled to within about 120 yards of the wood when we were spotted. I threw a 36 grenade and we then retreated hastily back to the platoon. In the meantime, Lieutenant Wilson had moved the platoon forward and I almost mistook him for a German patrol, but he spoke just in time to stop me firing a burst from my Sten gun. All this had taken quite a bit of time and dawn was about one hour away.

We had to move quickly and it was decided that I take the leading section (Cpl Anderson) and put in an attack on the right side of the wood. Lieutenant Wilson would follow with the remaining 2 sections ((L/Sgt Pratt and Cpl Hodgson) and P1 HQ and put in a second attack if ours failed.

No time for crawling this time. We took a fairly wide detour round to the right, moving quite swiftly, and then approached the wood in extended formation. We were about 20 yards from the edge of it when we fired on a point blank range. It was still dark but there was sufficient moonlight to show up our shadowy figures. We threw ourselves to the ground. I rallied the section and gave the order to move in with all weapons firing just as soon as the 2 x 36 grenades to be thrown by the section 2 i/c and myself had exploded. This we did charging forward firing and yelling for all we were worth. The Germans withdrew from the wood rapidly leaving one dead and, judging by the blood we later found here and there, some wounded with them.

Lieutenant Wilson and the rest of the platoon were quickly on the scene and took control, deploying the sections in defensive position to ward off any counter attack. After dawn he organised a patrol which he led himself to recce and clear strips of area between the embankment and the wood which offered good cover to the enemy in the way of shrubs and thickets. He returned with two prisoners.

The wood by the way was about 200 yards long and about 50 yards deep. We were within shouting distance of the foe. We dug in and prepared for a long threatening day.

Our prisoners had to be dealt with. They were in the way and in any case Bn needed them for interrogation. A volunteer was required to simply escort them to the Bn, crossing open ground in full view of the enemy. The theory being that they would not shoot at our soldier for fear that they would shoot at theirs. It worked!

During the whole day, we were mortared and on several occasions the Germans tried to infiltrate and test our defences. These probes no doubt were in preparation for a serious attack. We kept them at bay with small arms fire including a 2 inch mortar. We also found it necessary to bring down our own artillery, sometimes within 25-30 yards of our own positions. The BZs and our 88 sets proved very useful indeed.

The day wore on and it became obvious to us that a determined attack by the enemy at dusk would probably succeed. It was then decided to pull out in daylight (early evening), a section at a time at tactical intervals. Lieutenant Wilson to take the first section and Sergeant Chadwick the last one. Artillery fire would divert the attention of the enemy.

It was a crawl through the cornfield until we reached the cover of the hedgerow and each section made its own way to the Bn area. There were no casualties.

The success of the operation was due chiefly to our audacity and to the element of surprise. We alerted the enemy on the left side of the wood and then had the cheek to attack two hours later on the right. I don't think he expected that.

I would have liked to have mentioned more names but after 42 years the memory wears a bit thin. Unfortunately, I didn't keep a diary at the time!

Written by Major Herbert Chadwick, 1986

****

 ***Dorothy Volkert, a young US Army nurse in World War Two aboard an Army Hospital Ship, looks back on what it was like dealing with injured servicemen. These young men some with very serious and often life changing injuries were in great need of reassurance and emotional care as few knew how loved ones and friends would react to them when they arrive home.***

<u>Coming Home</u>
Army Hospital Ship *Charles A Stafford*
September, 1946

I put my pen down and lay aside the charts – time to make rounds again. I turn on my flashlight and try to keep from scruffing my combat boot clad feet in the relative quiet of the dark ward. I hear the usual sounds of the night: snores, groans, an occasional curse. Nothing surprises this young army nurse.

I clasp the iron rail of the bunks to keep from stumbling as the ship rises and falls in the rough rolling sea. As I move through the aisle a hand reaches out and grasps mine. I look down into the dark eyes reflected in the beam of my light. *'I need to talk'* a young patient whispers hoarsely.

I look quickly up and down the aisle to see if all is quiet, then bend over the tousled head and nod.

'I'm scared' he says.
'Of what?' I reply, stooping low so I can hear him and see his serious expression.
'My wife. Will she be angry at me? Will she hate me? Will she even want to see me when we get there?'

211

The young man then shares with me how he has never told his wife that he had lost an arm and a leg in battle. While he was hospitalised in Germany, they had written often but had never discussed the extent of his injuries. Their letters had been full of plans for the future that wouldn't be affected by his 'minor' injuries.

What can I say? I'm not prepared to advise - only to care. I continue to hold his hand and allow him to sob for a few moments. His hand relaxes and he closes his eyes and drifts off to sleep.

The next day our ship docks in Long Island and he is carried on a stretcher down the long ramp to a waiting line of army ambulances to be transported to a stateside hospital.

I never saw him again, nor would I ever know the outcome of his fears. I realised all I had been able to do for him was let him know I cared.

We began preparing for another shipload of wounded service men, all facing their own fears for their futures. All we could do was to ease their pain and anxiety to the best of our ability, to give them comfort, encouragement and appreciation.

Now, some 70 years later, this old army nurse veteran still thinks often of those young men, and wonders how their lives turned out. I've never forgotten them, their anxiety and especially their courage.

Perhaps, given our limited treatment options of the times, one of our strongest healing tools was our ability to care and to express it to our patients. We must not discount its continued importance today.

Dorothy Volkert, Illinois, USA

US Army Hospital Ship *Charles A. Stafford* circa 1944-1946.
Becky Volkert collection

Chapter 3 - By Sea

The battles for the seas in the Second World War were as crucial as those of land and air. With huge naval strength historically, it was inevitable the British fleet saw conflict in all theatres from the Altmark incident and disastrous Norwegian campaign in the spring of 1940 through D-Day and the defeat of the Japanese in 1945. However, the type of role changed significantly as set piece naval battles between vast navies disappeared and more emphasis was placed convoy protection, anti-submarine warfare and combined services operations as part of larger military actions. The role of aircraft carriers grew in importance but, as seen in the war against Japan, all large vessels proved vulnerable to air attack, not least the *kamikaze* strategy.

The Royal Navy was critical in the evacuation of the BEF from Norway and Dunkirk, and as a deterrent to invasion in the months following. The high profile evacuation of the allied troops from Dunkirk gave rise to the romantic notion that the so-called '*little ships*' that rescued most of the troops, it was the Royal Navy that ferried substantially the larger part, taking significant losses in the process. The Navy suffered a blow to morale and prestige when the HMS *Hood* was sunk in May 1941. Success in the battle of Taranto in November 1940 when British Naval forces successfully attacked the Italian fleet saw the first use of carrier-based aircraft to attack using Fairey Swordfish from the carrier HMS *Illustrious.*

The attack on the US Pacific fleet base at Pearl Harbor by the Japanese Imperial Navy, using the blue print learned from the British at Taranto a year earlier, was a decisive moment in the war. Although not sinking the US aircraft carriers which were at sea on trials, it brought the USA into the war, making it a global conflict with the industrial might of the USA greatly bolstering the allies. HMS *Repulse* and HMS *Prince Of Wales* were sunk by Japanese aircraft on 19th December 1941 when they attempted to intercept landings in British Malaya and for a while the Japanese were dominant in the region.

The Royal Navy was vital in interdicting Axis supplies to North Africa and ensuring allied supplies to Malta. It also guarded the sea lanes that enabled British forces to fight around the world. From 1942 in the Battle of the Atlantic, it was responsible for much of the North Atlantic and Arctic convoy system, and for defeating the U-boat threat. The defeat of the German capital ship fleet, including *Tirpitz*, *Bismarck*, *Prinz Eugen*, *Scharnhorst* and *Gneisenau*, having caused heavy losses to allied shipping in the North Atlantic, was crucial to the continued supplies of food, fuel and munitions to England.

Naval supremacy was vital for the allied invasions of North Africa, Sicily, Italy and Normandy. In Operation Neptune, the naval component of Operation Overlord, the Navy supplied 958 of the 1,213 warships taking part and the majority of the landing craft.

The Royal Navy undertook numerous other roles that often are overlooked, including mine laying and clearing, protecting home waters through coastal command. Specialist commando raids and undercover operations formed part of the RN's remit, not least the Dieppe raid, the Bruneval raid, and Operation Frankton, the so-called

'Cockleshell heroes' commando raid on German merchant shipping.

In the war against Japan, the growing strength of the US Navy over time saw successful major battles such as Coral Sea, Midway and, as the US forces island hopped towards the Japanese mainland, numerous amphibious landings.

During the war it had become clear that aircraft carriers were the new capital ship of the Royal Navy. It had also become obvious that the USA had become the dominant sea power.

****

Lawrence Taylor describes the 'miracle of Dunkirk' when 338,000 troops of the BEF and allied forces were rescued from destruction and captivity. Hundreds of small pleasure, fishing and other boats alongside ships of the Royal Navy, under heavy and relentless bombardment from the Luftwaffe managed to extract the troops from the beaches of Dunkirk. While almost entirely without equipment, these troops lived to fight another day.

'Jump on anything that floats'
Operation Dynamo 26th May - 2nd June 1940. The Little Ships.

On 14th May 1940, just four days after the German *Panzers* broke through at Sedan, the BBC made an announcement from the Admiralty. All owners of self-propelled pleasure craft, between 30 ft. and 100 ft. in length to send all particulars to the Admiralty within 14 days from today.

A phone call from the Ministry of Shipping, early on 27th May, to Douglas Tough of Teddington asked if he would be agent for the collection of small craft along the Thames. Soon over one hundred of these craft were assembled at The Ferry Road Yard, where Tough's employees worked to make them all sea worthy. A list of boat owners capable of taking the boats down to Sheerness was compiled, and the flotilla of small ships set off down the Thames Estuary. When they arrived at Sheerness, the boats were refuelled and many handed over to the Royal Navy. However, there were not enough naval crews, so many civilians took their boats over to Dunkirk. Three routes were designated for the evacuation.

On 26th May 1940, Vice Admiral Dover Bertram Ramsey signalled 'Operation Dynamo is to commence'. Ramsey dispatched Captain WG 'Bill' Tennant to Dunkirk on HMS Wolfhound to begin to supervise the evacuation, and with the imminent fall of Calais, proposed a second route (Route X) for ships to progress to Dunkirk, thus avoiding German artillery at Calais. Initial plans called for the recovery of 45,000 men from the BEF within two days, at which time German troops were expected to block further evacuation.

Tennant remarked 'The sight of Dunkirk gave one a rather hollow feeling in the pit of the stomach', he then set to work dispersing his staff along the beaches east of Dunkirk. He soon realised the method of using small boats to ferry men from the beaches to awaiting ships was too slow. The alternative was two long piers protecting the dredged

217

channel leading to the docks. They became known as the West and East Moles. A message was sent by Tennant, via *Wolfhound*, requesting a personnel ship to sail to the longer East Mole to evacuate soldiers. The honour of the first ship to begin lifting troops from the mole went to the ferry, *Queen of the Channel*. Just before dawn on 27th May she got away with 1,000 troops on board. On her way back to Britain, a near miss from a bomb broke her back and she was lost. All on board were rescued.

Captain WG Tennant

By the night of 28th/29th May, with more ships coming to the mole, Captain Tennant estimated up to 200 men an hour were loading. Alas on the evening of 29th May, the *Luftwaffe* mounted a heavy attack on the mole.

On 29th May, the Royal Navy Paddle Minesweeper *Crested Eagle* was assisting the evacuation of troops from the East Mole. At 6 pm she was tied up next to the mole along with destroyers HMS *Grenade* and HMS *Jaguar*, six trawlers, and the troop ships *Fenella* and *Canterbury*. The final German air raid came in at around 6.00 pm and was pressed home with great determination.

HMS *Grenade* was hit, and on fire was towed from the harbour. She remained afloat until blowing up several hours later. The trawler *Calvi* was hit and sunk, along with the Isle of Man Packet Company's *Fenella*. HMS *Jaguar* was hit as she headed away from Dunkirk, drifting back towards the beaches, she was taken under tow by HMS *Express,* and after transferring her soldiers, limped back to Dover.

At the time of the attack, *Crested Eagle* was carrying about 600 troops in addition to her crew. She was set on fire by four bombs as she passed the beaches at Zuydcoote; one missed, the second hit just forward of the bridge, the remaining two set the ships fuel on fire. She was run ashore by her captain Lieutenant Commander Booth. The survivors were machine gunned while they struggled in the water as the ship continued to burn. She remained a landmark for the small ships heading for the beach, but over 300 of those on board were either killed or drowned.

Losses on 29th May were appalling, fifteen British and four French ships were lost. At the end of the day Ramsey recalled all eight of his modern destroyers; only 50,000 men had been evacuated from Dunkirk.

As the Dunkirk perimeter began to shrink and attacks on the East Mole increased, the arrival of the little ships off Le Panne and Bray Dunes became vital. Piers constructed from army vehicles stretched out across the gently shelving beaches. The shallow draught civilian boats edged alongside, taking on troops and ferrying them out to the larger ships waiting sometimes one mile out at sea.

Commander CH Lightoller (RNVR).
Sundowner
On 1st June, Cmdr. Charles Lightoller left Southend aboard his vessel *Sundowner*. His crew of son Roger and Sea Scout George Ashcroft called in at Ramsgate to collect charts, and set course for Dunkirk. As a Second Officer, Lightoller had survived the loss of RMS *Titanic*. He served in the Royal Navy in the Great War and was twice decorated for gallantry. En route to Dunkirk, *Sundowner*

narrowly missed a mine and then was attacked by three German aircraft. These were at once driven off by a Royal Navy destroyer. Next, Lightoller picked up the crew and three naval ratings from the motor cruiser *Westerly* taking them back to Dunkirk.

Sundowner reached Dunkirk at mid-afternoon. Although licensed to carry just 21 passengers, Lightoller and his crew embarked 127 soldiers. On the return journey, Lightoller evaded gunfire from enemy aircraft, using a technique described to him by his youngest son, Herbert, who had joined the RAF and been killed earlier in the war. Gerald Ashcroft later recalled '*We attracted the attention of a Stuka dive bomber. Commander Lightoller stood up in the bow and I stood alongside the wheelhouse. Commander Lightoller kept his eye on the Stuka till the last second - then he sang out to me 'Hard a port!' and I sang out to Roger and we turned very sharply. The bomb landed on our starboard side.*'

For his actions during the evacuation, Charles Lightoller received a mention in dispatches in 1944. His actions inspired the character of '*Mr Dawson*' in Christopher Nolan's 2017 film, Dunkirk.

With so many little ships now off the beaches, Ramsey sent Rear Admiral William Wake-Walker to Dunkirk. Dubbed Rear Admiral Dunkirk, Wake-Walker was to try to organise the off shore embarkation - Bill Tennant would remain Senior Naval Officer for the beaches and docks and the long queues of soldiers stretched into the sea.

As the last days of Operation Dynamo approached, increasing raids by the *Luftwaffe* persuaded Captain Tennant to call for no further evacuation during the hours of daylight. With the BEF evacuated, Churchill ordered Ramsey to send his ships back to evacuate the French. On the night of 3rd/4th June HMS *Malcolm* loaded on the last troops. She was not the last destroyer to leave - that honour fell to HMS *Shikari*.

****

Alan Roberts' father, EHA Roberts, served in the Royal Navy in the Second World War. He was taken prisoner during the ill-fated St. Nazaire raid in March 1942 and in captivity until almost the end of the war. In this extract, he tells of the RN's role on convoy escort duty. Supplies of food, munitions, equipment and fuel to Britain were close to critical level at times due to the actions of U-boats and the major German battleships and protecting the convoys was of paramount importance throughout much of the war.

Convoy Escort Duty

On one occasion, we headed across the North Atlantic close to Nova Scotia to join a convoy of 37 ships heading then for Gibraltar. Although there were reports of contacts with German U-boats we successfully took all our convoy to Gibraltar without loss. I was the ramming number in the aft 6" gun turret during this trip. Every action station slept in the turret on the steel deck, quite comfortably.

After reaching Gibraltar we joined Force H with other cruisers and destroyers searching for U-boats in the Western Med and for the *Scharnhorst* and *Gneisenau* in the Eastern Atlantic, not seeing much action. The convoys, three days ahead and three days behind us, from Nova Scotia lost many ships from U-boat action, so we were really lucky. We soon left Gibraltar heading for Chatham and as my two months aboard 'to experience sea-time' was finished, I was due leave, on docking to proceed to HMS *King Alfred* in Lancing (it was Lancing College in peace time).

An occasion which stands out in my memory was when on an 'N Patrol', one night our telegraphist reported that he could hear over the Asdic the sound of heavy propellers, and as a convoy was not then due, I listened to the Asdic and thought it very strange. I asked Ted to make several changes of course so that we could ascertain the direction of the ships, which caused the Asdic indications. This was easterly, i.e up Channel. Reporting to Ted, he authorised breaking radio silence and immediately we were ordered to return to port. It was as well we were so ordered, as the heavy ships were the *Scharnhorst* and *Gneisenau* having broken out from Brest, hoping to make their way to the North Sea. Had they encountered us, we would have been blown to kingdom come. I have never discovered how these enemy ships were able to escape through the Dover/Calais straits, when sailing orders were non-existent at that time. Radar must have picked them up on the screens.

Captain Attack must have advised his Senior Command of this after having instructed us to return to port and therefore suspected probable enemy. Yet Fleet Air Arm Swordfish planes did not engage the enemy until they were close to the Straits. Being south of Portland Bill when we broke radio silence there was plenty of time to engage before they reached that far up Channel. All I can say is *'mine is not to reason why'*. We knew the Army Captain in charge of radar stations along that part of the South Coast and unfortunately, we were unable to contact him before we were ordered away from Weymouth to Falmouth a few weeks later.

$$****$$

Bill King tells the history of his father Tom's war in the Royal Navy in the Second World War. In this instalment, Tom was serving on HMS Active providing protection and escort duty for convoys bringing vital supplies across the Atlantic to Britain. The U-boat menace was at its peak in this period, with huge losses to merchant shipping.

Battle of the Atlantic

On 15ᵗʰ July 1940, HMS *Active* together with four other destroyers of the 13ᵗʰ Flotilla left Gibraltar and returned to Britain coming under the command of the Home Fleet and based on Devonport (designated HMS *Drake IV*). *Active* underwent a short re-fit and one of her banks of quadruple torpedo tubes was removed to give her a high angle anti-aircraft gun. After the re-fit *Active* was assigned to the 12ᵗʰ Destroyer Flotilla and detached with the cruiser HMS *Cairo* and the tribal class destroyers *Bedouin, Tartar* and *Ashanti* for escort of the ships of the 1st Minelaying Squadron during Operation SN14, laying off the northern end of the North Sea Mine Barrier. In September, *Active* returned to anti-submarine defence in Western Approaches based in Liverpool and was involved in escorting north Atlantic convoys and in carrying out anti-submarine hunting. On 23rd September 1940 Tom was awarded his third Good Conduct Stripe.

The period of the autumn, winter, spring of 1940-41 was one of the worst periods of the war for the British. Now that France had fallen all the major west coast French ports became bases for the German U-boats. Until the fall of France, the U-boats had been confined to operating from their North Sea and Baltic bases which had limited their operations largely to the North Sea and the British east coast. Now the Biscay ports of Brest, Lorient, St Nazaire and Royan became the home ports of the U-boat fleet, enabling them to make longer sorties and bringing the south and west coasts of the British Isles and the whole of the North Atlantic within their area of operations.

Although the convoy system was in operation, the number of escort ships was too few to provide effective escort and many convoys sailed with only one or two escort ships. Frequently the escort comprised one destroyer and one corvette for the period of the voyage and the escort augmented for the passage into and out of the Western Approaches. Outbound Atlantic convoys from the Clyde and Liverpool were escorted to an area approximately 300 miles west of Ireland and inbound convoys were met and escorted from that area for the final part of their voyage.

The area to the northwest of Ireland became the U-boats killing zone. The larger Type VII U-boats which were now forming the backbone of the U-boat fleet could stay at sea for up to one month. They carried ten torpedoes and could re-fuel and rearm from supply ships and specially adapted supply submarines, which allowed them to operate for longer patrols. The U-boat tactics evolved to attack the convoy at night and on the surface.

Radar which could identify surfaced U-boats had not yet come into use. ASDIC was only useful when the U-boat was submerged and with so few escorts operating the chances of successfully detecting and attacking was minimal. Another successful U-boat tactic was the introduction of the 'Wolf Pack' in which one U-boat, finding a convoy, would track the convoy without attacking and 'home' other U-boats on to it. Then the *'Wolf Pack'* would attack the convoy from a number of different directions and completely overwhelm the escort screen. Individual U-boat 'Aces' such as Kretschmer in U-99, Schepke in U-100, Lemp in U-30, Endrass in U46, Topp in U-57, and Oesten in U-61, notched up huge tonnages in ships sunk. At the same time, U-boat sinkings by the escorts was minimal - only three U-boats were sunk in the six months between 1st September 1940 and 1st March 1941. This period was known by the U-boat crews as 'The Happy Time'. In October 1940 the U-boats sank 352,407 tons of shipping.

Active was continually involved as part of the escort for convoys from Liverpool and the Clyde and in meeting inbound convoys from mid-Atlantic. On 27th October 1940 the British merchant ship *Diplomat* was sunk by the

German submarine U-104 128 nautical miles west-north-west of Bloody Foreland, Ireland, in position 55°42'N, 11°37'W. HMS *Active* carried out a search and picked up 39 survivors.

Tom would have been at the ASDIC set throughout this operation.

In early November *Active* was part of the escort for inbound convoy HX-83 in the Western Approaches. One ship from this convoy was sunk by U-99 commanded by the U-boat 'Ace' Otto Kretschmer on 5th November. *Active*, with Tom at the ASDIC set, would have been hunting this U-boat 'Ace'. On the same day, the following convoy HX-84 with the sole escort of the armed merchant cruiser HMS *Jervis Bay* was attacked by the German pocket battleship *Admiral Scheer*. The *Jervis Bay* immediately went into the attack but was no match for the heavily armed battleship and was sunk in 24 minutes. The valuable time gained in this gallant action allowed the convoy to scatter and although five ships were destroyed the remainder made port. Captain Fogarty Fegen of *Jervis Bay* was awarded the Victoria Cross posthumously. Tom often spoke of this action and the admiration the crews of the escort group felt for the crew of the *Jervis Bay*.

Pamela Leworthy joined the WRNS in 1943. She describes her story and experiences as a new recruit. She trained as an Air Radar Mechanic, and largely operated and maintained the RADAR on trawlers, which were generally converted to minesweepers. By kind permission of her son, Chris Leworthy.

A newly hatched Wren

On 22nd August 1943, the WRNS in its wisdom, having decided that the intake of 8th August should train as Air Radar Mechanics, sent the twenty or so newly hatched Wrens to spend four months at Walthamstow Technical College in order to learn the basics of radio theory and workshop practice. Thus was born Class ARM21.

We wrote reams of notes on fault finding procedures, made our own C spanners and mastered the intricacies of the soldering iron (electric ones not allowed!). It helped with the fault finding if one remembered whether the anode, or possibly the cathode, went positive, or possibly negative, at the outset of any radio operation. As very few of us had previously been introduced to Ann, Cath, or even Di Ode, it gave rise to various horrors and silent hysterics. But some of the girls were brilliant, outdoing sailors working on the same course at the same time

New Year's Day 1944 started us on four months' further slogging at HMS *Ariel,* which at that time was near Warrington in Lancashire. Radar, a title culled from the USA and previously having been referred to as Radio Location, or Radio Direction Finding, was so secret that on no account could it be discussed with anyone. Our books were locked in the classrooms at the end of each day, and on leave, the instruction when I asked what was the category indicated by the badge of wings bisected by a shaft of lightning was to say airily *'oh, something to do with wireless '.*

We took our final exams which reduced us all to quivering jellies, and some to tears, and together with two weeks unravelling IFF (Identification Friend or Foe) we passed out as Leading Wrens. Our 'buttons', when we became Petty Officers, followed a year later.

Having trained as Air Radar Mechanics on an ancient Swordfish aircraft, and an even more ancient Walrus, the rest of ARM 21 departed to various Fleet Air Arm stations, while I was posted to HMS *Devonport* to work with the Royal Navy.

The HQ of Maintenance and Shipping control in the dockyard was an old French battleship, FS *Paris*, which was distinguished by a very tall tower with the clock face painted on with figures from 1 to 10. I was never quite able to find out the significance of this, but I believe it was something to do with gunnery targets. After the war we watched her being towed back to France, very slowly, and in a dignified manner. Sad we were to see her go.

When I first arrived in Devonport, I found myself meekly carrying the toolbox of the Sub-Lieutenant in charge of radar for M/S and A/P vessels. (minesweeping and auxiliary patrol ships) – there were 25 or so converted trawlers, each with crews of about 50 men and four officers, mainly RNVR and RNR. The Sub Lieutenant left shortly afterwards having been drafted to Australia, I was asked if I would carry on until he was replaced, which never happened, so I carried on – regardless.

The 286 radar set was reasonably simple and was used for navigation and defence purposes. But occasionally, when the set was turned on, all the ship's lights went off. The electrics were, to say the least, whimsical and frolicsome. My trusty soldering iron played its part from time to time, and the valves expired regularly. (This was 'BT' – before transistors – but the electricians and I coped somehow).

The trawlers had picturesque names – *Ruby, Pearl, Kingston Andalusite, Kingston Chrysoberyl, Skomer, Lindisfarne, Gweal, Cornelean, Minalto, Cambridgeshire, Guardsman,* among others, and there was also *Ellesmere,* a whaler. The crews, somewhat surprised at having a young Wren on board, were very kind and I soon conquered my nervousness. As soon as I leapt among them, in bellbottom trousers, armed with my toolbox and statutory WRNS shoulder bag, never a wicked word was uttered – well hardly ever – and then only by mistake.

Occasionally I was called to other ships – a French corvette (they gave me a delicious lunch!), an LCT or two, and once, a captured German trawler. The whole vessel was filthy, the radar was unworkable, the acorn coffee dregs were indescribable, even to look at and I had to be deloused afterwards. Most undignified!

On the larger vessels I boarded, QH, which the RAF called Gee, was installed and many happy hours were spent in calibration. PPI (plan position indicator) was also used on some vessels, and is still in existence – but now in glorious colour. There were Wrens working on large gunnery sets (385, I believe) on the breakwater but I was very attached to my little 286s and was grateful to avoid the three miles out and three miles back each day in a small boat.

There were some sad moments amongst the many happy ones. Working on board *Ellesmere* one Saturday, a sailor asked me to send a telegram to his wife, whose birthday was on the following Monday, as they were about to sail on Sunday. I was then told that the '*Ellie*' had been torpedoed and sunk outside the breakwater. There were no survivors. All I could think about was that the widow would receive two telegrams on her birthday, one from her husband and one from the Admiralty. Tragic.

One FAA Wren radar mechanic friend, Isabel Squires, was killed when the aircraft in which she was testing a set crashed. She was 21 years old.

Another friend from ARM 21, Joy Pidgeon and I have recently arranged to have a tree planted in the WRNS plot in the National Memorial Arboretum in Alrewas, Staffordshire. It is dedicated: '*To those who did not come back*'

As I worked on trawlers for almost two years, I came to know those on board very well, and although I may have missed the hustle and bustle of an FAA station, Devonport had its many moments (I seem to recall an extremely long conga snaking along the Hoe on VJ Day). I value very much, and still do, the affection and friendship of those whom I have known for almost 60 years. Incidentally, one of them married me.

Historian Bill King recounts the wartime experiences of his father, Tom King, who was a career serviceman in the Royal Navy. The St Nazaire raid was an audacious attempt by the RN with commandos to prevent the fearsome German battleship Tirpitz from having a port on the Atlantic coast for repair and re-fit. The Tirpitz was regarded as one of the biggest threats to British merchant shipping and the convoys bringing vital supplies to Britain.

St Nazaire Raid

Having arrived at Falmouth, Tom was put in charge of a small team engaged in organising the installation, calibration and maintenance of the ASDIC equipment fitted to the various coastal forces craft based there. These were Motor Launches (MLs), Motor Torpedo Boats (MTBs) and Motor Gun Boats (MGBs). About 12th March, a number of additional Coastal Forces boats arrived - eight MLs from the 28th flotilla, four MLs from the 20th flotilla and a further four MLs from the 7th flotilla. The group began an intensive programme of exercises during which they sailed out into the English Channel on anti-submarine sweeps. They were joined by the specially modified MTB74 and MGB314. These ships were all painted a drab shade of mauve known as 'Plymouth Pink' as a form of camouflage. They were being made ready to take part in Operation 'Chariot' the raid on the French port of St Nazaire where the huge '*Normandie*' dry dock was located.

The '*Normandie* Dock' was the only dry dock on the Atlantic seaboard capable of accommodating the German battleship *Tirpitz* should she break out from her base in Norway to attack the Atlantic convoys. It was imperative that this dock was put out of action and the operation could not be performed by bombing raids. A combined operation was mounted involving commandos transported by sea in the eighteen newly arrived coastal forces boats and an old destroyer to ram and blow up the lock gates at the entrance to the dry dock.

On the 25th March the heavily modified old destroyer HMS *Campbeltown* (ex USS *Buchanan*) arrived and joined the force. The force sailed on the afternoon of 26th March. All the preparations for the raid had taken place in complete secrecy.

Tom had had the task of maintaining and calibrating the ASDIC equipment fitted to the MLs and saw the force sail. All the ASDIC gear was stripped out of these ships to make extra space for the commandos of the raiding force. Tom had regarded these as 'his' boats. The raid took place on the night of 27th-28th March and was a complete success achieving all its objectives. However, the *Campbeltown* had been sacrificed to ram and then blow up the entrance to the *Normandie* dock. Most of the MLs had been shot to pieces on the river Loire and had burned out with most of the landing force killed or taken prisoner. Only three of the eighteen coastal forces boats retuned to Falmouth where their crews were given a heroes' welcome.

****

Lieutenant. ECA Roberts served in the Navy in the Second World War. His son Alan Roberts tells his story of involvement in the St Nazaire raid with extracts from Lieutenant. Roberts' diary, written some years later in the 1970s. The raid itself achieved its objective in the successful blocking and the destruction of the huge dry dock gates by HMS Campbeltown; in so doing it prevented the dock from being used again by the German battleship Tirpitz for repair and re-fit. As in all actions, few are without casualties of war; only a third of those on the motor launches made it back to England and Lieutenant Roberts was one of many taken prisoner. He tells of his capture and transportation to the POW camp.

St Nazaire Raid - Into Captivity

So to Falmouth where we were joined by twelve other MLs making two complete Flotillas. Assembling there was the troop ship 'The Princess Josephine Charlotte' with Commandos aboard. What was this all about? The other MLs came from Dartmouth and Appledore. We had not long to wait before the officers were requested to assemble aboard the 'Princess Josephine Charlotte', where a large scale model of the St. Nazaire dry dock and its approaches, showing the Old Mole, and beyond were the U-boat pens.

We were then told that run crews were not to be informed that it was intended that an old destroyer was planned to ram the caisson of the dry dock having 500 tons of TNT in depth charges set in concrete from its stern to the bridge, with time fuses to be set on delay for approximately 8 to 10 hours, with an explosive charge set in its stern to prevent the destroyer slipping astern after it struck the caisson. The old destroyer, now named HMS *Campbeltown* and given

233

the one-way passage, was an American lease-lend vessel. Originally a four-stacker, its insides were gutted to reduce its draft, as it had to cross over the mud flats leading to the *Normandie* Dock, some six miles from the mouth of the River Loire. This could happen at one time only in the year, at high water springs, or not at all. To take off the commandos from the *Campbeltown*, as it was named, after they had done their demolition and attack procedures, the 16 'B' Fairmile MLs, which had assembled at Falmouth, also took commandos. An MGB 74 was to be towed to act as an HQ ship and an MTB carrying torpedoes was also to be towed to use its torpedoes if the *Campbeltown* failed to do its intended job.

We were due to reach the dock gates at 1.30am. It was now 1.20am, ten minutes to our target and still two miles to our target. The *Campbeltown* had grounded several times. Huge beams of search lights lit up the sky and raked the boats.... We just kept on going... Two signal stations on shore flashed up their challenges. Our signaller was a German speaker and sent a reply in German Morse code saying that '*we are a friendly force under orders to proceed to the harbour*'. One German battery opened fire across the *Campbeltown's* bows. Our signaller flashed back '*we are being fired on by friendly forces*'. The firing stopped briefly. However, had we really been a German force, as soon as we had been fired upon, we would have stopped, but of course we were English pretending to be German and so we increased speed, going as fast as the big old *Campbeltown* could possibly go. The Germans weren't fooled any longer; they opened up and began firing at the *Campbeltown*.

It was 1.34am, just four minutes later than planned, the *Campbeltown* crashed into the gate of the *Normandie* Dock. You can imagine the noise the flying debris, the sky lit up by red and green tracer flames, machine guns firing. The commandos, the demolition and protection teams disembarked down the scaling ladder, making their way to their planned targets.

Meanwhile out in the river the motor launches were trying to land all their commandos, there were lots of targets to destroy, the pumping station, the winding station, bridges, the submarine pens etc.

The motor launches were suffering severely…. highly flammable and made of wood. To be honest, they were sitting ducks out there on the river, being shot at from every angle, many caught fire and drifted helplessly.

Part of dad's launch caught fire. The fire spread so rapidly that the order to abandon ship was given, but before dad could do so, his launch's small magazine blew up, taking him with it. He plunged into the icy water.

'The force of the explosion embedded me feet first in the mud of the river bed. I slipped with regret out of my newly issued sea boots and leather flying jacket. I surfaced unhurt but deaf from the noise of the explosion. I was soon joined by Able Seaman Ball, he was in a bad way, his leg was shot up and he was losing blood. We swam with me trying to support him to the sea wall, we were quite disorientated. Above the sea wall was a line of Germans with their rifles pointing at us. I thought we were for it. Much to my gratification a rope ladder was thrown over the

wall.... I tried to climb up but fell back.... I hung on for dear life and reached the top.'

'Surprisingly a German appeared with my clothes dried and I was able to dress and be mustered with others ready for interrogation. In due time I was interrogated by an English speaking Hun asking my name, rank and number etc. - which was all we were instructed to give when in Falmouth. He was rather irate as I confessed to knowing nothing at all. I did as I was ordered. Eventually he got fed up and dismissed me. He called in another rank, a chap I did not know, but I was able to listen to what took part and was very surprised and worried when the young fellow said that the English had a secret weapon which of course, the German was most interested to hear about. After many persuasions the youngster advised that it was a rifle that fired round comers. What a sense of humour. After this, another truck ride to what I believe was a building in La Boulle, where I met up with others in my plight. Much talking took place. At one time Commander Beatty was brought in with nothing more on than a blanket, which he exposed with a grin. We had heard, a while before, a hell of an explosion which was considered to be the Campbeltown blowing up. Beatty was able to confirm this. He told us that when he was being interrogated the German had said to him, after he had admitted being Captain of the Campbeltown, how foolish the English were to think that they could damage the dry dock with such a flimsy ship. At that moment the explosion took place.'

Of the 16 MLs and MTBs, only 3 MLs managed to escape. The MGB got out but was sunk by one of the accompanying destroyers, having taken off Captain RD Ryder and the rest of his HQ, staff and crew. The *Campbeltown*, of course, had sailed with us from Falmouth and we were joined by the destroyers *Atheston* and *Rochdale*. Of the 611 who took part, 169 were killed, 215 became POWs and only 227 got home. The Naval casualties were 105 killed, so much higher than the Commandos, 64, as we were literally sitting ducks, and I became a POW having had to swim for it.

So eventually we were all trucked off to Reims to a filthy camp, where our stories were told, between ourselves. Summing up these left no doubt in our minds of the successful conclusion to our mission. All the food we had was soup, sauerkraut, and bread but thankfully we were not here long before we were trucked to a railway station, the officers being seated in carriages and the other ranks in cattle trucks labelled '*40 hommes*'. A long slow journey to prison camp in Germany, passing through Aachen on, I believe, Easter Sunday.

En route, before entering Germany my flotilla SO, Lieutenant Commander Billy Stevens was restless to jump train and take his chances of escape, but no possible chance arose, with the guards being constantly on the alert. At an odd stop or two we were allowed out of the train and most of us did a '*pump-ship*' on the line then. Soup and bread were the only sustenance throughout this trip and eventually we arrived at the Merchant Seaman's camp called Milag Nord and were put into a section wired off for us. The only contact with the rest of the camp was through the food staff.

Coastal Forces POWs.
Alan Roberts' family archive

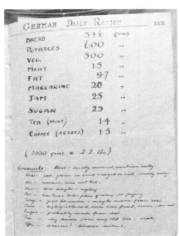

POW Rations in Stalag.
Alan Roberts' family archive

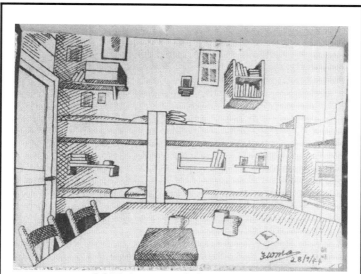

POW Accommodation in Stalag.
Alan Roberts' family archive

HMS *Active*.
Wright and Logan Postcards: Bill King collection

ML191 (similar to the ML's used in Operation Chariot –St
Nazaire Raid Horseshoe Club.
Wright and Logan Postcards: Bill King collection

HMS *Active* at 'Action Stations'.
Bill King collection

HMS *Active* somewhere in the North Atlantic 1941.
Bill King collection

 *This is an extract from the memoirs of Captain Mervyn Wingfield, DSO, DSC, RN, published as 'Wingfield at War' in 2012. As an experienced submarine commander, Lieutenant-Commander Wingfield, aged 34, was instructed to take the surrender of the U-boat fleet in Norway at the end of the war. Captain Wingfield took the surrender of 90 U-boats, escorting 25 of them to Scapa Flow. Courtesy of Richard Wingfield, Captain Wingfield's son.*

Surrender of U-boats in 1945

When Germany surrendered there were over 150 U-boats in commission despite the appalling losses sustained – 784 out of a total of 1,171 having been sunk. Few forces in history can have taken such a beating and still retained their fighting spirit. I was sent to Oslo, Norway, soon after VE Day with the title of Senior Officer (Submarines) Norway, to organise the surrender of the 90 odd U-boats in Norwegian ports. I crossed the North Sea in good style, accompanying Crown Prince Olaf, who was to represent his father King Haakon at the victory celebrations. These took the usual form of parades and marches but there were a few unusual features. There were quite a few girls in the ranks and many of the rifles had wild flowers stuck in the barrel. There was even an orange impaled on one soldier's bayonet.

We duly took over the U-boats at Oslo and other officers in my party did the same at Bergen and other ports where there were small flotillas. At first we armed our sailors with carbines but the senior German Officer, *Korvettenkapitän* Schnee, told me it was quite unnecessary.

242

'My men are disciplined. We have been told to surrender by Berlin and we will carry out our orders. This will be a well-organised operation and we would not like it to be marred by any shooting. Your men appear unfamiliar with their weapons and might easily cause an accident.'

Schnee was an impressive figure with whom I became quite friendly. He had several Iron Crosses as well as the *Ritterkreuz* with diamonds, which he had won for sinking a large tonnage of allied shipping. *'Many other U-boat commanders received high decorations in the early part of the War when any fool could knock up a good score, but I won all my medals in 1941 and 1942 when things were pretty difficult for us'* he told me with an engaging lack of modesty.

He said we were making a mistake in taking over the U-boats which would be useful to us when we had to fight the Russians, which we certainly would within six months. He insisted that despite their losses, the morale of the U-boat men was high and they were furious at having to surrender just when their new super U-boat, the Type XXI, was ready for service.

I took over one of these as my flagship and I soon realised how lucky we were not to have had to contend with the Type XXI. They were much faster, more heavily armed and could dive twice as deep as the old Type VII C which they were to replace. If the Germans had concentrated on U-boats instead of wasting effort on battleships and vast fleets of bombers, the war would have finished in 1942. I believe they only had 40 operational boats in September 1939. If they had had 200, Britain would have been starved into defeat.

Schnee told me that the Type XXI which I had picked up was a bad choice. The Captain had been a teetotaller and allowed no liquor on board, unlike the other boats which were well stocked with French wine and Dutch gin.

There were enormous stocks of champagne in the German equivalent of the NAAFI in Oslo, all stamped *'Reservé à la Wehrmacht'*. We used to send a car every day to the storehouse for a few cases which were *FREE*. At least they were free until the Army Commander, General Browning, found out about it when he issued an order which is probably unique in Army history.

'The free issue of champagne is to cease forthwith. In future a charge of one shilling and sixpence for each bottle is to be made, which will be given to Army charities.' In fact, we quickly got tired of the stuff and when a Polish destroyer arrived with a good stock of beer, we were happy to do a swap, bottle for bottle.

We were well supplied with staff cars requisitioned from the Germans. Mine was a very nice Mercedes open tourer with which I explored some of southern Norway. One evening in the hotel an RNVR officer asked me if I would like him to take it to the UK in his landing ship. *'All you have to do is park it on the dockside near my ship and then report it to the Military Police as stolen. I will leave it in some convenient car park when we reach UK and you can collect it. Worth £50, don't you think?'* He said he had done it several times and the system worked perfectly. Sorely tempted as I was, bearing in mind the shortage of cars in England, I foresaw difficulties in registration and licensing, and politely declined the offer. Now I don't suppose I shall ever own a Mercedes. Too bad!

Except for a few German technicians who were retained to assist our own men in sailing the boats back to the UK, all the U-boat crews were sent off to a POW camp to await repatriation. I went to the station where a special train was being loaded with the crews. Schnee was there, every inch the Prussian officer, wearing a long grey great-coat and sporting a monocle. He was a little annoyed with the Norwegian Authorities who apparently expected the officers to go in cattle trucks with the men. I am pleased to say I was able to put this right and proper carriages were provided. Schnee thanked me and said goodbye. *'Here is the address of my schloss in Silesia. I hope you will come and stay with me when all this trouble is sorted out,'* he said, adding *'You had better have my pistol. I shan't be needing it where we are going.'* The train drew out. It was a very well conducted surrender.

Next day I took my handsome new Type XXI to sea for a short trial, to find that they were brutes to handle. To be technical for a moment, I must explain that the propeller shafts pointed outwards 10° from the fore and aft line and the propellers were in-turning. Thus when going alongside starboard, in order to swing in the stern, one had to go astern with the starboard screw – exactly the opposite to every other ship in the world.

I got the hang of it in the end and proudly sailed from Oslo at the head of my flotilla of some 25 U-boats. We had no mechanical trouble thanks to our Germans, all of whom were keen to join the Royal Navy! In the wardroom we had the squadron engineer officer who had been in U-boats all the war until recently when he had been on duty at the construction yard in Hamburg. I asked him about air raids

245

by the RAF. He said they caused no trouble. Few bombs fell anywhere near the U-boats under construction and, anyway, what better air raid shelter could you have than the hull of a U-boat on the stocks?

We joined up with the other U-boats from Bergen and Kristiansand and made an impressive entry into Scapa Flow. Immediately a horde of would-be looters descended on us from the Home Fleet ships. But they were too late. I had told our people that every rating could have one thing and every officer two things. I allowed myself three. (These were two pairs of binoculars, one still in use, and a typewriter which I sold for £15 despite the fact that it had German characters.) So the souvenir hunters went away empty handed.

We laid up most of the boats at Cairn Ryan and the rest at Lisahally on Loch Foyle in Northern Ireland. The allied governments had agreed that Russia, America and Britain should each choose ten U-boats to keep and the rest would be towed out to sea and scuttled. For this, a tri-partite commission of officers from the three countries was appointed to make the selection. I led the RN team and in due course we all embarked in the cruiser *Liverpool* which provided us with accommodation during the week or so it took to make our choice. Our inspections were fairly perfunctory as the RN did not particularly want any U-boats, but the Russians were most meticulous and boarded every boat. Eventually our job was complete and we were disbanded.

Note: Korvettenkapitän Adalbert Schnee (1913-1982) commanded five U-boats and sank 23 ships (95,889 tons) and damaged 3 others (28,820 tons). Schnee held the Iron Cross 1st and 2nd class, the Knight's Cross with Oak Leaves and diamonds. In September 1944 he took command of the U-2511, the first Type XXI boat to go on war patrol.

Type XXI U-boat U2502, my flagship on the voyage from Oslo, is secured alongside a Royal Navy ship in Rothesay, Scotland in 1945. Also visible is a smaller coastal U-boat.
Richard Wingfield collection

Chapter 4 - War Against Japan

The attack by the Japanese on the US fleet at Pearl Harbor in Hawaii on 7th December 1941 was the turning point of the Second World War. It would not be an overstatement to say that this day was the first day of the end of the war, albeit that it took almost four further years until the final Japanese surrender. So why was this so significant and how can it be interpreted as thus?

For over two years, Britain had stood largely alone as German forces had conquered most of both western and eastern Europe. Britain had seen its armies roundly defeated in Norway, Northern France and North Africa: British forces had narrowly escaped annihilation through the 'miracle' of Dunkirk, and had seen the heroic victory by The Few, supported by many others during the Battle of Britain, and had started to experience the terror of the *Blitz* across British cities. Growing losses to shipping and vital supplies in the Atlantic due to the formidable U–Boat forces had threatened Britain's ability to feed itself and to produce sufficient armaments to keep fighting.

With this backdrop, Winston Churchill had been using all his political and personal guile and charm to persuade, cajole and pressurise US President Roosevelt to support the fight against Nazi tyranny.

Roosevelt, while personally a tacit supporter of Churchill and the British cause, was constrained by an American electorate and US laws determined not to let the USA get involved, directly or indirectly, in another foreign, European war just over 20 years after the previous conflict. Unofficially Roosevelt did help with lower scale 'below the radar' support with the supply of 50 ageing destroyers and other materials on the lend lease programme in return for the rights to some British colonies, particularly in the Caribbean.

'Pearl Harbor', as it is colloquially known, changed all that at a stroke with the surprise attack on the major naval harbour containing much of the US Pacific fleet. The attack, by aircraft from the Japanese carrier fleet under Admiral Yamamoto, in a matter of an hour or so sank or seriously damaged 9 warships, destroyed 180 aircraft and killed over 2,400 service men. Fortunately for the US Navy, the carriers were out of Pearl Harbor on exercise and avoided the attack.

The following day, in a speech to the US Congress, Roosevelt described this unprovoked attack as *'a date which will live in infamy'*. Conversely and with hindsight, Japanese Admiral Hara Tadaichi summed up the Japanese result by saying, *'We won a great tactical victory at Pearl Harbor and thereby lost the war'*.

The USA declared war on Japan the following day and Germany declared war on the USA shortly afterwards. A global world war involving all the major powers of the world was underway.

For Britain things did not change overnight or indeed for quite a time. Losses to U-boats continued to escalate, bombing of British towns and cities were nightly occurrences and the RAF's bomber offensive was only making a modest impact. American war industries would take many months to gear up their production lines to produce the equipment and munitions and to train the men to make a major difference.

In the immediate term, the war escalated dramatically. In a matter of weeks, Japanese forces surged across much of south east Asia, by land, sea and air, in a remarkable display of aggressive, dynamic military force inflicting great damage, terror and brutality on military forces and civilian populations alike. Within 2 days of Pearl Harbor, the British warships, HMS *Repulse* and HMS *Prince of Wales* were sunk off Singapore and within a few months the Imperial Japanese Army captured the Philippines, Burma, the Dutch East Indies (Indonesia), the Malay Peninsula, Rangoon, Singapore, Jakarta and numerous smaller islands and states. At its peak the Japanese Empire controlled over 20 million square miles of territory in Asia and the Pacific region. By mid-1942, Japan was poised outside Australia ready to strike and Darwin had faced its first bombing raids.

The allies were in a parlous state, with British colonies falling swiftly and in humiliating style. Hong Kong fell in December and Burma invaded in January 1942. The following month Singapore fell ignominiously to an unexpected attack overland, with huge British forces surrendering under General Percival in a matter of days - 140,000 British, Australian and Dutch troops were taken into what turned out to be a dreadful, indeed infamous, captivity. This is often regarded as the lowest ebb for Britain in the war.

Further defeats followed – the battle of the Java Sea, huge losses in the Philippines and the Japanese pushing further through Burma to start knocking on the door of India. The appointment of Douglas MacArthur as Supreme Commander in May 1942 saw the tide start to turn over the following months. Resistance stiffened - the first bombing raids on the Japanese mainland by carrier-based aircraft saw the first signs of fighting back. US industrial output and extensive recruitment and training of servicemen across all disciplines started to shift the balance of power.

The battles of the Coral Sea and then Midway, where the two navies fought in the air from aircraft carriers saw the first defeats of the war for Japan. Thereafter, from mid-1942 onwards, US forces gradually, and with significant losses, fought their way from island to island overcoming determined, well dug in resistance. Guadalcanal and Guam were symbolic of the fierce fighting across the region.

In Burma, the British and American forces eventually halted the advance. Initially Orde Wingate's Chindits, and then under Lieutenant General William 'Bill' Slim, the allies fought back in extremely difficult conditions. The enemy was as much the environment as it was the Japanese. Dense jungle, hot humid conditions, torrential rains, steep mountains, with few roads able to take motorised transport and all manner of tropical diseases made both fighting and resupplying the 14th Army incredibly difficult. In all, with huge support from Indian forces, the army fighting in Burma peaked at about 2 million soldiers.

Decisive battles were won at Imphal and Kohima, as Japanese supply lines became overstretched and the allied air forces restricted their movement. Dubbed the 'Forgotten Army', the remarkable bravery and losses incurred by allied forces in Burma were often overlooked as the threat of invasion of Britain receded and VE Day saw the end of the European War. Many veterans of this campaign felt bitter and let down by this attitude and lack of recognition for their valiant service.

Towards the end of 1944, the US forces on land, sea and in the air continued their inexorable journey towards the Japanese mainland. First, the Philippines were re-taken then numerous islands such as Iwo Jima and Okinawa, both of which were bitterly fought over and have become iconic names in US military history.

Pressure remained on the Allied leaders to try to end the war swiftly and with minimum of allied casualties. With the technology of the atomic bomb being successfully tested, the decision was made to foreshorten the Pacific war by dropping the atom bomb on Hiroshima. On 6th August 1945, the first bomb was dropped, and when requests for surrender made to the Japanese government were ignored, a second atom bomb was dropped on Nagasaki three days later. Casualties from the two blasts were enormous, with an estimated 120,000 people killed in the two cities. Japan surrendered within a few days, with the Imperial Emperor speaking to his people - it was the first time they had heard an emperor's voice. The surrender document was signed by the Japanese forces in Tokyo Bay on 2nd September 1945.

Over the following months the full scale of the horrific conditions and atrocities which had been inflicted on allied POWs and civilian populations under Japanese control came to light. The Bataan death march, and the construction of so-called Death Railway between Thailand and Burma are but two examples. Many died in captivity, and many more suffered for much of their lives, never forgiving the Japanese and refusing to talk about their experiences.

This brought to an end almost six years of war, costing up to 80 million lives – civilian and military - from across the globe.

****

 *Wilf Bainbridge describes the experiences of his father, George, as a POW of the Japanese in the Second World War. A musician, George managed to survive the horrors of four years of captivity by playing music to fellow prisoners. George was imprisoned in Chungkai POW camp in Thailand. It would normally house 11,000 prisoners and the men worked on the so-called Death Railway between Thailand and Burma.*

From Blucher to Burma

My father, George Bainbridge was born in a small hamlet called Blucher to the west of Newcastle upon Tyne countryside on 10th June 1915. His own father was a coal mine employee, and his mother, a housewife with musical ability, who played the local chapel organ as George dutifully pumped the bellows. He clearly had his mother's musical talents and as a boy won various awards in local singing competitions. Schooling as was usual in these times ended formally when he was but 14 years old and just as he left education the great depression of the 1930s loomed.

Faced with few work opportunities and no doubt some boyhood enthusiasm encouraged by his chum Eddie Humble, they decided that they needed to consider their futures. Clearly choices were diminishing and after weighing up the options they both decided to become soldiers and so it was on 16th June 1931 aged 16 years and one week my father and his pal joined the Aberdeen based 2nd Gordon Highlanders who were recruiting in Newcastle upon Tyne.

With each other for company the adventure began. It had only been 13 years since the ending of the Great War and so the prospect of another major conflict was not on anyone's horizon, not least for two 16 year old boys. As a boy soldier not long out of school, he first attended Ballykinlar, Northern Ireland, for his Army Certificate of Education which was completed in October 1931. Clearly Army life was good for him as he won the Battalion Boys Champion Athlete Cup for 1933. After training at Aldershot he was sent to Ranks on 10th June 1933.

More education followed to achieve his second Certificate, but his break came when on 4th December 1934 he was appointed as a bandsman. Resurrecting his natural musical talents, this opportunity would actually be his saviour and see him through life as will be told hereafter. From this point he attended the Royal Military School of Music, Kneller Hall, until the end of 1937. During this time in the Regimental band he performed at home and abroad including an event for the King of Denmark as part of the British Exhibition including a Tuborg beer plant tour it seems as I still have the presentation brochure.

Embarkation for Gibraltar at the end of 1934 saw him there for two years. Here the company also met up with the 1st Battalion Band which is recorded in a formal photograph. In the last month they departed and spent this time in Egypt and returned to the UK in August 1936.

With the talk of war escalating and strategies starting to be put into place, the 2nd Battalion Gordon Highlanders were sent to Malaya and on to Singapore where he ended up on 9th April 1938, all to defend British interests in the Far East. My father spoke nostalgically of his fondness in those peaceful times where they were able to enjoy this new found haven wearing tropical uniform. With its exciting departure from westernism, the exotic culture, pleasant climate and leisure activities, it became a very enjoyable place to be living. A few of them even bought a share in a Ford V8 Pilot car – something completely unimaginable and unattainable for him had he still been back in Newcastle upon Tyne. Being a proficient sportsman, the ability to swim, play tennis and football in these climes was delightful. He even took up photography which again would carry on throughout his life. He also seemed to have acquired a taste for certain spicy foods whilst away from these shores for when I was young and ready-made curry became widely available, I was surprised when he took to creating his own custom recipes occasionally – clearly a hark back to better times, but mother did not approve.

History well records the demise of Singapore as the Japanese advanced and invaded unexpectedly from the jungle. He told me that the vegetation was so dense that you could not see through it and a man had to hack his way through for every step that he wanted to take. The circumstance of his capture was fairly brief as he said that they engaged in firing mortars when they were ambushed, surrounded and captured.

So on 15th February 1942 began four long years incarcerated at the hands of the Japanese for whom surrender was the lowest form a soldier could become. The only upside was his urgent promotion to unpaid acting sergeant.

And so followed their new 'home', Chungkai Camp as a Japanese Prisoner of War. There followed an unimaginable term with excruciating conditions that only the fit and lucky would survive. Forced to build the infamous Burma Railway it is said a life was lost for every sleeper. A bowl of rice per day and jungle conditions like no other combined with disease and fatigue became the norm. Salvaging and making everything they could to make life a little more bearable was done and whatever could be done to help save life was a priority. Notably those men who were able to provide blood, including my father, received a citation to the effect given this was such a risky challenge.

Father spoke so little of this time of his life, understandably, but I do recall him describing a time when all working prisoners had been lined up, for some misdemeanour, and every tenth one was shot – ironically he was able to teach me effectively how to count in Japanese, something I still remember to this day and have used during my career with a global Japanese company!

Life in Chungkai was no life at all but the spirit, resources and talents of the men were remarkable. Keeping a diary was absolutely banned and would attract severe punishment or death; however, some light relief was found in the creation and performance of stage entertainment and a theatre was made using the spectrum of skills present in the camp.

For some unknown reason my father was known in the Army as 'Bill' and early on the creation of *'Bill Bainbridge and his Band'* found himself as Band Director and they became much valued and appreciated. Making instruments from whatever became available and writing music from memory and collaborative writing of well-known and new stage shows the Chungkai Theatre became *'famous throughout the Prisoner of War Camps throughout Thailand'* – Major A H Rycock, Feb 5 1945.

Personal effects were few and with uniform basically deteriorating, clothes ended up consisting of a linen jock strap and a beret that survived. Momentos that were saved and retrieved consisted of hand drawn and pencil coloured theatre show flyers, posters and programmes and these were mounted in a scrap book soon after the war and latterly were loaned and copied by the Gordon Highlanders Museum, Aberdeen. One interesting item is a hand drawn portrait rolled and kept in a bamboo tube which is a flattering likeness of father but he would quickly point out that the artist always made the men look *'healthier'* in sketch as they were all woefully underweight and thin. Indeed upon release he weighed little more than 7 stone and at almost 6ft this must have looked absolutely painful. I know that when he eventually returned home, if he was asked if he would like a bacon sandwich he would reply *'yes please, I'll have two!'*

Contact with the outside world was rare during their time as POWs and afterwards he said that they hardly ever saw any Red Cross parcels. He did however allude to the fact that there was 'one guard' that seemed okay, or at least better than the rest.

As Victory in Europe was declared and the focus on the war with Japan developed, he said that as it became closer to ending the war, the mood amongst the Japs changed noticeably. But this also became a dangerous situation and the POWs became anxious in case things changed for the worse. As happened, one morning the prisoners woke to find them all gone and liberation had arrived at long last. The journey home was not without its incidents and flying out on a DC-3 Dakota it was struck by lightning - father refused ever to fly again!

Eventually he returned home on 19th October 1945 to his mother, father and sister – and one of the first things he asked – *'Is our neighbour's girl Peggy married yet?'*

The answer was no and the rest as they say is history.

It was on 12th April 1946 that my father George Bainbridge was transferred to the Reserves and his civilian life began and the music, literally, played on, until his premature death on 14th February 1978 aged 62.

 *Elizabeth Lockhart-Mure wrote a book – 'Front Line and Fortitude' about her aunt's service as a WAS(B) 'Wasbies' in Burma in the Second World War. Captain Maria Pilbrow MBE, alongside many others served as Wasbies, providing support such as mobile canteens to the front-line allied troops fighting in Burma. They were normally just behind the front line and living in very basic jungle conditions similar to the fighting men. The Second Army serving in steamy jungles of Burma under General 'Bill' Slim was the largest British and Commonwealth army of the war, numbering over one million men. The Wasbies serving tea and cakes and other basic items to the troops with a cheery smile was a small taste of home, which many hadn't seen for years.*

The Wasbies 1942 - 1946
The Wasbies – who were they?

After my aunt Maria's death, I found a battered little diary, some notes and an MBE, together with its citation, tucked away, untouched for years in her desk drawer. I was intrigued, I knew nothing about The Women's Auxiliary Service (Burma) (known colloquially as the *Wasbies*).

I knew Maria had been a Wasbie in Burma but not much else, as she never spoke of her war years. After reading her notes and talking to people I felt I should research the Wasbies a bit more, only to find that very little was known about them.

This set me on a long journey to rectify this lack of recognition of a small group of feisty women who meant so much to the men of Field Marshal (then General) Sir William Slim's Fourteenth Army in Burma during the Second World War. Now known as *'The Forgotten Army'*, the 14th Army was the largest Commonwealth Army ever assembled, numbering over 1,000,000 men under arms.

The Women's Auxiliary Service (Burma) was formed shortly after war was declared against Japan in December 1942 after the bombing of Pearl Harbor. Initially they performed cypher duties for the British Army in Burma, but this was short-lived as they were repatriated to India, where they were disbanded, when Burma fell to the Japanese.

However, Ninian Taylor, an indomitable woman, who was to become the new Wasbie Commander, suggested to the military hierarchy that a canteen service could be established to support the troops of Burma Command. The suggestion was accepted with the Wasbies operating under the umbrella of the British Army.

The idea was to provide a taste of home in the form of tea and cakes (known amongst the troops as *'Char and Wads'*) along with basic items such shaving soap and razor blades, cigarettes and matches, tooth paste and bootlaces to mention just a few of the items which men who were operating away from base would need.

Once the idea was accepted recruitment began. A small group of brave women of all ages responded – they were from all walks of life: from military wives and daughters, colonial expats and missionaries, and they were willing to give their all to support the men in this campaign. Initially there were only 80 and they were spread over a vast region.

The climate was extreme and inhospitable. The girls toiled endlessly alongside the soldiers and airmen, week in week out, often not far from the front line where they were fighting against an unseen and ruthless enemy. Temperatures were either in excess of 110°F with humidity to match, or drenching monsoon rain and deep mud.

In addition to the extreme climatic conditions, the troops often suffered from jungle sores, malaria and dysentery along with other obscure tropical diseases. Along with this, everyone was plagued by flies, mosquitos, ants, snakes, leeches and other parasites. The girls took all this in their stride, always with a smile and time to chat, even if they had run out of supplies and had nothing else to offer the men. Their cheerful faces and presence were considered a huge morale boost to the men during a time of darkness and drudgery in a strange country far away from home.

Canteens

Static canteens were operated either from bombed out houses or large mess tents at base camps, transit camps, airstrips, railheads and seaports. The women also operated a mobile facility in the field, using specially converted Chevrolet vans, often travelling high into thick forested mountain terrain or deep in tropical jungle, often close to the front line, within the sound of gunfire.

It wasn't unusual for Wasbies to come across little hand-written signs attached to trees reading, *'Wasbies Please Call'* or *'Wasbies Welcome'*

In her diary Maria writes, *'One long night we attended a railhead, meeting arriving and departing troops, where we served thousands of men. Apparently over 800 gallons of tea was made, with water boiled in 40 gallon drums and served out of tin baths'*.

The Wasbies lived alongside the troops in *bashas* (local rattan dwellings), derelict houses or under canvas. They were not treated any differently to the men and nor did they expect to be.

In December 1944, Maria was promoted, to head up her own Canteen, No. 16, which was to be attached to the 36th Division under the Command of Major General Francis Festing (known to his men as *'Front Line Frankie'*). This meant she would remain with the Division for the duration of their offensive to reclaim Rangoon (Yangon).

The 36th Division was the only division to rely solely on airdrops for their supplies. An amusing anecdote in Maria's diary relating to their airdropped 1944 Christmas food provisions for the men reads as follows:

'During dinner we heard that when the pig was 'dropped' from the supply plane, its basket had broken and it had rushed off into the forest and had to be found and caught. One of the Christmas turkey baskets hadn't landed so well either, and one of the birds broke out, disappearing into the undergrowth with its parachute and broken basket trailing behind it....'

Being attached to a specific Divisional HQ, and therefore moving forward at the same pace as the men, the Wasbies were to experience the aftermath of a battle zone for the first time and Maria comments in her diary:

'It was very hot and dry, and for the first six miles we passed through countryside which had been shelled and bombed continuously and had been completely destroyed during the ferocious battle. The forest had been torn apart by the bombing, leaving the trees looking as though someone on a bulldozer had gone on a completely mad rampage. There were parachutes, with their loads still attached, suspended from some of the trees, and an atmosphere of complete devastation and destruction prevailed. The entire area was a total shambles. It was scorched, dusty and ugly and as we passed by, it seemed so abandoned and forlorn.

Along the sides of the desolate road there were a number of little crosses with tin hats hanging on them indicating the graves of men who had been killed, British, Indian and Gurkha. It was just so ghastly to see; a heartrending reminder of the recent savage battle.

The stench of death and acrid smell of burning still lingered; it was the first time we had encountered battle death so closely and it was a sobering and distressing sight. Taffy still insisted it was no place for women and he wouldn't budge on this. I don't suppose for one moment it was, but we were proud of our new role and wouldn't have it any other way, and the men really did make us feel so greatly valued.'

It was while Maria was with the 36th Division that she was Mentioned in Dispatches and both she and Gay Tucker were awarded an MBE.

The Women's Auxiliary Service (Burma) went on to assist with the repatriation of Far East Prisoners of War, including those who had been on the Death Railway. Some remained in Burma; others, including Maria went on to the Dutch East Indies to assist with repatriation of POWs including women and children. Others went on to Japan to do the same.

The Wasbies were finally disbanded in May 1946 - nine months after VJ Day.

Many poems were written to and by the Wasbies – here are just two:

A poem written by a member of the 10th Gloucesters
To the WAS(B)

Now this 'ere canteen a short way up the road,
Is run by the Wasbies *as most of us know.*
You are either served by a blonde or brunette,
Who have never been seen without a smile yet.
I think all the boys with me will agree,
That they always get a good mug of tea.
Only one drawback - not enough chairs,
But we can always sit upon the stairs.
So to the Wasbies who work till half nine,
The boys agree you are doing the job fine.
We wish you good luck and a very big cheer,
And hope you'll be with us this time next year.

A poem written by Wasbie Nancy (Bubbles) Clayton

TREES

I wonder if I'll ever see
A tree that's wholly notice free
A tree that may in summer wear
No mention of the Field Cashier
A tree with nothing to suggest
That Military Police may nest
A tree that doth not know too well
The M.D.S or P.O.L
A jungle where there are no grounds
For 'WAS(B) AREA: OUT OF BOUNDS'

And trunk ne'er carries legend plain
To bring one home to 'HQ Main'

Based on the book 'Front Line and Fortitude' from the diaries of
Captain Maria (J.E.) Pilbrow MBE, written by E.J. Lockhart-Mure.

****

Carole Sach's father William Pritchard served in Burma in the Second World War with the Royal Norfolk regiment. Carole tells of her research - piecing together details of his experiences and service in the harsh and frightening conditions of jungle warfare against the Japanese. Her father had a life-long hatred of all things Japanese.

<u>Fighting in Burma - William Pritchard</u>

My dad served in Burma with the Royal Norfolks. I always knew that he was in Burma because when I was growing up he used to go to the Burma reunions at the Royal Albert Hall in London; he used to go with Uncle Bert, Albert Nesling, who was dad's friend in Burma and my godfather. He lived in Bournemouth and was also in the Norfolks. When I got to about 7 or 8, I used to beg dad to take me with him, promising that I would be good sit on his lap and only ask for one orange squash; as Dad left I would be sobbing. Mum said he found it very upsetting so the Burma Reunion was given a new title in our house *'the big boys' party'* and I still call it that to this day. He stopped going in 1980 as he said it was full of old men and they were getting fewer and fewer as the years went by. I think Uncle Bert still went.

Dad never really spoke about his time there; he would tell me stories in dribs and drabs I could not ask him… I had to wait for him to tell me.

The first story I remember him telling me was about the fishes; I think they were in India and he said that railway lines were built on high embankments and that when it rained it was like a fast shower (I have actually experience this myself as we went to the Amazon Rain Forest in 2017 and it came down like power shower). He said that when it rained fishes came out of the ground (I wonder if he was talking about mudskippers) but of course being the British Army and not wishing to miss an opportunity the soldiers would catch them and cook and eat them. He said when the water subsided they went back into the ground.

A few years later he told me the chicken story. Dad and uncle Bert had somehow got hold of a chicken; there was much discussion while out on patrol on how they were going to cook it. So after the patrol had finished dad managed to get hold of a terracotta pot. They put the now dead chicken in the pot along with some vegetables that uncle Bert had got hold of and began boiling, and dad got hold of a large spoon and was stirring the stew; they had put the pot directly on the fire, again much talking of how much they were looking forward to eating it. After a few hours of cooking and dad stirring they decided that it was ready, as they lifted the pot off the fire the pot came apart. What had happened was as dad was stirring the pot it was getting hot and being terracotta dad had weakened the pot, so as they lifted off the fire it went everywhere. So I said to dad what did you do, his response was we ate off the jungle floor. He then went on to tell me about the ants and not to leave your boots outside your tent as in the morning the ants had eaten all the boots and nothing was left.

So now I am in my teens and the stories began to change, so this time he told me about the Japs hiding in trees and calling out to the British Soldiers *'Tommy Tommy, where are you Tommy, Tommy, Tommy over here'* he said it went on all night and I asked what happened if you replied he said *'bang you're dead'*. He said that some of our soldiers would go mad (we now know that this is psychological warfare, but at that time we did not know).

He then told me about him and Uncle Bert one night, they dug trenches at night to sleep in, and one night he said that the whole Jap tank corps drove right over the top of them. They did not know they were there. He said that they were too scared to even breathe, a very lucky escape.

He said to me once that you could smell the Japs before you saw them as they carried dried fish with them and that you could smell it. He also told me, that if captured, they would shoot the privates and just take officers prisoner (I am not sure how true this is, whether it was a rumour that went around the army out there, I have no idea).

He later told me about a patrol he was on, and in the middle of a field was an arm waving so they fanned out and went into the middle of the field where they found a dead soldier (not sure if it was British or Jap) and he had a wire attached to the arm making it wave, one of the group kicked the wire and got his foot blown off, so dad said when they saw dead soldiers they never touched them as they could have been booby trapped.

About 1979, and I was at work now, and someone had told me that day that when the troops came back from Burma they had to do an extra three months as some of them had caught VD out there and they could not send them home to their wives in that state. I came home one night and I remember sitting round the table eating dinner and made this statement. Dad went mad, he was furious and he said, yes that is correct because some of them could not keep it in their trousers and thanks to them he had to do an extra three months as well. He then went on to say that Burmese women were really beautiful, but once they got to about 30 they became like old hags, but he did say when younger were really lovely.

I know that the guys out there called Slim *'Uncle Bill'* well that was not my dad, he was always referred to as *'ole man Slim'* and that is how I refer to him as well.

Mum told me one night they were in bed and dad was looking at his feet and said *'these feet have marched half way round Burma.'* She said it was like the flood gates opening and he told her everything he saw and experienced. When he finished she went in the toilet and was very sick. I don't know what he told her, she would not say, but all she said was *'I really wanted him to stop, but felt it was better for him to try and get it out of his system and I felt I could not stop him.'* I told my aunt this (dad's half-sister) and she said that she had asked dad when he got home *'did you kill anyone?'* the only response she got was *'well I am here, aren't I?'* so in dad's speak that meant yes.

Dad being dad, he used to go into the American camps and when they found out that he had been in Burma for two years they were amazed as they only did six months out there and then they were shipped home. So dad was able to eat in the American camp where he said the food was far superior to the British rations; he actually told me he knew where the Americans had buried six tons of curry powder. He also used to go to their concerts and saw Bob Hope.

He told me Vera Lynn came to Burma and did a concert, …she was singing away and then all of a sudden she asked for the house lights to be put on and when they came up all she could see were officers. She then said *'I have not come to sing to you,'* pointing at them, she said *'Where are my boys?'* so they shouted out as they were in the gods, and dad said the rest of the concert she sang to the gods never looking down once.

He always said to me that they ate bully beef in Burma, I did not know what that was until one Sunday evening I was making a corned beef sandwich dad wandered in and I asked him if he wanted a corned beef sandwich. His response *'I bloody ate enough of that in Burma, I am not eating that again bloody bully beef, what do you want to eat that for?'* So that is when I found out what bully beef was.

Mum told me that before I was born in 1960, dad would occasionally get malaria attacks, but once I came along they completely stopped, she did not know why but they did. Whether it was because he had something to focus on she was not sure, but the malaria attacks ceased and I never knew my dad to have an attack.

There was nothing Japanese allowed in the house, except for when I was 21 (in 1981) I wanted a music centre and the one I wanted was made in Japan, so mum had to ask dad if it was ok and I heard dad's response and it was *'it's my war not hers'* so I got it the only Japanese thing in the house.

Dad then told me he was wounded on the way down to Mandalay. Unfortunately, I went completely mad and really lost the plot and after that he stopped talking about his time in Burma. Perhaps as I grew older he would have started again, but he died in 1983 just before my 23rd birthday.

It is unusual for someone to be at the precise place and the precise time when an historic event takes place. Catherine Leatham (née Jenkins) recounts the story of her father Corporal Allan Jenkins who was present and directly involved in the ceremony of surrender by the Japanese forces in Singapore in 1945. Not only was this of major significance in the war against Japan, but it was a poignant moment in the light of the humiliating defeat of the British forces 5 years earlier, when surrender under Percival took place without great resistance. Tens of thousands of British troops went into captivity and an horrific period in the camps, with many not surviving. Allan Jenkins was present when the Japanese surrendered – certainly an 'I was there' moment for this young serviceman.

Japanese Surrender of Singapore 1945
Corporal H. Allan Jenkins RAF Regiment 1940-1946

As is often the case with Burma veterans, my father spoke very little of his experience fighting against the Japanese in the Second World War. Since his death in 1981, when I was 16, I have found out only a little about his time in the Far East but have since resolved to research and find out as much as I can. I want to pass these on to my children and their children so that his stories, and the stories of countless others will not be lost and that this 'Forgotten Army' will be remembered for all time.

My father was born in Swansea, South Wales, in 1920 and served in the RAF Regiment (2965 Squadron) from May 1940 to March 1946. He enlisted as a ground gunner when he was 20 years old and upon leaving RAF, he was a Corporal (Gunner V). From his records I can see that he was overseas from 14th December 1944 to 16th March 1946. In this time, he was awarded:

1939-45 Star, Pacific Star, Burma Star, Defence Medal, War Medal 1939-45

The squadron was formed at Secunderabad (Light Anti-Aircraft) in August 1944, being deployed to Imphal, Meiktila, Toungoo, Rangoon, Penang, Butterworth, Singapore and finally Tanglin, where it disbanded in March 1946.

From a few press cuttings we have, we know that my father was granted the honour of hoisting the RAF ensign over the Seletar airfield when the Japanese surrendered it back to Allied command in 1946.

This extract is from an unknown newspaper, possibly South Wales Evening Post:

'How he hoisted the ensign over Seletar air base at Singapore on its being taken over after the Japanese surrender is related by a Swansea airman, who is shortly returning home. He is Corporal Hayden Allan Jenkins of 8, Penygraig Road who enlisted in the RAF in 1940 as a ground engineer.'

'There were 15 of us detailed to go to the base including a group captain and a flying officer of the RAF,' says Corporal Jenkins. *'We drove up to the gates of the airfield and the rest of us waited whilst the officers held a conference with the Japanese. When the officers came out the Group Captain ordered me to hoist the RAF colours on the station mast. The Regiment detachment of which I was*

in charge stood at the present arms and the Japanese officer in command, an Admiral, took the salute. The Japanese did not seem to mind our taking over possession,' he added *'and in fact were more interested in the British ranks than anything else.'*

And on Monday 10th Sept, 1945 of South Wales, Evening Post:

'Jap Admiral salutes Swansea man's signal

A Japanese vice-admiral stood to attention and saluted as the RAF ensign was hoisted by a Swansea man on Seletar airfield, Singapore Island, for the first time since 1942.

The ensign was raised by Allan Jenkins of Penygraig Road, Swansea while a detachment of an RAF Regiment presented arms and Group Captain Geoffrey Francis DFC of Dorchester took over the station from Vice-Admiral Kagure, says the Air Ministry.

The preliminary parley took place in the office of the British commanding officer, which had been used by the Japanese airfield commander. All the Japanese in the office were apparently unmoved by the surrender. They laughed and chatted among themselves and were interested in trivial details such as the uniforms and ranks of the British officers.'

A certificate of retention was given to my father saying that he was permitted to keep: *'One Samurai-Sword and two knives (of no intelligence value)'* and the certificate is signed by the Commanding Officer of 2965 Squadron RAF Regiment. He was also allowed to keep the flag, which we still have. The knives were identified as Naval Tantos, issued to Naval Officers and dating from 1900 - 1945. We gave the knives to the RAF Museum, Elvington but very sadly we have only recently been informed that they were stolen several years ago.

A letter from the Headmaster of Brynmill Boys' School, Swansea, A R Davies, dated 28th October 1946 shows that he gave the Samurai sword to the school.

'The boys of the school have been thrilled with the sword and the officer's belt - and when I told them the tale of how the sword had been handed over to a Brynmill Boy, they were extremely proud.'

We know little more, other than documentation stating that the first ship back into Singapore at 1400hrs on 5th Sept 1945 was MV *Derbyshire* - we believe my father was on this ship and the photo shows his arrival back into Singapore. My grandmother saw a newsreel in a cinema in Swansea of this ship's arrival and recognised my father, so wrote to the news company to request a photograph, which we still have.

He left for home in the UK due to return on 17th April 1946 on HMS *Winchester Castle*, arriving on 20th April 1946. Entitled to 72 days leave, his last effective day of service was 1st July 1946.

We have several letters of reference about my father, written at that time and one is particularly heartfelt, sent to my grandmother in December 1945 from a shop-worker whom my father had befriended during his time in

Singapore. I'm not sure what prompted him to write but he states:

'I can say Mr Jenkins is humble, polite, considerate and has the welfare of the civilian peoples at heart. He used to help the civilians if it is within his means and power whenever they came to him. He is a gentleman. I have met many a serviceman, but seldom have I come across one of Mr Jenkins' qualities. He has that pleasing personality that won him many friends.'

In his Service and Release book, his Squadron Leader has written:

'One of my most efficient NCOs. Smart, clean and very reliable. He will be an asset to any future employer'.

****

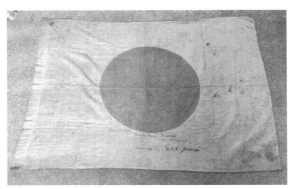

Allan Jenkins acquired this flag at the time of the Japanese
surrender in Singapore in September 1945.

Jenkins family collection

The Chungkai Theatre became *"famous throughout the
Prisoner of War Camps throughout Thailand"*.

Bainbridge family archive

The Wasbies at Work.
Lockhart-Mure family archive

The Sergeants Mess VE Day Celebration Day Dinner Menu.
Sachs family archive

Chapter 5 - Home Front

On 3rd September 1939, only minutes after Prime Minister Chamberlain confirmed to the nation that Britain was at war with Germany, the air raid sirens sounded and thousands scuttled to air raid shelters expecting bombs to rain down at any minute. As it was, this was a dummy run, a practice, a precaution for terrifying things to come. However, it was an important moment and it signified the day when life would change for every person in the country.

It brought home the reality of war, which over the following six years saw the *Blitz* across many cities, mass evacuation of hundreds of thousands of urban based children to safer locations, rationing, which did not end in full for 15 years, the Dig for Victory campaign, the formation of the Land Girls and Timber Corps, the enlistment of millions of men and women into the armed and auxiliary forces and war related industries based in Britain. The roles varied from the Local Defence Volunteers (renamed as the Home Guard), munitions workers, aircraft spotters or observers, drivers, nurses, firefighters and so many more. Brilliant mathematicians were recruited from the universities to go to Bletchley Park, while others such as cartographers were called up to draw maps for Bomber Command.

Day to day life changed visibly too.

The mandatory carrying of gas masks in anticipation of gas attacks, stadia turned into recruitment centres and afterwards to POW camps, iron railings torn down and appeals for saucepans to make planes, the '*black out*', parks and gardens turned into vegetable plots, Anderson and

Morrison shelters in millions of gardens and the underground stations used as protection against the bombing. Alongside these the rubble, and detritus following the bombing, beaches becoming out of bounds with miles of barbed wire and obstacles across the coastline, and the pill boxes scattered across the countryside in anticipation of invasion.

Britain adopted the principles of 'Total War' at a very early stage, having seen the threats from some years out and begun their preparations. Whilst not widely publicised for fear of 'upsetting' Hitler, much had been prepared and planned and was 'ready to go' on the home front well before the serious issues of the fighting started on huge scale in 1940. By contrast, in Germany, 'Total War' was never really adopted by the home population for over three more years. In Berlin and elsewhere life had gone on much as normal for the home population, except for the political control, and the removal of *'undesirable elements'*. The belief of 'Total Victory' led by the propaganda of Josef Goebbels provided a culture of complacency at home, so while the *Wehrmacht,* the U-boats and *Luftwaffe* were winning, few plans were being made should things change.

However, when the tide did turn the life and challenges faced by the home German population were remarkably similar to those faced by so many civilian populations across the globe in the 1940s. Survival, getting by, trying to protect your loved ones, feeding one's family, and wondering when or if ever you would see again your father, son or brother fighting in some distant land. The tales of resilience coupled with either good or bad fortune were the same for the populations of all nations. Emily Cameron from Wandsworth was widowed in October 1914 with four sons under 8 years old to bring up in an era of no welfare state, NHS or recourse to state benefits. Such was the struggle for many on the Home Front.

In the First World War, the recruitment of the local and Old Pals battalions from the same town, all serving together could see the menfolk of whole communities wiped out in a single action. In the Second World War, the civilian casualties were on a much greater scale and not just from bombing. Many examples exist, including an estimated one million civilians perishing from starvation in Leningrad during the siege, while during the *'Honger Winter'* of 1944 in Holland 20,000 people starved to death as fighting raged over their country in the latter stages of the war.

Similarly, these stories and experiences in their most basic form have been the same for civilians of all countries at war over many centuries. The fundamentals of finding food and shelter, trying to keep safe, worrying about your loved ones were the same when, generally speaking, it was the menfolk away fighting. No communication was available in the way we know it today in peacetime, with many months or years going by without knowing the fate of family members.

The contribution of the civilian population on all Home Fronts was huge, as were the trials, tribulations and hardships they had to endure. In the main these were met with fortitude, resilience, resourcefulness, good spirit and humour – whether British, German, Russian or whichever nationality. However, these experiences, most notably following the Second World War, lead to massive social change. Society did not want to be dictated to by the upper classes, women were not willing to relinquish the independence they had gained through war time work, and everyone believed that for the sacrifices they had made, they deserved, of right, good quality housing, good sanitation and a health system open to all. The General Election of mid-1945 resulting in a resounding defeat for Prime Minister Winston Churchill by Attlee's Labour Party reflected the new mood and the first changes to the social order.

****

David West describes his life as a youngster living in London during the Blitz in the Second World War. He tells of his fear as they heard the bombers fly over. Then came the move to Lincolnshire to get away from the bombs, to the new world of countryside and undisturbed nights. The family relocated to a village called Spilsby, living just outside an RAF airfield. This changed David's life forever as it started his love affair with the Lancaster bomber.

Outbreak of War - Living in London

Living in London, my early impressionable years were dominated by the outbreak of the Second World War. Sandbags around our school, gas mask practice, an Anderson shelter installed in our garden, windows covered by tape, barrage balloons floating in the sky and the nightly blackout are among my earliest memories. Regular warnings about the growing threat of bombing and my father's sudden departure to join the army added to a general sense of foreboding.

Fear really took hold as the local air raid siren started wailing on a regular basis. Initially daylight raids dominated, but soon it was relentless, night after night, activity that became so wearing. The sinister sound of the siren at night will never leave me, even today when I hear a wartime recording my scalp tingles with a subconscious fear.

It was usually around midnight when the local siren would start and within minutes my mother would appear at our bedroom door. An Ever-Ready cycle lamp provided just enough light for us to put on dressing gowns before making our way to the Anderson shelter at the bottom of our garden. In the chill night air two elderly ladies would usually appear out of the darkness from next door to join us.

Lighting candles in the shelter provided some welcome comfort as my sister and I would climb onto our wire beds as the resident spiders dashed for cover. The shelter always seemed damp and cold with a strong smell of sand and fresh concrete. At least we had a feeling of being out of harm's way. Looking out over the top of the shelter door our house looked so dark and forbidding as though it might at any moment be destroyed by a bomb.

All too soon the sinister drone of the German bombers could be heard getting ominously louder. Searchlights started roaming the night sky followed by the boom of anti-aircraft guns. Even as young children we knew that hearing the approach of the bombers was the dangerous time. I remember an overriding feeling of fear wondering if bombs were going to land near us. Even my mother, who would normally be so calm, seemed to be agitated during such moments but as always tried her best to calm us. When the bomber's drone started to diminish we knew if we heard the whistle of bombs they would impact somewhere beyond us.

Sometime after the war I learned that most German bombers had two engines that ran in and out of balance with each other. This characteristic, technically known as heterodyning, created a droning sound that at the time seemed so sinister. Although all this took place so many years ago, I have never been able to determine if the *Luftwaffe* deliberately created the sinister droning sound - à la *Stuka*! Recently somebody explained that British aircraft sound detectors could not determine where the bombers were if the sound was not consistent, maybe this is the explanation. If I ever hear a wartime recording of German bombers with their distinctive sound, I immediately sense the fear endured during the raids.

Life was beginning to be dominated by growing evidence of local bomb damage and there were the inevitable crop of gruesome stories going around, although some were of course rather exaggerated. There was one in particular I will never forget. A bomb had exploded at a fair distance away from a trolley bus but two passengers sitting upstairs at the front were both dead, although they were still sitting there without any sign of injury. Somebody said it was a classic case of being killed by a shock-wave which I now understand but at the time I was quite frightened.

Each night the bombing was became harder to bear until one day my mother said, *'we would soon be leaving home to live in a safer place far away from London'.* My sister and I eventually learned that we were going to live with aunties in Lincolnshire. Although we had absolutely no idea what to expect, Lincolnshire meant nothing to us, we were promised a more peaceful way of life away from the dangers of war. Little did we know at the time that although initially it would be so, the war was destined to dominate our lives once again.

Moving to Lincolnshire

It was a strange feeling to be leaving our London house without any real idea what to expect, wondering if we would ever return. Despite this, I felt a sense of adventure and excitement. The feeling increased as I helped my mother pack our cases and we caught a big red London petrol bus destined for Kings Cross railway station. I climbed to the top deck to see as much as possible of London's bomb damage and with so much destruction on view I could not help morbid thoughts wondering how many people had been killed and how they had died.

Arriving at Kings Cross station was a revelation, I felt overwhelmed by a sense of drama and anticipation. The impressive station building seemed to provide a stage for so many people, some in service uniform, arriving and leaving as many made their emotional goodbyes. This all took place with the drama of express trains arriving and leaving via smoke filled tunnels. Grimy but magnificent LNER steam engines coupled to express carriages were so impressive, I quickly developed an ambition to be an engine driver. So much to see then the excitement of getting on the train as my mother said *'we are about to leave'.*

284

Once on the train I found a place standing at a side corridor window so I could see as much as possible. Soon the train left the smoky tunnels and gathered speed passing suburban stations and an endless number of sidings filled with engines, carriages, and goods wagons. Soon the excitement grew as the sight of London's war weary suburbs was replaced by green fields and hedgerows that somehow seemed to promise a brighter future. Eventually the train left the main line and headed towards Lincolnshire. Many years later I learned that this was the East Lincolnshire main line heading from Peterborough towards Grimsby via Spalding, Boston, and our ultimate destination Firsby near Spilsby and Skegness.

Gradually the scenery changed as the train made its way through miles of flat farming land that is Lincolnshire. Spalding and Boston behind us, my mother said, *'the next time the train stops we will be at a place called Firsby where we will be getting out'*. Stepping off the train was like entering a new world. This was such a strange experience for as soon as we stood on the platform there was a sense of a new peaceful existence with no signs of the war. Compared to the London we had just left the air seemed so fresh and invigorating. Met by an aunt, her hair brushed back into a bun, there was a short walk before we arrived at her house. The house that would be our home for the rest of the war.

What a change, plenty of fresh food from my aunt's garden plus a good supply from local farmers combined with undisturbed nights free from wailing air raid sirens. On the other hand, the outside Elsan toilet was grim, always full and there was no bathroom! A tin bath in the kitchen was the only means for children in the house to have any sort of washdown. Drinking water had to be obtained by regularly dropping a bucket on a cord down a well outside the back door, not an easy task and many pairs of glasses were lost during the process.

We gradually came to terms with living with three aunts and the joys of country living. The eldest aunt ran the one and only village shop in the front room of our house. My sister and I would longingly look at the jars of sweets in the shop, but our aunt never succumbed, it was wartime. I believe we had the only telephone in the village based on how many people would visit to make a call. Interestingly my aunts had a superb large radiogram, being the main wartime news source and provided many opportunities to become familiar with the smooth voices of Bing Crosby and Frank Sinatra.

****

Here I am a London boy enjoying summer in Lincolnshire. Winters were so different, and I still had to wear short trousers during a mile walk to school.

David West collection

Gerhard 'Gary' Biss escaped Nazi occupied Vienna as a youngster on the Kindertransport six months before the outbreak of war, leaving his family behind. He wrote his memoirs 'Who Do You Think You Are?' which described his early life, his escape to England and his colourful career. The Kindertransport rescued some 10,000 young unaccompanied mainly Jewish children from Nazi Germany, Austria, Czechoslovakia and Poland. Many relocated to the UK and to some other western European countries. A scheme backed by the British Government, these children were transported by train and on arrival in Britain were housed in foster homes, hostels, schools and farms. Often they were the only members of their families who survived the Holocaust. Extracts provided by kind permission of Gerhard 'Gary' Biss.

Brief History - 'Ready for the invasion'

Briefly, I am one of about 10,000 *Kindertransport* people who came to this country just before the last war. I was born in Vienna during the first Depression (and it looks like I might leave this world during the present Depression – who knows?)

I arrived here in March 1939, having been thrown out of my school because I was Jewish and had to put up with some abuse on a daily basis as a result. I wasn't really Jewish, as the Jewish blood was on my father's side and the law states you are not Jewish unless your mother is. However, Hitler didn't care about that. You were Jewish if you had any Jewish blood in you going back in my case to my grandfather, who hanged himself just before the *Gestapo* arrived. My father meanwhile dashed off to Switzerland (pointing two fingers at the *Gestapo*) and remained there for the rest of his life.

I tried to have a word with Herr Hitler for as you probably know he was Austrian and at one time lived not far from me. I finally briefly caught up with him and waved to him when he came through Vienna in 1938 when he invaded Austria. Well, it was hardly an invasion as everybody was very pleased to see him. I didn't have my gun with me at the time (well I was only six years old).

I was adopted by a British family and then evacuated (as were all other children at the time) after the war started. But they had a lot of trouble with me, so my adopted mother brought me back to live near Croydon Airport which was later bombed, as it was a sort of Heathrow at the time.

I started my own gang of kids ready for the Germans. We had a transport section (a wheel barrow) a First Aid Section – a young girl who had taken a Red Cross First Aid Course, and an ammunition supply of about 100 electric light bulbs ready to throw at the Nazi tanks. We were called the Avenue Guards. I was the top-ranking officer and gave instructions when we prepared to throw our electric light bulbs at the Germans.

We had all the usual air raids at the time of course, but it was not until late in 1944 when we were finally completely burnt out when a canister of phosphorous bombs hit our roof and completely destroyed the house. Luckily, we all got out. In fact, an individual bomb went right through my bed and landed in our hall. Luckily, I had just got downstairs.

Oh, and I must just mention our cat.

It was usually my duty to let him in at night so he could sleep in our kitchen in the warmth. It was a cold March 24th 1944, when I put out our light (remember Dad's Army – *'Put That Light Out'*) and opened the kitchen door to let him in as usual. But he just looked at me with those glistening eyes in the dark.

So, I asked him again. *'Are you coming in, or not, because I'm not going to stand here in the cold much longer?'* Again he just looked at me, his eyes glistening in the dark and then he just turned and trotted away to the end of our garden where he turned again and looked at me as if to say you must be mad staying in that house because it's going to be blown to pieces tonight. Who says animals have no sixth sense? We went into a requisitioned house and as this was damaged by a *'Doodlebug'* we were invited to live with some friends in East Croydon because they had a cellar which we could all sleep in.

My adopted father was in Dad's Army (the Home Guard to the uninitiated) and I was told not to touch his rifle. One day he exploded an imitation bomb in the garden which resulted in damage to my ear.

Careerwise, I finished up with a Ship Owning Company in the City of London, but then of course (having become British) I was obliged to do my 2 years National Service in the Royal Air Force. Did the usual training at Padgate and finished up in Spitalgate, near Grantham, at the

Headquarters of Technical Training Command and the home of a future female Prime Minister. As I was proficient in shorthand (having attended Clark's College) I was appointed to assist a Squadron Leader who dealt with the paper work for Courts Martial. I even attended a couple.

I returned to the City of London and after some time joined the P & O Lines on board one of their big tourist ships and naturally visited many ports and places around the world. Later I found employment in no less a place than Saudi Arabia of all places. All I knew about that country was that they had plenty of camels and plenty of oil.

I worked there for the next 20 years mostly in Riyadh the capital, but also on an Air Base in the north of the country in Tabuk.

I later returned to Riyadh just in time for the first Gulf War with rockets flying in both directions, but managed to get through it all unharmed. Of course, our own forces were there as were the Americans.

It's funny the things you remember. But I particularly remember the day when an American female soldier walked into a local cafe in Riyadh and asked for a coffee and something to eat. She obviously was not aware of local customs in such matters and the owner advised her that she could not be served because she was female and that this was a male only section.

She replied in her broad Texan accent: *'Look here Mate, I've b......y well come here to defend your country and if you can't b......y well give me a cup of coffee I'll b.......y well shoot your b......y head off'.* At which point she drew her pistol from its holster and pointed it at the cafe's owner.

'OK! OK! Friend', came the quick reply, *'.............. do not worry, I will serve you; Inshalla'* (which in Arabic means 'God willing').

She sat down with two other female soldiers amid the many local men who pretended not to notice what had taken place and continued to sup their drinks. *'Cheers Mate,'* she said on the way out. *'I'm just off to kill a few Iraqis for you'.*

****

Karen Wiles, a local historian specialising in the Home Front in the Second World War, reflects on the 'miracle of Dunkirk' 80 years on. She tells of the poor condition of many of the troops, both mental and physical, and of the support they received on arrival back in England.

80th anniversary of Dunkirk

Everyone knows about the evacuation of Dunkirk and the brave fleet of little ships who saved the 338,000 men from the beaches and everyone should remember it. The arrival of the men back to Britain is usually the end of the story, but here's an aspect of that important part of our history that very few know about or remember.

As Operation Dynamo was planned the women of the Women's Voluntary Service were called on to what turned out to be their ultimate test of endurance and selfless devotion to duty.

While the little ships sailed away from the docks the women of the WVS set up canteens at all the main ports along the coast and major rail junctions across the country. This was not a simple story of serving a few cups of tea, this was an operation on a grand scale. It was not just the WVS members local to the ports, members were transported from far and wide to help. Stocks of food were depleted at the ports as thousands of refugees had already been fed there so WVS centre organisers arranged for the transport of tea, coffee and food to be sent to the docks.

When the first of the little ships returned the exhausted and traumatised men were taken to cinemas, churches and halls of every type. The women took over and often as the men fell exhausted they would remove their equipment, shoes and socks, wash their feet, wash and mend their uniforms while they slept. They provided them with food, tea and coffee, cigarettes and postcards to write to their loved ones. One lady in Kent was commended for arranging for 10,000 postcards to be sent on behalf of the returning men. After a brief but necessary rest the men would be placed on the trains which would transport them all across the country to their homes or barracks. As soon as one batch had left another arrived, it was relentless and a short way across the Channel they could hear the bombs falling on the thousands left behind and see plumes of smoke from the French coast.

Just one team of six or seven women were allowed into the actual docks to help the crews of the little ships and the men too badly injured to be transported right away. For days they worked bringing hot drinks, food and giving comfort to the injured. Headquarters pleaded with the powers that be to allow extra helpers to go into the docks but because of security and danger their requests were denied. Finally, it was considered too dangerous to continue as the raids moved closer to the mainland and they were moved back.

It was not just the rescued men who were helped, the WVS opened a hostel for relatives of the seriously injured men. A property was lent and all equipment donated and run by the volunteers of the WVS.

As it was not just the British men who had been evacuated, but with French and Belgians there was a need for translators and again the WVS stepped up with teams of French speakers to help.

I mentioned that the ladies of the WVS had set up canteens at major rail junctions, well this was to serve the numerous trains transporting the troops to their homes or barracks. Here tea and sandwiches were passed to the men in the trains as they stopped briefly at the junctions. This did not go unnoticed, Major-General Montgomery commended the ladies of the WVS at Frome for feeding 15,000 men every 24 hours for a week.

Assistance was also given to Montgomery when his 3rd Division arriving back from Dunkirk was scattered over several towns and villages with no transport for the staff to keep in touch. Within an hour, 15 cars and drivers had been set up with a rota in place to transport the staff wherever they needed to go for a fortnight until their own transport was in place.

So you see the story did not end with the arrival of our troops back on British soil, so when you next see a multi-million pound blockbuster all about Dunkirk. Please give a thought to the women who exhaustively and selflessly worked in the background who will not be forgotten.

****

Bob Payne, as a young boy living in Bury St Edmunds in Suffolk, tells of being 'shot-up' by a German plane one night.

Lone Plane Attack 1942/43

I lived with my grandmother, my mother and a sister at 51 St Andrews Street in Bury St Edmunds in a flat above a butcher's shop. My father was in the RAF in North Africa at the time.

One night our sleep was disturbed by the siren and the drone of a German plane circling round, we knew it was German as the engine noise was out of sync. We used to go into the cellar when the siren sounded, but we had heard the siren so many times we did not go into the cellar with the haunches of meat as it was cold down there and we assumed the plane was looking for the USAF base at Rougham just outside Bury where they had B-17 Flying Fortresses.

Suddenly, the engine note increased and was getting nearer. Then there was a terrific noise as the plane opened up with cannons and machine guns. I was terrified and froze, I could not move a muscle. Fortunately, it missed our house, but two doors away, where an old man lived and who had been warned by the Air Raid Wardens not to show a light, his house was shot-up. The ARPs had to knock his door in and found the man still in bed shaking. He was alright but frightened so much he had wet the bed. His windows were broken at the back of the house and his greenhouse did not have a pane of glass left in it unbroken.

Next morning, we inspected the damage and the cannon and machine bullet holes in a public toilet the other side of the road. The only casualty was the Playhouse Cinema manager coming out of the cinema with the day's takings at the wrong time and getting a bullet in the leg according to the local paper.

****

Betty Jackson recalls living as a teenager through the bombing by the Luftwaffe of her village in Lancashire and how the family narrowly escaped a direct hit.

A Lancashire Girl's Wartime memories

I was born in the village of Adlington, near Chorley, and we had an Andersen air raid shelter into which my mother would take me and younger brother Peter when the air raid sirens sounded. The shelter was situated in the bottom of our garden and was partly underground, and I remember we had a couple of steps to go down to get into it.

As for my father, all men had to do some sort of home guard duty or be a warden for certain areas. He was connected with the police and worked with a regular police officer and he had to do two nights duty a week.

Adlington sits below Rivington Pike, the top of which has a sort of castle that as a youngster, even before the war, I had

296

found rather dark and a bit frightening, and weirdly at school I remember being told by my classmates that this was some sort of beacon which was lit by spies to inform the enemy.

Other rumours abounded, the army had taken over or were the Americans there? There was a barrage balloon which we could see, so could there be anti-aircraft guns? The fact that there was no admittance made it even more sinister and we as young ones used to let our imaginations run riot.

What we did not know at the time was that we were on the flight path for *Luftwaffe* bombers as they returned from dropping their bombs on Liverpool and then flew back to their bases across the North Sea.

It was on the 27th November 1941 and the '*all clear*' had not yet gone but it had been quiet for quite some time although we had heard the droning of German bombers, the Dorniers and Junkers, as they made a rather distinctive noise. However, I believe it was about 1am and mother decided we had had enough, so we went back into the house and were sitting at the kitchen table having a warm drink. The next thing I remember was being on the floor covered in dust and when it settled, we could see that the roof had fallen in.

As my dad was on duty that night at the other end of the village, he was shocked to find us in the Ambulance Hall in Railway Road, being tended to by St John's Ambulance personnel. I remember being given tea and biscuits and my mother washing my face.

We later found out how lucky we had been in that the Germans had dropped two parachute mines which fell either side of the street. Fortunately for us one failed to go off while the other exploded in a field nearby. Had they both exploded then that would have been it for us.

In the aftermath, when we were eventually allowed back to see the damage to our house, my little brother Peter, who was only seven years old, refused to go as he was still in a state of shock.

****

Having moved away from London to Lincolnshire to avoid the Blitz, David West describes his new life based on the fringes of RAF Spilsby and the noise and excitement of seeing his first Lancaster bombers and how he 'befriended' F - Freddie He also tells of his remarkable aunt Thurza who set up a canteen on the boundaries of the airfield to supply refreshment and snacks to the returning airmen.

RAF Spilsby and My First Lancaster

Enjoying our peaceful country life, we suddenly became aware that everything was about to change as enormous Euclid trucks and tractors started tearing up the local countryside, removing hedges, trees and anything that seemed to get in their way. It soon became known that an aerodrome was to be built as local roads were dominated by lorries carrying great loads of ballast and building material. During summer holidays my mother and aunt arranged cab rides for me in Ford and Bedford gravel tipper trucks, no health and safety issues in those days. The trucks were always overloaded as they laboured along the country roads and I soon became a Bedford fan as from my perspective they had superior sounding engines.

Eventually the contractors departed leaving three great runways surrounded by a perimeter track with numerous dispersal points, three enormous hangers, a control tower, and numerous outbuildings. Spilsby aerodrome, as it was to be known, had arrived. Aunts and my mother were horrified to realise that our house was rather near to the end of the shortest runway, so much so we had a red warning light on a pole placed at the bottom of our garden. Some aircraft dispersal points were also quite near so there was a general feeling of anticipation spreading throughout the village. Soon a wind socket appeared, and everybody felt the aerodrome was about to be occupied.

I will never forget when the big day arrived. Cycling along a local lane I heard a terrific noise that got louder and louder by the moment. My first instinct was to get away but there was no time. Suddenly an enormous aircraft appeared over the hedgerows, wheels, and flaps down, four great engines roaring, gun turrets catching the sunlight and a huge bomb bay dominating its black underbelly. Moments later it touched down on a Spilsby runway. What a dramatic sight, then there was another and another and another until, as I was to learn later, 207 Squadron's Lancasters had arrived. We noticed that the Lancaster parked at the nearest dispersal to our house had large red identification letters EM-F on its side. It soon became general knowledge that this was the aircraft, F for Freddie, in which Wynford

Vaughan-Thomas made his famous broadcast over Berlin. EM were the code letters for 207 Squadron.

Start of Operations and F-Freddie

Our lives changed dramatically as within days 207's Lancasters were taking off night after night as Bomber Command's operations against Germany intensified. As a new friend and I became aware a raid was on we would dash to our local EM-F for Freddie's dispersal, usually in time to see the crew arrive. As they climbed into F-Freddie, the atmosphere heightened with the sound of engines bursting into life. Aircraft from inland could be heard climbing into the evening sky and the drama of 207's Lancaster starting to take off added to the excitement. Once F-Freddie had run up each of its four engines and the air gunners were in their turrets, it was time for our Lancaster to go. Chocks away, a burst of power and it would join the final group of Lancasters on the perimeter track for take-off.

There was often a strange feeling after the planes had left, the peaceful countryside of old seemed to return. For a moment at least, birds started singing again and the evening train from Skegness could be heard chugging its way round the curve into Firsby station adding to a sense of country life returning. Then a fish train from Grimsby would hurtle through Firsby station on the way to London.

It wasn't long before the operational dangers faced by 207's young aircrews became very apparent as so many were failing to make it back to Spilsby. My aunt's house with its small shop and telephone was situated between the drome and Firsby's mainline railway station. We began to have increased contact with the '*Boys in Blue*', my aunt Thurza's term for the RAF personal. I was particularly fascinated by the aircrew, identified by wings on their jackets, but it was difficult to comprehend that all too soon so many would no longer be round. The dreaded comment '*Oh they've gone for a Burton*' (a phrase used when aircrew failed to return) became so familiar.

My energetic Aunt Thurza was profoundly affected by 207's losses and was determined to provide some home comforts for her '*Boys in Blue*'. Despite having lost her husband in the First World War, worrying about her son serving on HMS *Repulse* and daughter working in London she was determined to do something to make life more acceptable for the airmen. She organised a large hut for use as a canteen, obtained tables and chairs plus a supply of bacon and eggs from local sources. Amazingly my aunt would regularly cycle some 4 miles to the Spilsby market obtaining such items as a bread slicer, tea urn, crockery, cutlery. She had her canteen up and running in no time at all.

We heard F -Freddie had been attacked over Berlin so I would dash to
the dispersal to see the damage.
David West collection

This painting perfectly captures a typical early morning view from my
bedroom window as returning Lancasters approached our short runway.
David West collection

Valerie Penfold tells the story of Fred, her father, living in North Woolwich in the docklands area of East London during the war. The family had a baker's shop and during the Blitz, she and others were moved to Penzance in Cornwall.

Fred's War

The only thing young Freddie wanted was a quiet life, as he had a nice home, a wife and little daughter. He also enjoyed his work in a laboratory of a large gas company. All was well. In 1932, this was about to change. His aunt Polly ran a flourishing bakery nearby, employing three bakers, a roundsman, a housekeeper and a lady serving in the shop. Polly wanted to retire and the elders of the family thought young Freddie could take it on and possibly widen its scope. So the little family upped sticks and moved into the premises behind the shop. All went well for a few years as Freddie learnt the bakery business and dealt with the business side of the bakery.

When war came in 1939, the Government took over. Two of the bakers went to war leaving Fred, his wife Vi, one baker and a roundsman with a heart condition! Also came rationing, meaning the shop had to sell rationed goods: butter which came in large blocks and sides of bacon, which came in a side of bacon to be boned and sliced, then wrapped in waxed paper to weights suitable for rationed amounts. Cheese came in a large drum shape covered in a wax cloth skin, that had to be cut with wire cutters (which was no mean task!) then sliced and wrapped to rationed sizes. People who registered with the shop had a weekly order covering their needs which was delivered at the end of the week. This was a great change from the bakehouse being the centre of activity. The horse and cart went and the stables were empty.

This is when Fred's bright ideas started!

Every back garden was being filled with an air raid shelter to be covered with sandbags. Our hero decided to have his in the stables and rather than sand, his would be covered with sacks of flour, which might have stood the test of a bomb, but I doubt it. However, the opportunity never arose because when the *Blitz* was at its worst, London ran out of food and one of the largest well-known stores in London sent a van to this tiny part of the East End and bought every sack of flour - just how they knew it was there, I have no idea. I am also sure it was sold at the price Fred bought it.

The war was at a terrifying time, invasion was on the cards, the factories were bombed out of action, so the workers joined their families and set off to be with their evacuated children. North Woolwich became a ghost town, nobody needed the shop.

Fred bought his mother and his wife a fur coat and a gold watch with their names and identity number engraved on the back.

Then his big adventure started putting two deck chairs in the back of his van, loading it with clothes and food, boarding up the premises, and setting off for Penzance 300 miles away. They set off - him, his wife and his parents in the deck chairs. This must have been some journey, of course there were no road signs at all and Fred's sense of direction was not great. Comfort stops had to be made somewhere in the countryside of southern England, and in one of these the cat escaped and took to the hills. How long this journey took I have no idea, but arrive they did, as did Vi's sister and her husband. Nor do I know how many weeks they all stayed in this three bedroom house. The owners, Beatrice and husband, having one bedroom and the two sets of grandparents, the other two. Everyone else slept on the floors downstairs. One person was very, very happy, Fred's little daughter, now eight years old, had all the people she loved under one roof.

Of course, once the time of acute danger passed, they all returned to their normal life. Poor Fred had one more roll of the dice to create havoc. He was issued with a real fire extinguisher the size of a small tractor. There were instructions, of course, and it sat in the yard beside the empty stables. One sunny morning it had to be tried out of course, and following instructions it leapt into action - a vast jet of water rose over the stables, a sight to be behold! Unfortunately, Mrs Jackson, whose house in the next street was exactly behind the stables and whose garden was just in the line of fire from the hose had put her highly treasured eiderdown on the line to air. She also kept chickens who with the power of the water, panicked and escaped making hay on her eiderdown which had naturally blown down. She was not pleased and said so in volumes of rage. The culprit tried to keep a straight face and pointed out it was part of the war effort; she was not convinced!!

Life dragged on only cheered up by new products appearing for sale. Children saw a banana or an orange for the first time, but life was pretty dreary in the shop. Later the building was demolished to make high rise flats which overlook the new Docklands airport. Fred and Vi moved to a nicer area but ill health took over and poor Fred was on his own, still able to create chaos and mayhem to the laughter and stress to his daughter and grandchildren. He died at 89. I hope he knew how much his antics were cherished and how much love went his way.

****

 *Violet 'Vi' Molinari describes her life as a teenager living in East London during the Blitz. Across Britain, over 60,000 people were killed by the bombing and the V1 and V2 rockets, with many thousands more being injured or made homeless. Vi describes how she left school and started working in central London during this period and how she met the man who was to become her husband.*

Wartime Memories - a Teenager in London

The Second World War commenced in 1939 when I was 13 years old. I was living with my parents and sister in a terraced house in St. Bartholomew's Road, East Ham, and we soon had to dig up the end of the garden to make room for an Anderson air raid shelter, not imagining that within a year we would be sleeping in it every night. Our elderly neighbours, who we always called Mr and Mrs Wickens, asked to join us so my father and Mr Wickens had the top bunks whilst my mother, my sister Ruby, Mrs Wickens and I slept like sardines underneath. (We never did call them by their first names!). Visits to the toilet at the other end of the garden had to be fitted in between air raids!

One Saturday afternoon the sirens went and German bombers were soon overhead dropping bombs mainly aiming for the nearby Woolwich Docks. Our local Woolworths opposite the station took a direct hit, as did the Picture Palace opposite. A great many lives were lost that afternoon. In the evening the raging fires at the docks could be seen from our garden. It was terrifying lying down in the shelter with bombs dropping all around.

My father was a trolley bus driver by day and spent most of his nights on the roof of Marks & Spencer in the High Street putting out incendiary bombs.

All schools were closed and my mother asked the headmaster if I could be released from the School List and go to work. This was agreed and I was taken on as a junior by a company called Radiation in Queen Victoria Street, London, near the Mansion House. Air raids were occurring continually.

My sister who was 15 worked in London too so on my first morning we waited outside the Town Hall for a bus. We soon found out there were no buses as the streets of London were covered in hose pipes still putting out fires from the night raids. Eventually an open-backed lorry stopped and asked us if we wanted a lift. We both climbed on, had to stand all the way, and had a very hair-raising ride into town! My husband ever after when asked how we met said '*she fell off the back of a lorry*'! At least we saved our fourpenny bus fare!

At 14, I joined the Women's Junior Air Corps, which used to meet in our school on Saturdays and Sundays and was a preparation for if we later decided to join the WAAF. We held a dance at the Town Hall and I was asked to dance with a handsome boy who was smoking a pipe! He walked me home but I had to leave him at the corner as I could see my father standing at the gate! However, my friendship grew with Eric from then on. I eventually became a Sergeant in the WJAC and we put on *The Mikado* at the Town Hall resulting in me becoming a 'G & S' fan for ever more.

My first experience of office work was sitting pushing and pulling plugs out of an old-fashioned telephone switchboard. At three o'clock I was allowed to leave to enable me to get home and down into the shelter before the raids started again. One day I couldn't get to my office as a bomb had dropped outside the Mansion House and a double-decker bus was in the crater.

Eric was a messenger for the ARP and whenever he cycled past the road nearest our shelter when a raid was on he would whistle *'Blues in the Night'* to let us know he was okay.

After a few months the Radiation building took a direct hit and they opened a new office in Stratford Place, off Oxford Street, by which time I had become a shorthand typist, having taken a course on weekend afternoons.

I was then taken on as a secretary by the National Federation of Property Owners in Cannon Row, Westminster (next door to the old Scotland Yard). One of the bonuses of working there was being right in the front line to see all the royal processions in Whitehall and State visits such as President Tito. Another was being asked to type constituency correspondence for two Members of Parliament - John Hay, MP for Wheaton Aston and Sir Eric Errington, MP for Anglesey, which entailed many trips to collect and deliver their mail in the House of Commons.

By this time *Doodlebugs* had taken the place of bombs. You could hear them coming and when the noise stopped you knew they were dropping near or on you. One day a friend and I were sitting opposite one of our bosses in the ABC restaurant opposite Big Ben when we heard the engine stop. We all dived to get under the table and my boss and I hit heads which nearly knocked us out.

A couple of days later I had a phone call at work to say my home had been hit. A land mine had dropped demolishing two whole streets nearby. I rushed home to find that my mother, who had been going downstairs, had been found by a fireman standing at the front gate with glass sticking out of her head. She had been blown downstairs and right through the front door. The fireman took her to East Ham hospital only to find her sister also injured from her home in Forest Gate. This necessitated my mother, father and I having to move into a small house with my father's very elderly mother until our home had been rebuilt. Many years after my mother would find tiny fragments of glass coming out of her head. Our clothes having been destroyed, we were allowed a voucher in place of coupons for basic replacements, and I can still feel the horror of having only two jumpers to wear alternately for several months.

Food was very mundane – no sugar, sweets, fresh fruit etc. When my cousin came to tea on Friday evenings my mother made a special '*meat pie*'– a pastry base spread with damp Oxo then a layer of mashed potato!

VE Day was celebrated by huge crowds, bands, etc. round East Ham Town Hall. Eric cycled all the way from his army base in Wrotham, where he was in training as a potential officer, to be with us for the night. He was later sent to Liverpool to embark on a Canadian Pacific liner which had previously been on the transatlantic route. This ship took him to India where he served for three years in various places: Bombay, Calcutta, Ramgarh, Ranchi, Sialkot, Punjab - finally reaching the rank of Captain.

One letter from India asked his father to take me to the local jewellers to buy an engagement ring. I was delighted but quite embarrassed at being accompanied by a very elderly man but I ended up with a lovely diamond solitaire ring and left the jeweller guessing!

On return to England Eric was stationed in Norwich from where he was demobbed. Whilst he was in India I wrote to him every day!

My sister who had joined the Army at 18 had experience of serving in Belgium on the ack-ack guns and then in Germany. She was luckily unscathed and I envied all her experiences.

Looking back I think as a family we were extremely lucky - there were some awful and frightening times but also some very happy and funny ones.

Eric became my husband on 2nd June 1951 but sadly died in February 2018 after 66 years of very happy marriage.

 *Historian Steve Richards describes one of many instances when bomb disposal experts were called upon to defuse bombs and mines of all different sorts across Britain during the Second World War. Sub Lieutenant Hugh Syme was called out in December 1940 to go to Birmingham for his first ever job since joining the team. Bomb disposal experts came from all three services and it was extremely dangerous and lonely work, not least as, as the war went on, the Germans built in more and more complicated anti-handling devices to prevent easy disarmament. Syme went on to become one of the most highly decorated bomb disposal experts.*

Just doing his job - Bomb Disposal

It was 2:55am when the phone rang in the lodging room on Half Moon Street, London W1. Outside it was bitterly cold; the frost was giving a crisp and deepening coating to the slush of dirty snow in the street. It was barely any warmer in the room where the man reached out his arm from under the bed covers to pick up the handset. He propped himself on one elbow and grunted an acknowledgement into the mouthpiece.

A voice at the other end said, *'Birmingham's taking a hammering and Jerry has dropped parachute mines all over the place, a dozen of which haven't gone off... yet. Get your bag of tools, a car has been organised for you.'*

So started the day of 12th December 1940, for Sub-Lieutenant Hugh Syme of the Royal Naval Volunteer Reserve. Other naval officers were receiving similar calls which resulted in a rendezvous of eight officers and fourteen men, spread across seven cars, congregating at the White Hart in St Albans. The plan was to breakfast there and, once everyone had arrived and eaten, move in convoy northwards to Birmingham.

It is doubtful that Syme's churning stomach would have allowed him to eat much. This was the 37 year-old's first job since joining RMS (Rendering Mines Safe), a specialist unit within the Royal Navy.

It was after eight o'clock that the convoy of cars set off from the White Hart. They were under orders to travel at high speed and horns were used to warn other traffic of the priority to be given to the speeding saloons. The drivers were professionals, and they needed to be; black frost was an ever-present hazard. The cars arrived in Birmingham, but only the one which contained Syme had escaped mishap.

Birmingham was a mess. Officially, road and rail access in and out of the city was deemed to be dislocated. What the Royal Navy visitors smelled was a mixture of brick dust, soot and smoke. What they saw was rubble, hosepipes lying everywhere, iced over pools of water, smoking buildings, dazed people and officials doing their best to inject some organisation into what seemed like chaos.

It was a policeman who directed the convoy through the blocked streets to the Council House where the ARP Report and Control Centre was located. The city had just suffered its longest raid of the war, lasting thirteen hours.

Lieutenant Miller, Syme's senior, had established himself in a corner and, handing his men hot coffee, briefed them as to their assignments. Miller pointed to a pinned flag on the wall map and said to Syme, *'Take this one. It's in a suburb called Smethwick and it's outside the local Council House.'*

It was an anxious Syme that arrived at the barricade some distance from the Smethwick Council House. The time was 11:30am. Syme, his bag man and his mentor, named Gilbert Stubbs, proceeded beyond the barrier and headed into the deserted area. The mine had wedged itself by penetrating two feet into the paving flagstones which had turned inwards and kept the mine fairly upright.

The two naval officers and one rating made a lonely band. The area had been cleared across a 400 yards radius. Stubbs ordered the rating to leave the bag and return to the barricade. Having assessed the situation, he told his Sub-Lieutenant not to remove the fuse or time clock by hand. Instead he was to attach a line and, using pulleys, run it to the dug-out which was located 35 yards away around the corner.

Stubbs smiled at Syme, *'If you need me, I'll be at the barricade. Good luck old boy!'* And with that, he marched off.

When Hugh Syme had signed up for the Australian Navy less than 18 months previously, he would never have guessed that he would find himself here, alone, in a freezing cold, deserted urban district named Smethwick, a place he had never heard of until an hour ago. Completely alone (or so he thought); alone with a mine that could obliterate him in a second and devastate the buildings he was now looking at. He drew in the cold air through his nostrils and walked

313

directly towards the torpedo-shaped object. It was protruding drunkenly out of the icy pavement with its shroud lines reaching up to the telephone wires above.

For the next two hours, Syme worked steadily and, at times, not so steadily on the mine. If he had been permitted to send a postcard home describing his first day in action it might have read as follows:

'This was my first defusing assignment after my training. I was driven to a barricade near the Council House. It was extremely cold. On my way to the assignment people were calling out 'Good luck!' As I got closer to the mine, there was not a soul to be seen. I arranged the tools on the ground and set up a pulley to the telegraph pole and the bomb. My hands were raw with the cold and they stuck to the metal. I attached a cord to the bomb fuse and stretched the cord for 35 yards to a dug-out shelter. I padded the pavement with layers of Hessian where the fuse would fall. The telegraph wires and parachute lines had to be moved. I turned the tap on the bomb fuse and the safety pin popped home. I slowly unscrewed the keeper ring. I tied a knot around the ring. I walked to the dug-out, pulled on the cord and the fuse fell out. I counted to 20. I walked back to the bomb and picked up the fuse. The detonator went into my wallet; my souvenir. Now there was the hydrostatic clock which could have been booby-trapped. I tied a cord around this and repeated the same operation. As I approached the bomb once more, I noticed two young boys playing with the clock. I was totally aghast. They asked me what I was doing. They had been hiding in the bushes for nearly two hours. I shouted at them and they ran away. Then it was all over; the mine was safe. I returned to the barricade and

many people ran towards me. I was dragged into a nearby pub. A hat was presented to me brimming with coins and notes. I told them they couldn't give me money and that I was only doing my job, so they gave me beer instead.'

The Parachute Mine (or Aerial Torpedo)

These weapons were capable of destroying a row of houses with a single blast. The civilian population held the parachute mine in contempt because it was obviously indiscriminate, as it was impossible to aim them onto a given target. As with other German bombs, a sizeable proportion failed to explode.

The Germans adapted anti-shipping sea mines in order that they could be dropped by parachute. These were not the familiar spherical mine with spikes sticking out, but were akin to torpedoes. The parachute allowed little, if any, penetration and, together with the impact fuse, guaranteed maximum blast effect. These *Luftminen* were either 500kg or 1,000kg, designated LMA and LMB respectively. The LMA was 5 feet 8 inches long and the LMB 8 feet 8 inches.

As the parachute mines which the *Luftwaffe* dropped on British towns and cities were essentially naval weapons, it fell to the Royal Navy to deal with those which failed to explode. A naval unit operating under the name of Rendering Mines Safe allowed careful examination of their design to be carried out. In this way, development of countermeasures could be pursued in order to frustrate the effect of those dropped in the sea lanes around Britain's coast and in her river estuaries.

Lieutenant Hugh Randall Syme GC GM and Bar

Born on 20th February 1903 in Melbourne, Australia, Syme studied Civil Engineering, Science and Industrial Management. The Syme family owned *The Age* newspaper which his grandfather had started and for whom his father worked. For a time, prior to the outbreak of war, Hugh Syme also worked for *The Age*.

Being a yachtsman, he volunteered for service in the Royal Australian Navy and was posted to Britain. Syme joined a small unit of volunteers whose job it was to disarm and recover German mines. Within a week of him dealing with the Smethwick mine he was promoted to Lieutenant. The following June he received the George Medal after his work on a series of mines.

In all, Syme was responsible for rendering safe some 19 mines. Two assignments in particular stand out. In April 1941 he disarmed a mine that had penetrated 15 feet into stinking clay which threatened to breach an embankment alongside the reservoir at Primrose Hill, London. He burrowed into the embankment in order to get at the mine side on. This filthy and dangerous job took Syme four days. Had the mine exploded the torrents of water would have been devastating for the homes below. For this, he was awarded a bar to his George Medal in June 1942. The following November, and now nearly 40 years of age, Syme had to suspend himself upside down in a mud hole off the coast of Weston-super-Mare in order to deal with a previously unknown type of German mine.

He was awarded the George Cross in 1943 and so became the most decorated Australian naval officer up until that time. In January 1943, following the death of his father and uncle, he returned home to become a trustee of the family business. He attempted to return to Britain in order to carry on his work but the Royal Australian Navy prevented this, wanting him to set up a bomb disposal unit in Australia.

He left the navy in 1944 in order to manage *The Age*. Queen Elizabeth II awarded him the Coronation Medal in 1953. He declined a knighthood, however, on the grounds that he was simply doing his wartime job. He remained in newspapers and broadcasting until he died following a brain tumour on 7th November 1965. He was aged 62.

Steve Richards is the author of **The Luftwaffe over Brum**

An example of the 500kg LMA parachute mine which the Admiralty designated Type D.
Nigel Parker collection

Letters Home from an Evacuee

My mother was evacuated from Ealing with her school, Haberdashers' Aske's (including the teachers) to Dorchester, in 1939. This seems a little ironic, as Weymouth, being a major port, was under heavy attack by 1940. She wrote regularly, and sent her washing home by mail. Hard to believe, but she was actually 16, in spite of the most frequent topic of her letters being requests for a doll.

The 2 letters of interest are verbatim, including spelling and punctuation errors

Letter 1
21st September 1939

Dearest Mummy and Daddy

Thank you (Daddy) for the little note for me enclosed with Mrs Miles' letter, I was pleased to get it as I didn't know you were still both at home.

We go up to the county school every day to report, and he have been given heaps of homework –enough to keep us occupied for hours. We must go to school every Saturday too, but actual lessons do not start until Monday. I do not know what is happening properly yet, but I believe we shall be going to the school in the afternoons.

318

I am sorry to hear that you are not coming to see me until half term; I'm not homesick yet, but lots of the girls are.

I am afraid my expenses have mounted up considerably more than I expected them too, and am now rather short of money. I assure you I have spent the money thoughtfully, but we have had a number of things to buy for school (ie books). I have enclosed a further account with this letter, also some plans of the house and the rooms which I thought might interest you.

I have made myself a linen bag to keep my dirty clothes in, and will not send anything home until it is large enough to go cheaply for sixpence. I have a good store of clothes now, so there is no immediate need.

On Tuesday, Mrs Miles drove us into Weymouth with Ruth and the baby, and we had tea in their beach hut. We are not supposed to go into Weymouth, because of German attacks, but so many people are taken, I think they will abolish this strict rule. Here are some of the rules we have to keep here

1. We are not allowed to 'visit friends' in other billets without permission from the hostesses of those billets
2. We are never allowed to go out in less than twos.
3. Long walks require three people going together
4. No one is to leave their billet after 6-o'clock, unless accompanied by their hostess
5. No one is allowed in the streets, unless they are

319

wearing their hats, gloves, stockings and gasmasks.
6. School uniform is to be worn at all times, unless the hostess of your billet does not object to a change of clothing in the evenings.

You can imagine what we feel like taking Jenner (the dog) for a walk in our hats, gloves etc

Please let me know about buying the gas mask cover, as it is a nuisance having to carry it round all day. The only covers you can get here are 1/11d which I think is too great a price to ask for so simple a thing, don't you?

Ian is going back to school tomorrow. We saw some pictures of his school, and it is really enormous, and looks a lovely place.

The maid here is called Ada, and she is an extremely nice girl. She does not sleep in, her hours being 8.30 – 6. She is a guide, and yesterday she brought us some old 'Guides' to read, which was very kind of her.

Mrs Miles leaves us to ourselves a good deal on today, it being Ada's half day, we came in from school and made tea for ourselves. Mrs M and Ruth, go down to Weymouth for tea, while they can, so Pat comes here to have tea with Dorothy, Ada and myself, and we have great fun. Mrs M also has a bosom friend whom she has to see each night. We are left to put ourselves to bed every other night, but on the other nights, the friend comes here.

We take the dog for a walk every day, and meet Cynthia Sutton out with the baby at her billet.

The Buckland Newton people are not coming in until Saturday week now, so I am working almost on my own.

I am just going down to ask Mrs Miles if I may have a bath tonight, so I will stop writing and say goodbye now.

All my love

Jean xxxxxxxxxxx

Letter 2

This letter was written in June 1940 from her new billet at the Popes', a rather palatial house with a cook, a nanny and 2 housemaids.

Darling Mummy and Daddy,

I am sorry I have not written to you for such a long time, but really, there seems to be so much to do, and so little time to do it in!

Today, we had a fine time; a lot of people in Dorchester have offered their gardens out to the BEF's disposal, Mrs Pope included. We had a large notice on the gate 'All members of the BEF welcome in this garden'. We had eleven of them by teatime, and Dorothy and I had to hand round sandwiches, buns and cakes and cups of tea and help Mrs P make the tea. Nanny, Pamela, Flossie and Eileen[59] were

321

all out.

We heard some very interesting, also some very ghastly stories from the soldiers, who have just come back from France. There's not a spot of room for them in Dorchester and that's the fact. I saw about ten of them yesterday, sitting down on the pavement by a shop window because there was nowhere else. Dorothy saw one man asleep on some chapel steps! That's why so many people in Dorchester are offering them their gardens, a good tea, and in some cases, baths.

Do you know, about 1/5 of their company have arrived in Dorchester and they don't know what's happened to the rest! They've just come back from France round the Dunkirk region, and they all have horrible experiences to tell. They spent 48 (hours) on the beach at Dunkirk without any food or any sleep, and whenever they heard planes coming they had to dig themselves into the sand. The Germans followed them wherever they (the BEF) went, and gave them no peace at all. One of the men saved the life of a woman and her child, and in her thanks, she gave him a pearl necklace that wound round the throat and hung down four times. The poor chap put it in his kitbag, and when they were getting on the boat, they had to throw everything with them into the sea in case the Germans got them. All these men by the way are Lancashire men who were dumped in Dorchester, it being the nearest place for them. They

---

[59]The servants

look absolutely awful – they've lost half their clothes, they're tired and hungry, and most of their friends have been killed – it makes you think.

To change to a more cheerful subject! Yesterday, Vivienne and I took [illegible] and Pat out to Beckhampton. The weather was absolutely baking and we nearly died of heat; all the same, we had a marvellous time. We saw heaps of dragonfly lava in the ditches and we want to get some.

Of course, I haven't said a word about the most important thing yet, and that is about mummy coming down to see me next week. This is <u>absolutely marvellous</u>. But you should have come down before, and this should be the second time this term instead of the first.

This is all for mummy's benefit, so you, Daddy, need not read it if you haven't much time. It's about what I want mummy to bring when she comes etc

Please would you bring my talcom powder and my scent and soap set, also the 'Stein song' and 'Where the rainbow ends' record. Also, if you would let me borrow it, may I have your little gold chain you promised me, to put my identity disc on mummy? My round ornamental box with the peacocks on that auntie Maggie gave me my bathing costume and towel, the other box of tennis balls Daddy left me and anything else you think I might want. Oh, and my bracelet of course, And Geraldine[60] with her clothes

---

[60]The much requested doll

and Wendies extra one. Have you made Geraldine's pyjamas yet? It's Monday now, and I am waiting to post a parcel to you. Mrs Pope has just found a woman who will do our washing for us, so I shall have to unpack my beautifully tied up parcel, and sort out the things – oh dear

[....further plans for her mother's arrival] I do want to be with you as much as I can. Mummy I definitely do not <u>want</u> you to take Dorothy anywhere, but may Vivienne come out with us on Sunday afternoon if I invite her? I don't want to go to the pictures much, do you?

Tons of love from

Jean xxxx

Extract from accounts sent:		
	<u>s</u>	<u>d</u>
Handkerchief (1)	1	0
Exercise book (for school)		3
Birthday present (for Joyce)		6
Glacier mints for family		4
Linen		4 ¾
Cotton		1 ½
Stamps		6 ½
Total	3	1 ¾
1. She seems to have had an almost permanent cold, and later got chilblains, so the house was clearly not comfortable.		

****

Carole Sach recounts the experiences of her mother Joan Pritchard during her life in London and during the Blitz during the Second World War. During the war, the bombing of British towns and cities killed over 40,000 people, injuring and making homeless hundreds of thousands of others. For several years the people of these towns and cities had to live through the fear, the disruption and hardships of bombing and later in the war the V1 and V2 rockets.

Life in Romford in Second World War
Early years:

My mum Joan Pritchard née Waller was born in 1922 in Leyton, she moved to Romford in 1925 when my grandfather Frederick Waller opened his first shop, Frederick Waller Tailors Shop. Just before the Second World War mum went to work for the water works in South Street.

The Second World War years:

Nanny nicknamed the Germans as '*The Bothers*'- she meant another 'B' word but did not swear, so the '*Bothers*' it was. Mum said at the outbreak of war the headlights of the cars were blacked out and you only had a small strip of light to show where you were going and of course all street lights were out. At the beginning mum said they closed all cinemas and pubs in Romford down, but that was soon rescinded. Of course, Hornchurch aerodrome was just down the road and the pubs were always full of airmen. The dance halls were packed, but she never mentioned any of the names.

Mum said that they listened to Lord Haw Haw and one night he mentioned '*Our Dear Romford*' and what '*the*

Bothers' had done was to put parachutes on the land mines left behind at Dunkirk and release them over Romford. Mum said one had slipped its chute and it made an awful noise as it came down so she clenched her jaw and when it exploded she was in agony with her jaw for months: the Government had said not do this but to try and keep your mouth open.

So mum was now working at the water works, South Street: she did mention that she did fire watching but never really went into detail about it. I believe it was either on the roof of the water works or the Town Hall. When at work she said that when the sirens went off she would get a colleague to grab her typewriter and go down to the water works shelter. That way she could go on working while *'the bothers'* were bombing. She used to type all the reports of where the mains were hit in Romford during the bombings. Eventually the water works got her a typewriter and left it down there for her.

She said that one day one of the male colleagues came into the office put his head down on his desk and sobbed. She said she had never seen a man cry before, and the reason was that on his way to work he walked down Mawney Road and there was a little girl playing in the garden and he always gave her his sweet ration and said she was the prettiest thing he had ever seen. That morning they had found her head in the wall and her the rest of her body in the rubble. Around this time mum had a boyfriend and I think it was quite serious. His name was ether Jack Lamb or Jack Seal. Still, he was in the RAF but he was naughty and played mum off against another girl and he ended up marrying this other lady. Unfortunately, he was KIA and

326

my mum whenever she talked about him would sob uncontrollably about his death.

Then mum met a Canadian called Johnnie, not really sure of the surname, think it might have been Hayward. He was a parachutist. He did the drop over the Rhine, but he landed in a tree and broke his leg. He managed to get down and crawled under a bush and hid. He said he heard footsteps and took a chance and called out. Luckily for him it was one of our medics and he managed to get him evacuated back to the UK.

Mum said that many a Sunday night Johnnie would show grandad how to jump out of a plane by both of them jumping off the arm of the sofa. Johnnie was stationed at Farnham. Both mum and my grandmother always wrote to Johnnie's mother to let her know how he was, and mum said she really appreciated the letters. When Johnnie returned to Nova Scotia after the war, his uncle, whom he had left in charge of his fruit farm, had basically bankrupted him so he wrote to my mother telling her that he could not marry her. Mum said about a week later his mother sent a letter to her saying *'I don't know what Johnnie said in his letter but as he was writing it was breaking his heart.'*

So mum was in The Lamb one night and an RAF flyer came up to her and asked her if she would give him her dog. Mum said that pilots used to take small dogs up with them in the planes, so if they were KIA they did not die alone. Of course mum refused, she was not giving Bonnie for anything. He was strange one, he was a Cairn Terrier, and mum said that he would whine at the door to be let out, and they worked out that he was *'hearing'* the *'Bothers'* in their planes before the sirens went off so sometimes they were half way down the garden before the sirens started to go off.

During daylight mum said they would also stand in their garden and watch the dog fights over head. Mum said Romford was targeted a lot because of Hornchurch. She said one day she was getting off the bus - I believe it was Main Road, Romford - and a fighter belonging to the '*the Bothers*' came down and tried to machine gun her getting off the bus. She said he was so low she could see him smiling as he was trying to get her. She managed to get under the bus so that saved her life, but started a lifelong hatred of '*the Bothers*'.

Mum never really mentioned much about the Home Guard, which my grandfather was in. She told me only one story. Mum and nanny were under the stairs as their shelter in the garden had flooded, and could not be used. This, she said, a lot of them did and lot of people drowned in their shelters, because *'the Bothers'* when bombing were hitting the mains. My nanny was deaf, but could '*feel*' vibrations. Mum said it was an awful sound and they just did not know what it was that the '*Bothers*' were throwing at them now. Nanny could feel the vibration and she could not understand what was happening so they decided to open the door and to use the door as a shield between them and what was going on outside. Mum said when they opened the door and looked out at the Main Road, she said she thought she was looking into the jaws of hell. Every single tree down, the road was alight and she said there was this thing going across over the top of them with fire coming out the back and it was so low the trees were catching alight as it went. They slammed the door and ran back under the stairs.

With that the door opened and in came grandad, he had '*deserted*' his post in Raphael's Park and walked through that lot to get back to them. Mum said that he was stationed to guard Raphael's Park against the German parachutists in case they tried to land there. It was the rockets. I think this may have been the first attack of them on Romford.

One night when they were in the shelter, she said it was a bad raid, they could hear '*Fred, Fred, where are you, Fred?*' So they turned down the lamp and grandad had put a thick piece of black cloth at the entrance of the shelter. She said it used to get hot in there, but by having this thick material they could leave the door open and get air. So grandad peered out and it was his brother. His home had been bombed in Lodge Avenue, which is not so far from where they lived. Fred replied '*the Bothers have bombed us out*', so into the shelter came other people.

My mother's aunt had cancer and sometimes her daughter told me that when the warnings went off for a split second she thought she would leave her mum in the house in case it was bombed to put her mother out of her misery, but she never did leave her. My great uncle and his family ended up living with my grandparents and mum for 6 months, mum said she loved having her cousin with her. In fact, one night my great grandparents came over and mum and her cousin did my great nanny's hair and they were very pleased with the result. When they asked great grandad what he thought '*yea it's all right*'. Another time, they dyed their hair - my cousin's hair looked lovely, but mum's turned green (not fashionable in those days).

Mum said that on a Sunday evening the German Prisoners of War who worked at the farms at Harold Hill (mum said that there were two farms there) used to walk past the house at tea time and mum said grandad always said that every week these Prisoners of War were getting fatter while the rest of us were getting thinner. Mum said that some local girls went out with these prisoners and the girls were very unpopular within Romford.

She remembers at the end of war going to the cinema to see the news and the films of the camps. She said again grown men were crying and everyone was very upset. She did say that they had heard rumours, but could not believe it. She always told me you have grown up with it, so you have always known, but we just could not believe what we were seeing or the rumours.

She never really spoke about VE or VJ Day in Romford, shame as I would love to have known but never thought to ask.

Just as a side note, I had a friend in 1979, she was a work colleague and she was my friend although she was roughly the same age as my mum. And she came over on the *Kindertransport* from Berlin, she was a German Jew. She eventually ended up in Scotland, but she had to report to the police station every week, because she was German. She told me that she begged her parents to come with her, but they would not, and were murdered… not sure what camp. When the '*Bothers*' had finished all she had left was two aunts. She always went on holiday every year to Germany and I remember asking her how she could return to a country that had done that to her family, her response was '*it's my home*'.

Bob Payne as a young boy tells of his simple yet happy memory of VE Day.

VE Day

On VE Day, we did not have a street party but all the children were given an ice cream from a shop, my first ever ice cream. Afterwards, we went to the Odeon cinema to see Mickey Mouse and cowboys and indians films, it was wonderful.

****

Chapter 6 - Occupation and Resistance

The plight of lands under occupation is hard to imagine to those who have not lived through it or whose country has had that experience. Being under complete control of another foreign power where every part of one's life is dictated on a day-to-day basis is hard to comprehend. Where you can live, what you can eat, what you can read, who you can meet, where you can go, what you can buy and much else – all things we regard as part of everyday life and our basic rights are stripped away and determined by another party. On top of this the fear of being arrested, being informed upon by neighbours, internment and torture, deportation for forced labour becomes something which constantly prays on everyone's psyche.

Law and order invariably is normally determined by military diktat and rigorously enforced by the army or secret police, with penalties for non-compliance extreme, often arbitrary and meant to set out a clear example or warning to everyone else. Dissent or active resistance was treated even more harshly with hideous torture, death and whole families and associates or suspects being killed or deported, whether or not directly involved.

Large amounts have been written about the Nazi occupation of much of Europe and Russia. A strong and initially victorious military enforced a rigorous regime with four principle aims – to subdue the civilian populations, to eradicate the Jews and other 'undesirables', to extract the physical resources of food, raw materials and machinery from the occupied lands and to provide a slave workforce for the enormous Nazi war machine.

Controlling the civilian population was a combination of strict laws reducing the freedoms to the bare minimum. Very low limits of food, everyone being forced to register with the local police and a ruthless secret police – the SD, the SS, the Gestapo – seeking out dissenters, resisters and law breakers and inflicting extreme penalties to reinforce the compliance message. They were often accompanied and assisted by local supporters in this enforcement regime. In Holland, it was Anton Mussert and his fascist National Socialist Movement (NSB). In Norway, the collaborationist National Union Government, led by Vidkun Quisling, made his surname a byword for treachery. The much hated Milice in France was a political paramilitary organisation created by the Vichy Government to help fight against the French Resistance and to round up Jews for deportation. Every country has had its collaborators and informers who were hated, despised and often murdered, with or without trial by the occupied populations.

While not often recognised, the occupying German forces in the Great War enforced a draconian regime on civilian populations of Belgium and northern France, with quotas of crops, cattle, horses, manpower required from the local people. More widely reported in the Second World War, the excesses of the German and Japanese military apparatus in the occupied lands have been well documented, being even more harsh and extreme in some countries than others. Hundreds of thousands of people, were rounded up and deported to work in factories building defences, working in mines in terrible conditions and on starvation rations with an almost total disregard for human life. Other civilians were slaughtered in their thousands at the whim of local commanders. Hardly surprising that the 'retribution' inflicted by the Russian troops in Germany upon the civilian populations represent a catalogue of slaughter and rape.

Within these environments, where populations were totally controlled by the victorious armies, small groups of people were determined to fight back. Underground presses would print leaflets of dissent and defiance, small feats of destruction of railway tracks and engines, telephone lines and small attacks on occupying forces. Normally carried out by brave people, with no military background, and across all the occupied lands, these were small groups, poorly armed but with the overwhelming, some would say foolhardy, desire to fight back - whether the resistance was in France, Norway, Poland or the partisans in Russia.

In the Second World War, it was soon recognised that these groups could not succeed to any extent without support from Britain. The formation of the Special Operations Executive (SOE) within Churchill's instruction to '*Set Europe Ablaze*' as a first attempt to fight back saw arms, radios, specially trained agents – men and women - supplied across Europe to help the resistance groups. High risk and extremely dangerous, their activities saw attacks on the apparatus of the German war machine – whether German troops, munitions factories, transport and communications links. They also provided a means of getting military intelligence about German activities back to Britain. High profile successes such as the raid on the heavy water plant at Vermork in Norway, the assassination of Reinhard Heydrich by SOE trained Czech resisters, the disruption to the movement of *Panzer* Division *Das Reich* towards Normandy immediately after D-Day. These were accompanied by smaller lower profile 'day to day' attacks on the occupying forces throughout the war, some successful, some terrible failures. The brave but ultimately futile Warsaw Uprising in 1944 saw huge bravery but savage retribution.

Failure or capture brought terrible consequences not only for the participants, but for their families or whole towns and villages. Capture often brought imprisonment, torture, deportation and execution. In extreme cases whole towns were destroyed as a warning and retribution – Lidice in Czechoslavakia, Oradour-sur-Glane in France – but not uncommon was the arbitrary execution of ten, twenty, maybe one hundred civilians randomly selected as punishment for presumed complicity.

The toll taken upon civilian populations of the occupied lands was immense. Years of loss of freedom in many cases accompanied by increasing hardships as food rationing took its toll. In Holland, as the war was coming towards its end in 1944 and 1945, the conditions worsened. After Operation Market Garden, the failed attempt to cross the Rhine at Arnhem, the German occupiers gave the entire population of the town – tens of thousands of people – 48 hours' notice to leave. Young and old, able bodied or not had to take what they could carry and try to find some shelter wherever they could. Compounding this, where food was already in short supply, vast swathes of farmland were deliberately flooded in the west to prevent further airborne landings, reducing food availability to crisis levels. So when the harshest winter in decades arrived weeks later, over 20,000 people starved to death. Food supplies only started to improve once the Germans were forced back, and huge food relief drops –

Operation Manna (RAF) and Operation Chowhound (USAAF) – started in spring of 1945 and subsequent liberation.

While history often concentrates on the military events, the impact on occupied, civilian populations is often little known or recorded, but nevertheless is important on how the evolution of subsequent events, and political alliances form. The desire of the countries of mainland Europe for peace is a core facet and reason as to why many Europeans want to hold on to the institution of the European Union.

****

Auschwitz is a name that became known the world over in the Second World War to symbolise the absolute horrors and moral depths to which Hitler's Nazi regime had descended. Hitler had made it known that he intended to rid the planet of all Jews, which he blamed as being the race that undermined the German nation and Imperial German Army in the First World War and was the cause of Germany's defeat. During the war, over 6 million Jews and other 'undesirables' - men, women and children - from across many countries were rounded up, and transported to numerous concentration or extermination camps. These camps were located mainly in the eastern part of Germany and occupied eastern Europe where millions were murdered, brutally treated, worked to death or allowed to die of disease. At Auschwitz over 2 million people lost their lives in horrific and inhumane conditions. Polish historian, Alina Nowobilska, describes the first mass transport of Jews from Poland to Auschwitz in June 1940. Alina has dedicated this piece to her great great uncle, Leon Lipieński, prisoner number 555, who perished in Auschwitz on the 12th February 1942.

The First Mass Transport into Auschwitz

'*We had just arrived, and did not realise how awful the place would become, or the millions of murders that would be committed there! After these preliminaries had taken away any hope of saving our lives, we started our existence in that hell on earth created by the sadism of Hitler*'[61] 728 Polish men arrived at Auschwitz on the 14th June 1940, they were the first mass transport of prisoners to this hell on earth.

The history of concentration camps in the Third Reich can be traced back to March 1933, when the first concentration camp was opened, KL Dachau; there the SS developed a system that would be adopted by other camps over the next thirteen years.[62] The first camps were built to hold those who opposed the Nazi regime, communists and socialists. Concentration camp functions would change over time; many non-Germans would be sent to the camps; the German inmates would then become a privileged minority. [63] However, when discussing Polish political prisoners, Auschwitz becomes the place where the deadliest assaults were launched against Poles.[64] Auschwitz is known for the Holocaust but it began as a concentration camp for Poles.

---

[61] (Drecki and Drecki, 1992) p18
[62] (Langbein and Zohn, 2017) p33
[63] Ibid
[64] (Wachsmann, 2016) p236

The history of Auschwitz began on the 1st September 1939 as Poland was invaded by Germany. Just over two weeks later on the 17th September the Soviet Union invaded from the east. The September campaign cost 250,000 lives on all sides, and it was to show the brutal practices taken on by the invading forces that were yet to come, for example targeting civilians, aerial bombings and mass killings.[65] From the first day of the German invasion, Poles were being rounded up, imprisoned and executed in street executions; the terror was instantaneous, it was the only way to control the population. There were regular roundups, a policing hour and any resistance was suppressed. The country was to be economically destroyed, and all culture was to be wiped out. On the 2nd October 1939, Hitler said, *'All representatives of the Polish intelligentsia must be exterminated. This sounds harsh, but such are the laws of life.'*[66] Prisons began to overflow by the end of 1939, and prisoners were being sent into the Third Reich to already established concentration camps like KL Buchenwald, but these camps were not prepared for such a large influx of prisoners.

In December 1939, the President of the Katowice District informed Himmler that *'some of the existing prisons are filled to three times the capacity.'*[67] Prisoners were in extremely overcrowded cells. [68]The situation needed to be dealt with, therefore, in February 1940, Richard Glucks, the concentration camp inspector was ordered to inspect

---

[65] (Moorhouse, 2019) pxviii
[66] (Piper, 2000) p44
[67] (Konieczny, 1995) p.6
[68] (Borkowski, 1986) p13

potential sites for a new concentration camp, one of which was the former Polish military barracks in Oświęcim. By April 1940, the decision had been made that there will stand the new concentration camp, KL Auschwitz. Rudolf Höss, the first commandant of Auschwitz, arrived at the camp on the 30th April 1940 to ready the camp. Along with five other SS men, they obtained approximately 300 Jews from the town of Oświęcim to help with the preparation of the camp.[69]

The situation became worse after May 1940 after *'action AB'* came into force, it was the pacification of Polish intellectuals and intelligentsia. Imprisoned Poles would then be either shot or sent to a concentration camp in Germany. At this point, there were no concentration camps on former Polish territory.[70] Prisons began to swell even more after Poles began trying to cross the borders to join the free Polish Army in Hungary, Romania and France. Some made it; others were caught, imprisoned and tortured in prison. The Germans would call these men, *'tourists'*.

The first prisoners of Auschwitz were made up of men who were arrested for being *'tourists'*, for *'illegal'* underground activity, for being part of the scouting movement or from street round-ups. Some were even betrayed by friends or family, which led to their arrest. They were then kept in local prisons; many were tortured and interrogated. Over a few weeks in May and June, they were slowly moved to Tarnów prison, from where they would be deported. These men and boys who were slowly gathered at Tarnów were

---

[69] (Czech, 1989) pp11-12
[70] (Piper, 2000) p49

composed of predominantly teenagers and young men. At least 56 of them were under the age of 18, the youngest being only 14 years old. Approximately 450 of them, which is over half, were also between the ages of 18 and 24.[71] This number could be higher because the data is, unfortunately, incomplete. There were various professions onboard, teachers, railway workers, military officers, landowners, athletes, artists, priests, the majority were students or university graduates. Some of these men were related, for example, Edward and Zdzisław Drzał, both brothers, perished in the Lübeck disaster on the 3rd May 1945, or Kazimierz and Mieczysław Albin. Kazimierz escaped on the 27th February 1943 and his brother Mieczysław was liberated in KL Buchenwald, or Zbigniew and Edward Drecki. Edward perished on the 31st August 1941 after being severely beaten by a kapo and suffering with internal bleeding,[72] his brother Zbigniew survived and was liberated in KL Buchenwald. Some fathers and sons ended up on the transport together, for example, Stanisław and Adam Drohojowski. Adam perished on the 23rd December 1940 and his father Stanisław 3 months later on the 12th March 1941. Prisoners were also deported with their friends, for example, seventeen-year-old Stanisław Białaś was in the underground resistance, he was arrested on the 30th March 1940 alongside five of his friends. They all ended up on the same transport; however, only three out of the six friends survived the camp.[73] Friendship groups were formed before their arrest, in prison and at the camp. These helped the men to survive.

---

[71] (Strzelecka, 2002)
[72] (Drecki and Drecki, 1992) p33
[73] (Białaś, n.d.) p74

So what happened on that fateful day? On the 13th June 1940, the prisoners were taken out of their cells and forced into the courtyard of Tarnów prison. From there, they were taken to the local Jewish baths where they had the opportunity to bathe and receive some food from the local Red Cross. In the early hours of the 14th June, they were woken and forced to line up in rows of five. Orders were given to the local civilians that they were not to leave their homes and to stay away from the windows. The men marched through the streets in silence to Tarnów train station. [74] 753 men reached the station, 24 of them were removed for one reason or another, and the remaining 729 set off on their journey to the unknown, a dozen or so of them were Jews. The train was a regular 3rd class passenger train; the men boarded calmly and were not beaten by their escorts.[75] It was stuffy in the train carriage, they were not allowed to open the windows. Just before the train reached Kraków, a prisoner managed to escape from the transport.[76] The train arrived into Kraków just before noon, the Herald from the Mariacki church greeted it.[77] The train station was covered with Nazi flags, German soldiers were celebrating, and the speakers were blaring German music while informing that Germany had conquered Paris, Paris had fallen.[78] It was devastating for the men aboard the train; they had had hope; it was now shattered.[79]

---

[74] (Cyba, 1973) p237
[75] (Antoniewicz, 1972) p160
[76] (Hordyński, 1998) p12
[77] (Cyba, 1973) p238
[78] (Kielar and Flatauer, 2017) p1
[79] (Albin, 2003) p58

The train moved on; still the prisoners had no idea where they were going. The train then stopped at the Reich/General Government border; they at least knew they were heading west.[80] In the late afternoon, they reached a central station with the name 'Auschwitz', Oświęcim in Polish. The train then took a side track, slowly chugging and pulling the wagons over the unused and overgrown tracks. It finally stopped outside the old Monopoly building where SS men were waiting. The doors opened, and the men were pulled from the train and beaten with rifle butts, shouted at and kicked. They ran towards the building which was surrounded by barbed wire and guard towers.[81] The beatings were continuous. On the side was a group of 30 men dressed in stripes with green triangles on their chest, holding batons. Only a few weeks before the first mass transport arrived, on the 20th May, 30 criminals from KL Sachsenhausen arrived at the former Polish military barracks. These men were to become the first kapo, functionary prisoners of Auschwitz. According to Höss, they were hand-chosen by Gerhard Palitzsch for their brutality.[82] However, not all were brutal and sadistic like the infamous prisoner number one, Bruno Brodniewitsch or Leo Wietschorek, prisoner number thirty. Some like Otto Küsel helped the prisoners and used his position to help save the lives of his fellow prisoners. [83]

The 30 kapos began beating the newly arrived prisoners and helped the SS line them up, ready for a roll call. After the

[80] Ibid
[81] (Drecki and Drecki, 1992) p18
[82] (Höß, 2001) p108
[83] (Cywiński et al., 2017) p104

roll call, Karl Fritzsch, one of the SS Officers, made a speech where he stated that the prisoners were in a concentration camp and that the Poles had the right to live for three months, priests for one month and Jews for two weeks. The prisoners were then registered in the basement of the building, their personal details were noted, and a number was provided, they received numbers 31-758. At this point, prisoners were not yet tattooed; this only began in spring 1942. They had all their personal belongings taken away, and then they were forced to bathe and have their heads shaved. Prisoners struggled to recognise each other.[84] Their identity was removed, and they only became a number, no longer a name, they were dehumanised. At this point, prisoners were not given the same striped uniforms as the kapo; they wore their civilian clothing. Everything was done at a run, with constant beatings and shouting by the kapo and the SS men. After registration and disinfection, the prisoners were split into groups and chased to the first floor of the building where they were to sleep. The floors were covered with straw, and the men were tightly packed in. There was one bucket available for them to relieve themselves into, [85] but that quickly became full. It was stuffy in the rooms because the windows were closed and they were not allowed to open them. The men did not sleep as SS men and kapo would regularly run into the rooms and cause chaos, waking the men and creating clouds of dust which rose from the straw on the floor.[86]

---

[84] (Borkowski, 1986) p4
[85] (Albin, 2003) p62
[86] (Stojakowski, 1970) p61

343

The men spent two weeks in quarantine where they spent their time taking part in *'sport'*. Do not take this word lightly because it wasn't sport as we know it in the modern term. This was agonising exercise, barefoot, [87] where prisoners were forced to squat, do bear walks, the frog jump and forced to crawl along the ground among other exhausting exercises,[88] for up to 12 hours a day. They were extremely difficult, so difficult that even the youngest of them could not endure it. [89] If they did not do as they were ordered, then they would be beaten mercilessly. They were also taught to sing German songs, the problem being that some prisoners could not speak German, therefore understanding the words and singing them was difficult. If a prisoner was not singing loud enough or not pronouncing the lyrics correctly, they would be beaten mercilessly. Roll calls were also held for hours. [90] Just a few weeks after the first mass transport arrived, a prisoner by the name of Tadeusz Wiejowski escaped on the 6th July. He was aided by the local civilians who were hired to work in the camp. He was provided with civilian clothing, money, food and a green armband that civilian workers were required to wear. He walked out of the camp with the civilian workers and boarded a freight train to Spytkowice. [91]

It is what happened after his escape that was truly horrific and a perfect example of the cruelty that the SS inflicted upon the prisoners. Nearly every prisoner from this transport clearly remembers this day; it is imprinted in their

---

[87] (Chlebowski, 1947) p202
[88] (Malcherczyk, 1947) p311
[89] (Garliński, Foot and Polonsky, 2018) p22
[90] Ibid
[91] (Bicz, 1946) p2

memory.[92] The prisoners were forced to stand for a nineteen-hour roll call, through a freezing night and a burning hot day that burnt their shaved heads, many of them passed out. [93] The SS would mock the prisoners, beat them and humiliate them.[94] They were forced to kneel with their hands behind their heads, then stand to attention with their hands raised up, then their hands by their sides.[95] It was continuous torture. Also, prisoners were not allowed to relieve themselves, however many suffered from diarrhoea and other gastric problems; if they did relieve themselves, they were forced to get on all fours and bark like a dog.[96]

Five civilians were also punished for aiding the escape. They were interrogated in Block 11, denied food and water for seven days and imprisoned in the camp.[97] In November they were sentenced to death which was commuted to five years in a concentration camp and 75 lashes. Bicz was beaten till he passed out and spent seven months recovering in the camp hospital, he was then sent to KL Mauthausen where he was liberated. [98] His fellow civilians did not live to see liberation. There were also eleven prisoners punished with 25 lashes and deportation to KL Flossenburg. Most of the eleven lived to see liberation.[99]

---

[92] (Albin, 2003) p77

[93] (Drecki and Drecki, 1992) p21

[94] (Bałut, 1945) p7

[95] (Fingerchut, 1954) p2a

[96] (Bałut, 1945) p7

[97] (Bicz, 1946) p3

[98] Ibid p4

[99] (Muzeum Auschwitz-Birkenau, 2020)

This was only the beginning of hell for these men, 325 of them would survive, 292 would perish and for the remaining 111; nothing is known of their fate.

*I would like to dedicate this article to my great great uncle, Leon Lipieński, prisoner number 555 who perished in Auschwitz on the 12th February 1942.

****

Author and broadcaster Clare Mulley pays tribute to the brave women who served as agents in Special Operations Executive. Working in occupied Europe, these women carried various undercover roles such as couriers and wireless operators and some more leadership roles alongside the resistance organisations under the noses of German forces and the local collaborators. This was highly dangerous and risky work in a hostile environment and required people of exceptional calibre to carry them out. They needed all their ingenuity, courage and good fortune to survive: Sadly, many didn't make it and faced terrible deaths. Clare Mulley explains why the interest and admiration for these brave women has increased over recent years but why at the time their roles and achievements had been down played both by the authorities and the media.

Female special agents

The names of 75 courageous women from 13 nations are etched into a beautiful memorial at RAF Tempsford, home of the Special Duties Squadrons during the Second World War. These are the female special agents who volunteered for active service behind enemy lines as couriers and wireless operators, running escape lines and leading partisan armies. All were brave, and all deeply committed to the Allied cause, but they had little else in common. Although most were British or French, there were also women from the Soviet Union, Belgium, The Netherlands, Ireland, America, Switzerland, India, Australia and Chile, as well as two from Germany, sent in to support the domestic resistance, and two from Poland, including Krystyna Skarbek, aka Christine Granville, the subject of my last biography. Some were lucky, others not, many were beautiful which had its own pros and cons, some were plain, and one had a prosthetic leg. Most female agents were effective, at least for a short while, and Skarbek survived in active service for six years. The huge contribution of this diverse group of women came at a high price. 29 were arrested and 16 executed. One more chose suicide with her lethal 'L' pill.

Today there is increasing interest in these women. Over the last few years there have been many new biographies and anthologies about them and several memorials. Tempsford is important in that it is the only one that pays tribute to all the women by name. Its marble column stands on a granite plinth collectively honouring the two special duties squadrons that flew them into enemy occupied Europe, but there is no reference to the male agents. Perhaps now we need to ask why is it that we still distinguish heroines from heroes. After all, the Special Operations Executive, better known as SOE, was in many ways a great gender leveller. Selected women and men went through the same training, including in the use of guns and explosives, and silent killing, and were armed and sent to work alongside each other in the field.

It was, however, precisely because they were women, that these female agents were so valuable during the war. Unlike able-bodied men, civilian women travelling around France by train or bicycle attracted relatively little attention. This meant they were better-placed to serve as couriers between different resistance circuits or groups of Maquis hiding in the hills. Women transported messages, micro-film and radio codes, as well as heavy equipment such as weapons and wireless transmitters to arrange the delivery of agents and equipment, etc. Some of them, notably Pearl Witherington and Nancy Wake, went much further, commanding resistance armies of 2,000 men, and, among other achievements, Skarbek persuaded a German garrison on a strategic pass in the Alps to defect.

Skarbek, the first woman to work for Britain as a special agent, was employed in December 1939. Eighteen months would pass, during which time she served both across Eastern Europe and in the Middle East, before SOE was even officially established. The first female covert radio operator to be flown into France, Noor Inayat Khan, left England in June 1943. Even at this point, women in the British military were not officially allowed to carry guns or explosives. To circumvent this, SOE enrolled women into the FANYs, which officially operated outside of the Armed Forces but still theoretically offered some protection under the Geneva Convention in the event of capture, and provided pensions should the women become casualties.

Churchill had approved the employment of women in SOE, but their role was not made public until some time after the war for fear of a backlash. Meanwhile the women who had survived found their achievements were underplayed and their skills undervalued. While Skarbek's male colleagues were reassigned to roles overseas, after she turned down a series of secretarial jobs for which she was monumentally unsuited, Skarbek was dismissed as *'not a very easy person to employ'*. Meanwhile the official papers sent to her were accompanied by belittling notes such as *'Hope you are being a good girl!'* Even the honours the women received were less than their male counterparts, as women did not qualify for British military awards. Many felt bitter about this, but none expressed it as succinctly as Pearl Witherington. After being awarded the MBE (Civil), she famously commented that *'there was nothing civil'* about the work she had undertaken.

It was only in the 1950s that the women's stories began to be told. Having signed the Official Secrets Act, many of the women, like the men they served with, refused to talk. Others, such as Odette Hallowes, spoke out, or like both Hallowes and Violette Szabo, who had been executed at Ravensbrück, had their stories retold in biographies and films. And so the myth-making began. All too often, female agents and other women in the resistance have been honoured more for their courage and great sacrifice, than for their actual achievements. It has been judged more important that they tried, than that they succeeded. When the women did achieve, they still seem to have been feminised in the retelling, their beauty and sacrifices emphasised and their rough edges smoothed over. In order to be celebrated they have been, in effect, often recast as victims, rather than simply as heroes.

Ironically perhaps, today we need to reconsider the female special agents not only because historically they were marginalised but because, all too often, when given attention they have been judged as women, rather than as individuals doing an extraordinary job. If you have been in the business of special operations, it is clearly self-defeating to be elevated as a heroine if at the same time you are diminished as an independent agent.

Distinction or Discrimination: Honouring the female special agents of the Second World War | Clare Mulley's Blog - *a blog on some of the Second World War female SOE special agents, including Krystyna Skarbek aka Christine Granville, the subject of my second book, The Spy Who Loved.*

Clare Mulley is an award-winning author and broadcaster. Her first book, *The Woman Who Saved the Children,* won the *Daily Mail* Biographers' Club Prize, and *The Spy Who Loved,* now optioned by Universal Studios, led to Clare being decorated with Poland's national honour, the Bene Merito. Clare's third book, *The Women Who Flew for Hitler,* tells the extraordinary story of two women at the heart of Nazi Germany, whose choices put them on opposite sides of history. Clare is a regular contributor to TV, radio and podcasts, a popular public speaker, and reviews for the *Telegraph, Spectator* and *History Today* www.claremulley.com

****

SOE Memorial
Clare Mulley archive

Andrea Gibson, summarises the conversation with her mother Erica Kammerlander in February 2020 who was living in Muerzzuschlag in Austria at the time of the Russian 'liberation' in 1945. Erica was Jane Chadwicks' godmother and her mother's best friend. She is still going strong at the age of 95 at the time of writing. At the end of the war, much of Austria was initially occupied by the Russians, but under the terms of the international agreement, most was handed over to the British or the Americans as the occupying power.

Russian Occupation

After the war, Muerzzuschlag was first occupied by the Russians with the demarcation line being at the Semmering Pass. The Russians arrived and entered the peoples' homes and occupied them. My mum told me that they also knocked on their door and scribbled something in Russian language outside the door which informed the other Russian soldiers that this home was already occupied. My mum said that they were lucky as no one actually came back to live in the house and as there was the writing outside the entrance door obviously to inform others that this house was already occupied and they did not have to move out.

My grandfather was the only saddler in town, so the Russians expected that he worked all day long for them. He had to get up at 4 am and had to work until 10 pm. As no one was allowed to walk at this late hour they brought him home. He had to use all of the leather he had to make belts and holsters where they could fit their pistols in.

My mum also told me that women got raped and that my grandmother was always very worried. The Russians wore as many watches as they could fit on both arms and always wanted '*ura*'; in correct German language one would say '*Uhren*' ie watches.

My uncle was also kept as a prisoner of war by the Russians somewhere near Linz in Oberoesterreich, and was ready to be transported to Siberia. He was spotted by a railway worker who knew him as my uncle, and who also used to work for the railways in Muerzzuschlag. The railway worker informed the family at home and his sister went to rescue him. She took a railway uniform which she could smuggle to her brother and he could escape. This was very dangerous because, had they been caught, they both would have been shot.

My mother said that it was a great relief when the Russians left Muerzzuschlag and the English arrived.

****

 *Tom Dehn has kindly contributed a poem written by his cousin Paul Dehn, a special forces agent working with SOE in France in 1944. A square in the town St. Aubin D'Aubigne is named after Paul Dehn as a tribute to his role in the liberation of the town.*

SOE Poem - The Place de Paul Dehn
ST. AUBIN D'AUBIGNE
August, 1944

It was only a small place and they had cheered us too much
A couple of allies, chance symbol of Freedom new-found
They were eager to beckon, to back-slap, even to touch;
They put flowers in my helmet and corn-coloured wine in my hand.

The boy from Dakota and I, we had suffered too little
To deserve all the flowers, the kisses, the wine and the thanks.
We both felt ashamed; till the kettledrum clangour of metal
On cobble and kerbstone proclaimed the arrival of tanks.

Who saw them first, the exiles returning, the fighters,
The Croix de Lorraine and the Tricolor flown from the hull?
Who saw us moving more fitly to join the spectators,
The crazy, the crying, the silent whose hearts were full?

It was only a small place, but a bugle was blowing,
I remember the Mayor performing an intricate dance
And the boy from Dakota most gravely, most quietly throwing
The flowers from his helmet toward the deserving France.

****

Local historian, Nick Brazil, tells the story of David Dill, who as part of an SAS party was dropped into France in August 1944 to make contact with local resistance forces. He was captured and executed under Hitler's notorious Commando Order.

David Dill - South Stoke's War Hero

St Andrew's in the Thameside village of South Stoke is a beautiful parish church dating back to the 14th Century. But, as well as a rich historical interior including a fine font and some lovely stained glass windows, there is a more modern memorial to great heroism that is easily missed.

Mounted on the left hand wall next to the church entrance is a memorial plaque to Lieutenant David Dill who sacrificed his life under tragic circumstances when aged just 20. The inscription on the plaque simply reads:

> *'David Gordon Dill*
> *Croix de Guerre*
> *60th Rifles and 2nd SAS Regiment*
> *Born February 1st 1924*
> *Killed behind enemy lines in Germany November 25th 1944*
> *Aged 20'*

Behind this simple statement lies a story of great bravery and tragedy. On 12th August 1944, a small advance party of SAS troops under the command of Captain Henry Duce was parachuted into the Vosges. On the basis of an eyewitness account by a local civilian Yvonne Malaise, Lieutenant David Dill was part of this first group.

In the 1940s, this wooded and hilly region of Northern France was sparsely populated with farming villages and hamlets. The SAS mission was codenamed Operation Loyton and was designed to work with the local resistance in attacking and hampering German forces in Northern France. It was planned to last two weeks at the end of which the SAS forces would link up with General Patton's US Third Army. Unfortunately, this would not happen since Patton's Forces were delayed in Nancy by a lack of supplies.

Duce's advance force was tasked to make initial contact with the local resistance cells. They were then to reconnoitre the area for suitable enemy targets and locate a dropping zone for the main SAS contingent under the leadership of Lieutenant Colonel Brian Franks. They parachuted in on 30th August 1944.

In warfare, success or failure invariably hinges on timing and luck. In the case of Operation Loyton, the SAS ran out of both. Unfortunately, the Germans chose to reinforce this area of the Vosges against Patton's advancing Third Army at exactly the same time. As a result, the Germans became aware of the British Forces behind the lines much earlier than they might have otherwise. From then on the SAS were fighting a running battle for their lives.

Believing the British force much larger than it actually was, the Germans sent 5,000 men up the valley towards the village of Moussey. There followed a series of firefights and ambushes that cost the Germans dearly. Following the addition of six jeeps armed with heavy machine guns and twenty more SAS men, the British intensified their attacks.

Many German patrols were shot up with a high number of casualties.

On one memorable occasion, a patrol led by Captain Duce swept into Moussey with all guns blazing catching the *Waffen* SS just as they were forming up. The SAS men escaped after inflicting heavy casualties on the Germans.

David Dill must have been in the very thick of all this fighting and indeed he is mentioned in the memoirs of a French family who put the SAS men up during this dramatic period. Eight of the SAS soldiers hid out at a farm called Grandes Gouttes near Moussey for two weeks. The owners of the farm were Clement and Lucie Launay who chose to put their lives on the line to give shelter to the British fighters.

Their daughter Yvonne Malaise also lived there with them and it was she who shared her recollections of those dangerous times for the French website: http://www.resistance-deportation.org/spip.php

At the time Yvonne was a 22 year old teacher with a six month old baby. Her husband Lucien Villemin, a forest guard had been deported on 24th September 1944. Here are some edited sections of her recollections:

'*We have often talked about those men and their Lieutenant (David Dill), and of Captain Druce who I saw 2 times coming from meeting them. These paras usually went out for mysterious operations. They came back to eat and sleep, often very tired, sometimes with dirty or damaged clothes. Sometimes they did not come back. At the end of the first week of October a few of them came to take their food and said they were going to the American lines. They were upset, and anxious for the following days. They said 'see you soon in better circumstances and thanks for everything'.*

Since that moving day, my parents, my uncle and aunt (all deceased) and I asked the same and hard questions: did they reach the American lines, did they come back alive at home...?'

'I know now that none of them returned alive in England!

Still today we don't know their names, except recently the name of the officer, thanks to a photo given by Len Owens. So we are now sure he was Lieutenant David Dill.'

In fact, Captain Duce managed to cross back and forth through the American lines no less than three times carrying valuable information about German troop movements. It is said that he was accompanied by another soldier. Whether or not this man was David Dill is unknown.

But the fact that Dill was recognised as one of the officers with Captain Duce at the farmhouse by Yvonne Malaise indicates that he probably arrived in France with the Captain's advance party.

Operation Loyton was only planned to last two weeks but eventually stretched out for two months. By the beginning of October, the SAS's supplies were running out and with Patton's force stalled near Nancy, there was no chance of salvation from that quarter. It was at this point that Lieutenant Colonel Franks gave the order for the SAS force to break up into smaller units of three or four men and make their way back to allied lines. Some made it, but many didn't.

One SAS group of four men was ambushed by the *Waffen* SS. Three of the SAS commandos were killed whilst the fourth man Lieutenant Peter Johnson was injured but escaped. Another 31 men including Lieutenant David Dill effectively disappeared. It was not until the war had finished that the fate of these men was ascertained.

It must have been a matter of considerable concern and distress to Lieutenant Colonel Franks that he did not know what had happened to his missing men. After the war he went back to France and Germany with the SAS War Crimes Investigation Team to find out precisely what had happened to them.

He discovered that ten of his men were buried in the cemetery at Moussey. The SAS War Crimes team ultimately discovered that 31 others had fallen foul of Hitler's notorious Commando Order commanding that all captured commandos be executed regardless of whether or not they were in uniform. Accordingly, all the 31 commandos were murdered at various locations including Natzweiler-Struthof concentration camp in the Vosges and Gagennau in Germany.

David Dill was one of those men executed at Gagennau and he is buried at Durnbach War Cemetery in Germany. He was awarded the Croix de Guerre posthumously.

During Operation Loyton, 48 British soldiers were either killed in action or murdered in captivity. In addition, 210

French civilians from the Moussey area were deported to concentration camps where 140 of them died.

David Dill's memorial in that quiet Oxfordshire church is a reminder of the high price he and countless others paid to secure our freedom.

David Gordon Dill Croix de Guerre 60th Rifles and 2nd SAS Regiment. Born February 1st 1924. Killed behind enemy lines in Germany November 25th 1944 aged 20. He is commemorated in South Stoke Church in Oxfordshire.

Nick Brazil archive

Chapter 7 - POWs, Escape and Evasion

Film and literature since 1945 has in a large part romanticised or at least sanitised the stories, true or fictional, about prisoners of war, and attempts of escape and evasion. The reality, sadly, is somewhat different with POWs, whether escaping or otherwise, enduring great hardship and many years in confinement. For some imprisonment was a relief from the horrors of war, but others endured huge mistreatment and often death.

Over the centuries the fate of prisoners was in the hands of their captors. In the Middle Ages and before, 'taking no prisoners' was the norm, even basic medical treatment was not made available and few made it back home from whence they were captured. Some died of starvation, many of illness and of their wounds, some were worked to death and for many they were dispatched by the sword. Avoiding capture was a huge priority for the typical soldier or sailor.

It was following the Battle of Solferino in 1859 during the Austro-Sardinian war that Swiss businessman Jean-Henri Dunant witnessed the aftermath of the battle and saw the 40,000 soldiers left wounded on the battlefield without help, or even basic medical treatment. Appalled by what he saw, Dunant, who later won the first Nobel Peace Prize in 1901, devoted his life to improving the lot of wounded and captured soldiers. Only a handful of years later, this led to the foundation of the International Red Cross and then in 1864, the first Geneva Convention. Over the following 150 years most countries signed up to the convention which over time and in various reiterations increasingly gave wounded and captured soldiers basic rights of medical care, shelter, food, clothing and much else as well as defining in part what was an acceptable way to wage war. However, the reality on the ground could be very different.

In the Second World War, hundreds of thousands of allied prisoners in the west were housed in hundreds of prison camps across Germany and part of occupied Eastern Europe, with numerous nationalities housed together in separate parts of the camps. Treatment was generally good or at least acceptable. For many prisoners, time in captivity saw uncomfortable conditions in purpose-built prison camps, with mediocre food, beds of straw-filled mattresses, cold winters and hot summers and long periods of boredom. Across many POW camps, the boredom was relieved to an extent by activities organised by the POWs themselves – sports, academic lessons, theatre variety performances.

Hunger and boredom were the main features of captivity for many POWs with little to fill their time, the same diet day in day out, of worsening quality and amount of food as the war dragged on. This, coupled with just not knowing when their 'sentence' would come to an end, drove some prisoners to near insanity and to poorly thought through and irrational escape attempts or behaviour. Red Cross parcels arrived periodically to supplement food and basic needs and were greatly looked forward to.

The end of the war, as Germany was squeezed from both east and west, was a worrying time for the POWs. Not only were there genuine fears of random and arbitrary mass executions by fanatical SS guards, but as the Russians advanced from the east, tens of thousands of prisoners were force marched westwards to new camps ahead of the advance. Living off the land in often freezing conditions with deteriorating clothing, health and rarely any shelter, many died or sustained long term medical conditions.

Similarly, as the war went on and especially after the North African campaign onwards, huge numbers of German soldiers were captured by Allied forces. They would be shipped to Britain and housed in prison camps, normally in the more outlying parts of the country, while others would be transported to Canada to prison camps there. Work on the land under supervision was routine for the lower ranks, while officers were often housed in country mansions where either interrogations took place or their conversations were secretly bugged to try to glean vital information about German war plans, morale, and the strength of their armed forces.

Conversely, on the Eastern Front, the fighting between Germany and Russia, following Operation Barbarossa in July 1941, was a completely different story. With almost total disregard of the Geneva Convention by both sides, the majority of prisoners did not make it home. Mass killing, and starvation was the norm, and the brutality inflicted reflected the bitterness between the two armies. Partisans and any people or villages felt to be assisting them were summarily executed by the Germans. And as the war turned, millions of Germans were captured yet only a few thousand survived. The familiar photographs of miles and miles of bedraggled, defeated German POWs shuffling into the unknown on a vast bleak unforgiving Russian landscape were testament to the scale of the losses.

As is well documented, the Japanese treatment of POWs and civilians held the terms of the Geneva Convention in utter contempt, adopting the militaristic doctrine, the so-called 'Code of Battlefield Conduct' (*Senjinkun*) that prohibited them from surrendering and implied that those who surrendered should also forfeit the right to live. This resulted in such well-known acts as the allied prisoners working on the infamous Death Railway or in the copper mines on mainland Japan. Prisoners were worked and starved to death, given no medical treatment and generally brutally mistreated. More descriptions from survivors are given in the section War Against Japan, but suffice to record that death rates were six times higher among those held captive by the Japanese than those held in German POW camps.

Again generally speaking, there was a different attitude to the treatment of escaping POWs. Under the Japanese, escapers were put to death, often after extreme torture. Allied escapers in the west rarely ran that risk, and as a result there were ongoing attempts to make the holy grail – the so-called '*Home Run*'. Few achieved it but some well-known names - Airey Neave amongst them along with others of many nationalities too - got back via various routes normally from camps in eastern Europe. Many tried, but relatively few made it all the way home from inside the camps. Generally, films and books have concentrated on these valiant escapers rather than the hundreds of thousands enduring the drudgery of long-term imprisonment.

Examples of localised murder of captured allied troops during the retreat to Dunkirk in 1940 or at Malmedy in 1944 were relatively few and far between and normally perpetrated by fanatical SS divisions. Since the start of aerial warfare and particularly bombing of civilian targets in the Second World War, the risks of bailing out by aircrew over enemy territory were high, aside from injuries being sustained on escaping the aircraft or on landing. There were many instances of civilians attacking downed aircrew in German cities.

Through MI9 and resistance organisations, escape lines across Europe helped repatriate 3,000 aircrew and escapers to return to Britain by various hazardous routes moving from safe house to safe house run by local people at huge personal risk. Brigadier John 'Shan' Hackett of 4 Para was seriously wounded at Arnhem and only survived and escaped through the remarkable support and bravery of local Dutch families, resistance members and doctors. They hid and cared for him over nearly five months. He eventually was guided back to the advancing allied forces in February 1945.

At the end of the day, the decision whether a captured serviceman or woman was taken as a POW or died was often in the hands of the soldier on the ground, and the discipline imposed by his officers. This was always the case and as likely will forever be so too.

****

The Real Great Escape

The narrative of the Great Escape resonates through our culture as persistently as the score of the film. Just as most can complete Elmer Bernstein's entire tune if they merely hear its opening B flat and E flat, many of us can relate the tale denoted by simply the two words, 'great' and 'escape'. The story of the film, for those who missed it last Christmas, is that of a group of Allied prisoners-of-war imprisoned in a German camp set deep in a forest in occupied Poland. Hungry to get back to the fight and eager to prove as much of an annoyance to their captors as possible, the POWs mount an audacious plan to tunnel out of the camp in order to secure the escape of some 200 prisoners. Led by an ambitious RAF officer called 'Roger Bartlett', himself a veteran escaper and a survivor of torture by the Gestapo, the prisoners execute their plan with the utmost ingenuity, building not only three tunnels, but also producing perfectly forged passes and brilliantly tailored civilian clothes. Finally, the night of the escape arrives, and when the tunnel is broken, the POWs are shocked to find that it falls some fifty feet short of woods. Because of this, and other mishaps, fewer than 80 manage to break free from the camp, which is nevertheless a brilliant achievement. However, of these, only three manage to make it home, and the remaining escapers are recaptured as they flee through various parts of the Third Reich. At the end of the film, as fifty of the POWs are supposedly being driven back to the camp, they are invited to stretch their legs in a field, whereupon they are all shot dead on the order of a vengeful Adolf Hitler.

As films based on actual events go, the outline of *The Great Escape* is reasonably faithful to the true story of the mass breakout of prisoners from Stalag Luft III in Poland in March 1944. Although a few of the *dramatis personae* are drawn on real personalities, many are necessary composites in order not to overburden the movie with characters. 'Roger Bartlett', as played by Richard Attenborough, is perhaps the most accurately drawn, based on a Squadron Leader Roger Bushell, who did indeed play a leading role in organising the escape. Many of the details of how the civilian clothes and documents were produced are reasonably accurate, although the results in the film are distinctly more accomplished than their real counterparts. The relationship between the Germans and their captives is also well observed, and rings true to the reminiscences of the men who were there. However, as is to be expected, there is much in the film that is either sensational – a certain motorcycle chase comes immediately to mind – or simply wrong – the weather is exceptionally fine in the film, whereas at the time it was freezing and thick snow lay around.

From a historical point of view, the film contains two great failings. The first is tone. Much of the movie is comic, and although it is this quality that helps to make the film a classic, it does a disservice to the grimness of the real tale. It is in that grimness in which the second fault lies, which concerns the emphasis placed on the murders. Notwithstanding the incorrect depiction of the men's executions, the film – quite necessarily for a jaunty blockbuster – does not dwell on these killings. This ignores the fundamental fact that it is the execution of 'the Fifty' that distinguishes the real story of the Great Escape from the numerous other mass breakouts conducted by Allied POWs from German camps. Ultimately, the Great Escape is a story as much about a terrible crime as it is about heroism and ingenuity. If this seems wilfully mawkish, then it is worth noting that the other mass breakouts – no less great, no less ingenious – have all been forgotten. It is undoubtedly the murders that set this story apart.

The purpose of (my) book is to ascertain the real story behind the escape. Of course, there have been other books about the breakout, not least those by Paul Brickhill, himself a former '*Kriegie*' – the POW slang for POW, derived from the German for 'prisoner of war' – at Stalag Luft III, who wrote two accounts of the breakout; *Escape to Danger* in 1946, and *The Great Escape* in 1951. Both accounts are suitably exciting, but what they lack is objectivity and analysis. Furthermore, as he wrote them shortly after the war, Brickhill was not able to draw upon the vast amount of material contained in archives in Britain, Germany and the United States. As a result, his books contain many errors, many of which are forgivable, but some of which are clearly the result of needing to make the story commercially appealing. Many of the histories that followed Brickhill have built upon his somewhat shaky foundations, and as a result, the errors have been magnified, and many new ones have been inserted. Previous historians of the escape have relied far too heavily on the book that came before, and, with two exceptions, very little attention has been paid to the wealth of primary sources. Not one of these books offers a fresh perspective, or even raises any pertinent questions. As a result of the clumsy application of too much varnish, the true story of the Great Escape has been almost totally obscured.

Historians always like to claim that their work is a 'new history', and I do not claim to be exceptional. This *is* a new history because I have attempted to strip back all those layers of varnish. The best tool for that process is archival work, and I have been surprised – but not shocked – at the enormous disparities between the documents and the histories. What has also raised my eyebrows is the ubiquity of downright fabrication in the memoirs of some of the escapers themselves, which cannot be explained away as the product of faltering memories. Trying to resolve the differences between those memoirs, histories, interviews and wartime files has nevertheless proved to be an enjoyable task, not least because that is the job of the historian.

After removing the varnish, the next task is the restoration, and it is during this process that big questions need to be asked. In the case of the Great Escape, there are several. What was the real purpose of the breakout? What did it achieve? What was the motivation of Roger Bushell? What warnings did the POWs receive before they broke out? Was it really the duty of an officer to escape? How many men actually wanted to escape? How much assistance did the POWs receive from their German captors? Who were the men who carried out the executions of the fifty escapers? Was it right that these men were hanged after the war? Does the escape really deserve a place in our national consciousness? In short, was the Great Escape really that great?

Such questions may make some suppose I approached this subject with a preformed iconoclastic agenda, but they should be assured that I did not. My only object was simply to tell the story from scratch, as if the film and all those other books had never been released. This history, therefore, is based as much as possible on primary sources, and what those sources reveal is a very different tale to the one that we are used to. In addition, as well as presenting a narrative of the escape itself and examining some of the camp's leading lights, these pages also tell the story of the murders that followed, and examine the decisions taken by the men who pulled the triggers. After all, the story of the Great Escape is as much theirs as that of the escapers. Some of the conclusions I draw will doubtless cause discomfort, but my findings are based on evidence and not prejudice. Readers should also be aware that my approach emphatically does not make me a killjoy. The real Great Escape you hold in your hands is just as exciting and absorbing as the almost fictional version you currently have in your head. The only bad news is that nobody escaped on a motorbike, but then you probably already suspected as much.

****

Chairman of the Colditz Society, David Ray, describes the iconic camp for allied officers, Oflag IVc better known as Colditz Castle. Renowned for being the most difficult POW camp to escape from, David describes the various escape methods used and some of the prisoners who made escapes, both successful and otherwise.

Oflag IVc, Colditz Castle

Colditz Castle was unique in Nazi Germany during World War II in that it was a multi-national and multi-service prisoner of war camp. It was also meant to be escape-proof. Hauptmann Reinhold Eggers, security officer, wondered why the authorities had put '*all the rotten eggs into a place that was meant to stop people getting in while his job was to stop people getting out*'. It was a place of tension and atmosphere, where men of spirit were continually looking at ways to inconvenience the Germans and get home.

The easiest method to explain the escape history is to consider over, through and under the defences. A few examples will suffice. The famous glider, the brain child of a Royal Artillery officer, was constructed but never flown. It was going to be used as a last resort should the Germans start to eliminate the inmates or march them away from the fast approaching Americans. Frenchman Mairesse-Lebrun was catapulted by a fellow prisoner over the exercise wire in the park in July 1941. Under heavy fire he got away in singlet and shorts and eventually reached France via Gibraltar. Douglas Bader showed interest in climbing over the roofs of the castle with two other prisoners. The legless airman was eventually persuaded that there might be a more realistic way of exiting the castle. Mike Sinclair and Jack Best had sixty seconds to get out of a second floor window, across a terrace and garden and through a barbed wire fence. As the extra sentry came on duty they were scrambling down the final precipice. They reached the Dutch border before recapture. So much for *'over'* examples.

'Through' case studies meant appearing as a German civilian or someone in the Wehrmacht. French Lieutenant Boulay received a number of parcels from his wife. Gradually he built up a complete ladies outfit from hat and wig through blouse and dress to shoes and a handbag. Shedding his greatcoat on a walk down to the park he began to make his way back up towards the castle. His watch came off, a British prisoner, unaware of the transformation, drew the attention of a sentry to the dropped item and that was the end of that attempt. Airey Neave first tried to walk out of the main gate as an *Unteroffizier* but his uniform was poorly made and he was detained half way out of the castle. Five months later his disguise was first class and he got away as a German Lieutenant with a Dutch officer. The first home run by the British contingent.

'*Under*' must start with the French tunnel. The other nationalities as well as the Germans heard the work going on for months. It reached forty-four metres in length and reached eight and a half metres below the level of the courtyard; its route starting in a cellar and then progressing under the chapel and the sixteenth century foundations. Just four metres from breaking it was discovered. Three British prisoners tried to get out through the sewers. Unfortunately the drain got narrower and narrower. You can imagine what state they were in when a sentry detected a noise under a manhole cover in the approach yard. Six prisoners exited the castle into a clothing store by digging a short tunnel from the locked office of *Oberstabsfeldwebel* Gephard. Two got home; again a British officer and a Dutchman. Sadly the British officer was killed test flying over Wiltshire before the end of the war.

In a camp of characters, Flight Lieutenant Peter Tunstall stands out. He was court martialled four times, got off twice and served a total of over four hundred days of solitary confinement. On liberation he still owed the Germans twenty four days. At his final trial in Leipzig the judge spoke to him after the guilty decision had been reached. The war was entering its final phase and the judge realised the way the wind was blowing. Making sure they were not overhead, the judge said, *'If I give you twelve months the Allies will not be happy. If I give you three months the Nazis will be angry. Will you accept six months?'* Peter agreed. When the US forces liberated the castle on 16th April 1945 the prisoners had taken charge of the castle. The guards still patrolled but the inmates had the keys to the weapons and ammunition stores. The Americans had lost three platoon sergeants in the battle for Colditz. They were in no mood to treat any German with kid gloves. *'Any kraut you want taken out and dealt with?'* they inquired. The former prisoners said no, most of them had behaved pretty well over the last four and a half years. Two days later the prisoners were back in Blighty.

****

John Kelleher describes the daring escape attempt by his father, Denis 'DK' Kelleher, whilst a POW in north-east Germany. Captured at Tobruk alongside 33,000 other prisoners in January 1942, DK escaped in February 1944 and arrived back in England via Sweden a month later.

Denis Kelleher – Escape from Germany

This is the story of Denis Kelleher's daring escape from a German prisoner of war camp in 1944.

The youngest of six children born to Irish immigrants, Denis Kelleher (known to family and friends as 'DK') was 20 years old when Britain declared war on Germany. The son of a policeman, DK was living in Coulsdon, Surrey in 1939 and worked for the Metropolitan Water Board. Responding to the national call to arms, DK, who was a talented sportsman and doubtless keen for adventure, decided to join the Royal Navy.

On the evening of 21st June 1942, the second Battle of Tobruk was over when Major-General Klopper surrendered to Rommel, having spent four long days defending this vital port from lethal German attack; newly promoted to Field Marshal on the back of his victory, Rommel captured 33,000 allied prisoners, including 19,000 British troops: Denis Kelleher was one of them.

DK had almost avoided capture the evening before the surrender of Tobruk; having received orders to return to his ship, DK had boarded a small tank-landing craft. Unfortunately, within a few minutes of embarking, the vessel's engine was hit by a shell from onshore and began to sink. Having no alternative other than to swim to shore,

DK was subsequently captured and taken to the aerodrome, along with the other allied prisoners.

Between July 1942 and September 1943, DK was held in four different prisoner of war camps in Italy. In the last of these camps, Campo 19 in Bologna, there had been a mass attempt to escape but most of the escapees (including DK) were rounded up within hours.

In 1943, as the tide began to turn against the Germans, it was decided to move the officers to more secure camps in Germany. Despite several unsuccessful escape attempts by allied officers during transit to the station, they were eventually loaded into cattle trucks with no more than a bottle of water and a Red Cross parcel to last each man for the five day journey.

Over the next two months, the British officers were moved between several different camps until, at the beginning of November 1943, they arrived at Marlag und Milag O (the 'O' was for officer), near Westertimke in north eastern Germany. It was here that DK met his future escape partner – Lieutenant Stewart Campbell RNVR.

By January 1944, the two men had already come up with a plan to escape, despite the obvious risks. It was an audacious plan which required them to pass themselves off as Germans so that they could join the German ship SS *Waal* at Rostock. In order to do this and have any chance of convincing the authorities, DK and Campbell had forged *Ausweis* (identity cards) and a letter from the government-run employment service (the *Arbeitsamt*) in Wilhelmshaven to the harbour master in Rostock. The document stated that

Campbell was a third officer and DK a ship's engineer. To prepare them for pulling off this ambitious deception, the men had had six German lessons from fellow prisoner, Sub Lieutenant Jackson, who taught them how to ask for train tickets and enquire about platforms. In keeping with accepted procedure, DK and Campbell put their plan to the camp's escape committee and, after several attempts, it was signed off.

Two other prisoners keen to escape (McLister and Taylor) had noticed that one of the perimeter lamps was fused, leaving 50 yards of perimeter fence in the shadows. This could give the four men a vital opportunity to get through the fence unseen. It was still, however, a perilous plan since, as a result of multiple escape attempts, the prisoners had to be in their barracks by 1800hrs and the guards had been instructed to shoot on sight anyone trying to breakout. As an additional incentive, the guard responsible for any failing would also be shot.

It was arranged that both the barrack guard and the sentry patrolling the fence would be distracted by staged arguments amongst the prisoners although this was not actually needed since, on the night of the escape, the sentry guard was absent from camp.

At 1850hrs on 22nd February 1944, McLister cut the wire of the fence in just seven minutes, allowing him and Taylor to escape. After the next searchlight sweep, DK and Campbell rushed to follow them. In less than a minute, they were lying flat on the ground on the other side of the fence desperate to avoid the searchlight. With the voices of shouting sentries and barking dogs ringing in their ears, the two men crawled on their hands and knees for 100 yards to reach a cart track that ran parallel to the perimeter fence.

With the most dangerous part of their plan completed, DK and Campbell, dressed in their naval uniforms, adapted to look like merchant seaman's attire, headed for the local town of Tarmstedt to catch the last train to Bremen. With just 50 marks each as well as maps of the main towns and the harbour area in Rostock (the latter were provided by MI9), the men began their long and nerve-wracking journey back to Britain. The camp's escape committee had given them escape cakes for the journey (made from porridge, margarine, sugar and cocoa) and they also had a shaving kit, a towel and a bar of soap to enable them to disguise their escapee identity.

When the men arrived at Tarmstedt to catch the last train to Bremen at 2000hrs, they were dismayed to find they had missed it. Anxious to leave the local area before the alarm was raised, DK and Campbell decided to walk the 30 km to Bremen. After an anxious five-hour walk, the men arrived at Bremen in the early hours of the morning. Unfortunately, the next train to Hamburg was not until 0400hrs so they did their best to blend in with the locals by buying a glass of beer and settling down to wait in the station's waiting room.

On arriving in Hamburg, the men intended to catch a train to Rostock but, on seeing a train to Lubeck (a port further down the coast from Rostock), they decided against waiting for the Rostock train and head for Lubeck. Their papers were examined and, after an anxiety-inducing hesitation, the men were allowed to board the train.

Arriving in Lubeck at 0900hrs, DK and Campbell headed for the docks where they noticed a 400 ton Swedish collier but they were unable to board it due to a heavy guard presence. After a failed attempt to catch a connecting train to Rostock, the weary men returned to the docks only to find that the collier had now sailed. Exhausted and hungry, with no further trains that night, the men decided to spend the night in a nearby air raid shelter.

As they had now run out of money, a train journey to Rostock seemed out of the question, so in the morning of the 24th February, DK and Campbell tore up their forged letter to the harbour master at Rostock and headed once more to the docks at Lubeck.

Having failed to get aboard a Swedish ship moored in the harbour, the men wandered around the docks, increasingly desperate and hungry, taking cover from air raids and planning how to get aboard the Swedish ship, which had now been moved to a guarded area of the harbour.

After climbing over a barbed wire fence, unfortunately located next to a German minesweeper, and evading another sentry patrolling the quayside, the men ran up the gangway and onto the Swedish ship. On opening the door to the officers' kitchen quarters, DK and Campbell found two women, a matron and stewardess and introduced themselves as British naval officers. As the women spoke little English, they took the men to the ship's officer who explained he could not help them, as he would be shot if they were discovered. Just when it looked as though their luck had run out, the ship's cook, who spoke reasonable English, offered to help them as the British Navy had once saved his life.

Unfortunately, the ship was not due to leave the port for five days so the cook, and then the matron, at considerable risk to themselves, hid the men in their cabins.

At 0400hrs on 27th February, DK and Campbell were taken to the engine room to hide as the ship was due to be searched before departure; the men lay under the boiler in 3cm of water for over 70 hours managing to evade the guards searching the ship. Eventually, with the escapees still under the boiler suffering unbearable heat, the ship sailed at 0730hrs on 29th February. DK and Campbell were introduced to the ship's captain early the next day. As a precaution, he refused to hear any details about them and their escape, but allowed them to have a bath and gave them dry clothes.

Nine days after DK and Campbell had escaped from Marlag und Milag (two of only three men to ever escape from the camp), the Swedish ship arrived in Stockholm where the men were handed over to the police. As a neutral country, the Swedish police were able to hand the men over to the British authorities in Stockholm. With great relief, DK and Campbell arrived home in England on the 16th March 1944. DK was awarded the military MBE shortly afterwards.

Undeterred by his experience, DK, an Irish Amateur Soccer player, had cabled his club Barnet from Stockholm to announce that he was available for selection the following Saturday. Accordingly, on Saturday 18th March, two days after his arrival, DK played in the team's semi-final of the Amateur cup, scoring two goals and securing a win for Barnet.

Barnet went on to win the Amateur cup two years later in 1946 with DK scoring the winning goal. He was later selected to play for Ireland after the war and, in 1948, was picked to play association football for Great Britain in the London Olympic Games. DK went on to qualify as a Doctor of Medicine at St Mary's Hospital in 1952 and married Anne in 1953. The couple had six children together and Denis worked as a GP in South London until he retired in 1988.

Dr Denis Kelleher MBE died in February 2002 aged 83, almost 60 years after his capture in Tobruk.

****

Historian and writer Helen Fry, describes the role of MI9 and the escape lines that were built up across to Europe to assist allied prisoners and particularly airmen to get back to Britain or neutral countries. MI9 provided all manner of materials including maps and compasses, for both escapees and the brave local people who assisted them return via Spain, Switzerland, Italy, Sweden and elsewhere. It was a substantial organisation covering many people of numerous differing skill-sets required to help get 'our boys home'. It is estimated over 35,000 allied servicemen made it home through the escape lines network.

MI9, Escape, Evasion

MI9 is best known for the daring exploits of escape and evasion in the Second World War. The extensive and superb histories of MI9 written after the war by Airey Neave, and Foot and Langley are hard to better. However, new research from declassified files can now expand on their work to reveal just how important MI9 was for the wider wartime clandestine operations and even as an important intelligence gathering organisation. Its operations were not limited to Western Europe, but also the Balkans, Greece, Eastern Europe, the Middle East and Far East.

Formed by special charter on 23rd December 1939, MI9 was a branch of the British Secret Service responsible for gaining intelligence from prisoners, whether enemy prisoners-of-war or Allied personnel trapped behind enemy lines or in POW camps. It began as two branches: the first was MI9(a) which dealt with enemy prisoners and these were taken to special sites after capture and their conversations bugged for intelligence (later became MI19). This was the subject of my book *The Walls Have Ears*. The second was MI9(b) which aided British personnel to evade capture in enemy territory or escape from German POW camps (this later simply became MI9 after MI9(a) became MI19).

Stories like Airey Neave's escape from the infamous Colditz Castle in Germany – from which the Germans believed it impossible to escape – have become legendary. Historical examples of escapes, like prisoners tunnelling out of Stalag Luft III near Sagan or tunnelling under a wooden vault, have been immortalised in big screen films like *The Great Escape* and *The Wooden Horse*. Underpinning MI9's existence was a philosophy of *'escape-mindedness'*, a term first coined by its chief, Brigadier Norman Crockatt.

Crockatt knew that techniques in escape and evasion might not come naturally to personnel in the moments immediately after capture and disorientation. Therefore prior to going into action, personnel were trained by MI9 in aspects of escape and evasion techniques.

The organisation's role was broader and included the collection and distribution of information to British and Allied prisoners in POW camps via clandestine means, such as coded messages and smuggling escape and evasion devices into the camps. MI9's officer Christopher Clayton Hutton designed many of the ingenious gadgets in which silk maps and miniature compasses could be hidden. The MI9 gadgets were an extraordinary success story. Between 1942 and 1945, MI9 organised the manufacture and issue of 1.3 million round brass compasses, 1.6 million maps concealed in purses and pouches, and over 7,000 flying boots that converted into civilian shoes for personnel on the run. The rapid production of devices in such large quantities was essential to successful escape and evasion and survival.

Prime Minister Winston Churchill, himself a POW and escapee in the Boer War, understood the difficulties which prisoners had to bear. He sent a rallying message to British POWs to boost their morale: *'In this great struggle in which we are engaged, my thoughts are often with you who have had the misfortune to fall into the hands of the Nazis. Your lot is a hard one... never has the country been so completely united in its determination to exterminate Nazidom.'*

If there is a strong theme which emerges in MI9's history, it is the commitment and courage of thousands of helpers –

women and men – who led the escape lines, and acted as couriers and guides across Europe. They were prepared to work in secret, for an unnamed organisation in Britain whose name they did not discover until after the war. All were united in their efforts to free Europe from Nazi occupation. Through simple and ordinary acts of resistance, they made a crucial contribution to saving Allied airmen and soldiers, often at great personal risk and with severe consequences if betrayed. The risks were increased if they smuggled intelligence to MI9's agents or over the border from behind enemy lines. Although the escape lines of MI9 and MI6 were controlled by MI6's man Claude Dansey (the deputy of MI6), to keep the lines operationally separate, the daily coordination for the MI9 side was delegated by Dansey to Jimmy Langley and Airey Neave. But as they later admitted, the real risks were taken in occupied Europe, the Middle East or Far East. Men like Harold Cole and Christiaan Lindemans ('King Kong') sabotaged the escape lines for their personal gain, often for money, which led to helpers and guides being betrayed, tortured and sent to concentration camps or shot by the Gestapo.

Extraordinary Sacrifice

An inspirational part of MI9's legacy are some of the stories emerging about the women leaders and helpers. They displayed extraordinary acts of bravery, all trusted the mysterious organisation that they worked for and believed that victory over the Nazis was possible by their acts of resistance. They saved the lives of hundreds of airmen and soldiers. One of those women I interviewed in Brussels, and now in her late nineties, was Elsie Maréchal. Her

383

interview was transformational for me during the writing of my recent new book on the history of MI9.

I was moved by her story – her whole family and she herself were betrayed in 1942 with devastating consequences. Yet, her spirit of defiance – still evident today – came through as I asked her why she risked her life at the age of only 16 to shelter Allied airmen whilst working for the Comet Line. She replied: *'Under German occupation things became worse each day. Trains were leaving every day from Brussels to Germany, packed with food and supplies. Our nation was being robbed of food and coal. We had a shortage of food. I saw the posters and the Germans every day. I saw all the Jews with yellow stars – children taken from my school class to Auschwitz. We thought 'out with the Nazis!'*

As the Comet Line temporarily went down after a series of betrayals, Elsie spent 3 years in Nazi prisons and concentration camps. Through all this she never wavered in her support for the Allies. Elsie Maréchal remains humble about her wartime contribution but still displays the same fighting spirit as over 70 years ago.

The Comet Line was led by two other inspirational women: Dedée (Andrée de Jongh) from Brussels, then Paris, and Elvire de Greef – a Belgian woman who operated for MI9 with her family on the Basque side of the Pyrenees. It ran from Brussels to Paris and down to the Pyrenees.

Dedée trekked hundreds of miles from Brussels to the Pyrenees with her 'parcels' [as the airmen and evaders were called]. Although young she led the Comet Line until her arrest in 1943. She also survived concentration camps. Elvire de Greef was the unspoken heroine and leader in the south of France, instrumental in running Comet Line operations along the Pyrenees from 1940 until the end of the war. She arranged the shelter of escapees and evaders in safe houses in the region until they could be smuggled into Spain. Defiant in danger, she blackmailed officials to avoid arrest and organised for other members of the escape line to be broken out of prison. As the Comet Line went down, she continued to rescue airmen and smuggle vital intelligence, with other members of her family, to the Allies.

There was also Mary Lindell, a British woman married to a French aristocrat who became the first woman to be trained by Room 900 (a top secret part of MI9) and dropped back into France as an agent. She established an escape route near Ruffec. With a steely and tenacious spirit she aided many escapees and evaders in France and risked her life on many occasions, spending time in Nazi prisons. Although seriously ill in hospital, she discharged herself to be able to save the Cockleshell Heroes – the only 2 survivors of the commando raid *Operation Frankton*. Still wanted by the Nazis, she was arrested in 1943 and suffered terrible torture in prisons and concentration camps. Her spirit unbroken, she was described as one of the most colourful agents.

These women, and thousands of male helpers and guides, all played their part in numerous escape lines that included the Pat Line, the Rome Escape Organisation, the Shelburne Line and other sea evacuations. Many did not survive and paid with their lives for helping the escape lines.

The Legacy

Traditionally MI9 has been seen as an organisation that solely ran escape lines and agents, and this was indeed a large part of its work. But new research has revealed that MI9's role went beyond escape and evasion to engage in intelligence and counter-espionage work; some of it along the lines traditionally the domain of MI6. MI9's intelligence-gathering included debriefing returning airmen and soldiers and interrogating members of the escape lines who had to be exfiltrated by MI9 back to Britain. They all provided a vast amount of information from enemy territory that could be used in future training and printed in the MI9 bulletins. Amongst examples of intelligence gathered was that of a military nature on enemy defences, ports and sea defences, Axis fighting units, and general life and circumstances behind enemy lines. There had been no precedent for escape work *combined with intelligence* in the First World War. The official declassified history of MI9 in the National Archives states that *'clandestine escape work as a specialist form of intelligence was an entirely new development.'* Thousands of interrogation reports of returning escapees and evaders survive in the archives. No two escape stories were the same; each had a unique set of circumstances and useful information for MI9 as well as intelligence about the enemy.

The history of MI9 was as much about those who made up this highly secret branch of military intelligence as the daily workings and structure of the organisation itself. Its success was largely due to the diversity of people who came together quite by chance in wartime and who would probably never have crossed paths in peacetime. From its small beginnings in 1939, the organisation evolved into a highly efficient branch of military intelligence. The success of the escape lines would only be realised at the end of the war when it became known that, in spite of the dangers and difficulties of German occupation, around 35,000 Allied soldiers and airmen made it back to Allied lines because of MI9. New research now shows that MI9's legacy deserves recognition as an intelligence organisation and should be placed alongside the wider intelligence operations of the Second World War.

Helen Fry's new book *MI9: The Secret Service for Escape and Evasion* was published on 8th September 2020.

****

Roger Fowkes recounts the story of his aunt, Phyllis Hutchinson, who survived being torpedoed in the Indian Ocean on the way to Ceylon. Approximately 500 of the 600 people on board lost their lives. Rescued by a destroyer, this ship was then badly holed whilst ramming a Japanese submarine. Her personal account of the experience and her remarkable survival is given below.

On Active Service

On 12th February 1944, a convoy of troop ships, escorted by two destroyers and a cruiser of the Royal Navy, was proceeding through the Indian Ocean from Mombasa, the main port of East Africa, to Colombo, port of disembarkation in Ceylon. The convoy was transporting European and East African personnel, with necessary equipment and stores, for service with the 14th Army in Burma.

The commodore's ship in the centre of the convoy, an Egyptian vessel - the *Khedive Ismail* - carried, in addition to various other units, including contingents of WRNS and East African FANYS, a complete unit of matron and fifty-three nursing sisters to staff the 150th (EA) General Hospital destined to be the base hospital for the 11th (EA) Division. The convoy was expected to reach Colombo in about two days, and that morning, orders had been given as to disembarkation kit and the wearing of steel helmets.

It was a lovely sunny afternoon, with a few white clouds drifting lazily across a blue sky, the sea a clear blue green. Many people were resting in their cabins others sunbathing on the decks, a concert for the WOs and sergeants was in progress in the saloon, strains of music drifted pleasantly forth, and a feeling of peace pervaded the ship, war seemed utterly remote. Without the slightest warning of any kind the peace and the ship were rudely shattered by a terrific explosion occurring amidships on the starboard side, the result of a torpedo, fired from a Japanese submarine, which had suddenly surfaced about forty yards from the *Khedive*, right in the middle of the convoy.

The music ceased abruptly in the saloon, the crashing of fallen debris and an occasional scream took place, the bright sunshine was instantly succeeded by the gloom caused by dark smoke, and debris flying everywhere, there was the acrid smell of cordite, and the sensation of the great ship listing rapidly to starboard. Another torpedo crashed into

388

the bows and the ship broke up like so much matchwood and sank in less than a minute.

There was no time for lowering the lifeboats or attempting to muster, hardly time for the brain to realise that disaster had doomed the vessel, each person fought for survival, help of any kind was out of the question. In the saloon there was a mad rush for the doors leading on to the boat deck, unfortunately the furniture broke loose from the moorings crushing several people, then the deck gave way and they crashed down into the dark depths of the ship where they lay wounded and helpless, until the sea swept in; mercifully they did not suffer long.

Of the 600 people on board only about 80 Europeans and the same number of Africans managed to escape, nearly five hundred lost their lives. The survivors clung to bits of wreckage strewn about in the sea. Only one life-boat was flung clear of the wreck and that was crowded. There were many wounded aboard including the three Sisters, sole survivors of the unit of fifty-four which had set off from East Africa with such high hopes.

After a few hours one of the destroyers hove to and a motor boat was lowered which speedily picked up the survivors. They clambered up swaying rope ladders and sailors were ready waiting to help them on to the deck above, welcome cups of tea and cigarettes were handed out by the sailors on the destroyer, then all the European survivors were taken down to the wardroom, where clean sailors' clothes and towels were in readiness for them. The Africans were tended elsewhere. Before the survivors had time to change their sodden clothing a stentorian voice rang down from the top deck '*Get out and lie flat, about to ram submarine*'.

No sooner had they obeyed the command, lying packed like sardines in the barrow space outside the wardroom than there was a horrible rending sound on the starboard side as the two vessels collided. The lights went out, oil and water started seeping up and the destroyer listed heavily to starboard; a great rent having been tom in her side. The survivors scrambled up on to the top deck in time to see a large submarine drawing away from the side of the destroyer and gradually submerging. There was a rat-a-a-tat-tat of machine gun fire and the terrific noise of four-inch guns firing salvoes. The destroyer was a hive of activity with sailors working frantically to save the vessel, endeavouring to shut off the damaged compartments below, working the pumps, jettisoning heavy gear and manning the guns. It was hoped that the submarine was fatally damaged, but after a short time it suddenly surfaced and came straight for the damaged destroyer, where it lay like a crippled duck unable to move. Fortunately, a torpedo fired from the second destroyer struck it before it had time to ram, and it blew up, throwing a mighty column of water high in the air. There were no survivors.

The survivors of the *Khedive Ismail* and most of the crew of the destroyer *Paladin* were transferred from the damaged vessel to the second destroyer and the former was taken in tow. The next day both destroyers put in at the Maldives. The cruiser in the meantime, had escorted the other troopships safely away from the scene of disaster and returned the following day to effect temporary repairs to the damaged destroyer and to take off survivors and carry them safely to Colombo.

The officers and men of the Royal Navy were simply wonderful, so very kind and considerate, and set a grand example of courage. Let us hope that all those who perished in the *'Khedive'* and thousands of others did not die in vain. By remembrance of them and practising sympathetic understanding between ourselves and other nations, we can contribute to future world's peace.

Miss Hutchinson's personal experience of being torpedoed in the Indian Ocean in 1944
I have found that people are apt to categorise one as:- (a) an object of pity (b) heroic character. I am neither, merely a fortunate survivor; any pity or applause should be reserved for the unfortunate ones and the necessary wheels set in motion to prevent any possible recurrences of like nature.

I was standing on the boat deck amidships, on the port side of the late ship *Khedive Ismail*, about to go below to do some ironing on the afternoon of Saturday, 12th February 1944, when the first Japanese torpedo struck the vessel on the starboard side. The impact flung me forward on to the deck. There was a huge hole in the ship and I saw two of my friends disappear. The mast and the superstructure crashed, the ship rapidly developed a heavy list to starboard, thick smoke and debris obscured my view. I scrambled to my feet, grabbed a lifebelt slipping past me on the sloping deck and hastily donned it; I hadn't time to fasten it properly when the second torpedo tore into the bows of the ship. Nobody was near me to advise or help, a matter of seconds for the brain to realise that disaster had struck, instinctively I acted, jumping as far away from the ship as possible, remembering to hold the front of my life jacket to prevent it jerking my neck.   Time 2:40pm.

Flying debris must have struck the back of my head (as evidenced by a large egg-shaped swelling later).   I was unaware of it and have no recollection of entering the sea. Later I came to and found myself deep in the ocean, being dragged down by a terrific suction, rather like being in the grip of a giant octopus; I did not feel anything and was blissfully ignorant of the fact that I was drowning peacefully.

The dead body of a girl shooting past me partially restored my numbed senses, I was instantly aware of my danger, aware of the dark green gloom, the uncanny silence and the noiseless destruction of the great ship disintegrating in the water.   My spirit rebelled against the whole ghastly affair, strangely enough I never thought of death although I was perilously near it. I kicked out frantically and endeavoured to swim upwards.   I was soon conscious of a strange suffocating feeling in my chest; most uncomfortable.

I suppose I must have been on the edge of a vacuum because suddenly the suction ceased and I shot upwards. A pale greenish-white patch above my head grew rapidly larger and then came the wonderful moment when my head rose above it and I saw the sun high up in the sky. I dazedly thought how odd it was that I had not associated the patch of light with the reflection of the sun on the water.

I floated for a short time, trying to get a little air into my overtaxed lungs and to regain some strength as I was very exhausted.   Queer rumbling underwater explosions disturbed me (due to depth charges dropped by two destroyers I discovered later) had a weird effect on my body, a kind of vibrant shakiness and a sickening feeling of insecurity.

Again the instinct for self-preservation came to my rescue, objects came into focus again, an overturned boat about twenty yards away was the nearest solid thing. With a great effort I managed to swim to it and I shall forever remember the wonderful thrill of touching something solid and substantial again, as I grasped the hard wood of the boat and my cheek rested against it. There were nine Africans and another member of the EAMNS on top of the keel, two of the Africans leaned over, placed their hands under my armpits and heaved me up. I collapsed across the keel, water cascading out of my nose and mouth, I idly thought how disgusting such a performance was in front of the askari. Then I entered a peculiar state, time, past, present and future merged, I knew everything and I knew nothing, was unaware of physical pain or anything going on around me. As from a great distance I became conscious of the other sister calling my name, I was drowsy and didn't wish to be disturbed; the voice came clearer and I was aware of anxiety in the tone of it. I realised there were other human beings alive and to be considered; with a great effort of will I managed to reply that I was alright and so came back to life again.

Presently I pulled myself up into a sitting position and took stock of my surroundings - no trace of the *Khedive Ismail* except for a few bits of wreckage strewn over the sea, two destroyers scouting around dropping depth charges, which caused our craft to rock perilously, the cruiser and other merchant ships speeding away to the horizon. I looked at my watch - a Grana, shock proof and water proof - it had lived up to its reputation and was still going? Five minutes had elapsed since the previous time I had looked at it on the boat deck and warned my friend it was time for us to go below to use the iron, it seemed quite unbelievable.

The Africans were calm and stoical, bewildered ebony figures. I assured them we should soon be picked up, badly needing reassurance on that point myself. One wisely asked how long it would take us to reach land!

We were picked up after a few hours and taken aboard a destroyer where we received the utmost kindness and attention, no tribute can be too great for the Royal Navy; it is magnificent.

****

Part 3 - Post 1945 Conflicts

The formation of the United Nations following the Second World War was intended to ensure peace was maintained between nations by providing a forum for *'jaw, jaw rather than war, war'* as attributed to Churchill. To an extent, by avoiding world-wide conflict and further use of atomic and later nuclear weapons, the UN has achieved it aims, albeit narrowly at times. However, barely a second has passed when there has not been military conflict somewhere on the globe.

Civil Wars from the Hindu - Muslim civil war surrounding partition, to the Hutus and Tutsis in Rwanda, and in Bosnia and Kosovo, to the dictatorships of Pol Pot and Saddam Hussein to the wars by French forces in Algeria and Indo-China and the Americans in Vietnam to name but some.

Britain too has been involved in an almost continuous cycle of wars, civil wars, emergencies, rebellions and peacekeeping operations. She has acted mainly with allies but sometimes alone and there are very few years in the second half of the 20th century and the first 20 years of the 21st century in which British forces have not been actively deployed.

One of the first tasks facing British forces was the **Greek Civil War** from 1944-48. The conflict was an ideological one with its roots pre-war and exacerbated by the split in the resistance movements in the Second World War. The Greek Government was supported by the UK and the US in training and financing the Greek army, who fought against the military branch of the Communist party of Greece, supported by Yugoslavia, Albania and Bulgaria, in fact proxies for Russian power.

The Malayan Emergency 1948-1960 was a conflict between Commonwealth armed forces and pro-independence fighters of the Malayan National Liberation Army (MNLA), the military wing of the Malayan Communist Party. The creation of an independent Malaya in 1957 did not stop the insurgency which continued until 1960. 40,000 regular British and Commonwealth troops were involved.

Britain was involved as part of the United Nations in the **Korean War** from 1950 to 1953. The post Second World War border between totalitarian North Korea under Kim Il-Sung and capitalist South Korea under Syngman Rhee was not accepted by either regime, and conflict broke out when the KPA, the Korean People's army, crossed the border in June 1950. A multinational United Nations force succeeded in pushing the KPA back into North Korea, resulting in the entry of Chinese troops in support of North Korea. The KPA and the Chinese forces then fought their way south into South Korea by December 1950. The front then stabilised into a war of stalemate and attrition on land. In the air, the United Nations conducted large bombing campaigns and Soviet pilots flew KPA planes. At one stage the United States was threatening the use of atomic weapons but was dissuaded by European leaders who feared an escalation of nuclear war into Europe. An armistice was signed in July 1953 but there has still been no peace treaty. There were three million war dead and many of the United Nations forces who became prisoners of war were badly treated.

British forces were involved in Kenya from 1952 where some of the Kikuyu tribe rose in the **Mau Mau Rebellion** against the European settlers and Kikuyu loyal to the government. From forest camps, members of the Mau Mau secret society carried out attacks on civil authorities and settlers. British troops reinforced local forces in response. British military operations ceased by November 1955 but the state of emergency continued to 1960.

In November 1956, British, Israeli and French troops responded to the nationalisation of the **Suez Canal** by Egypt's President Nasser with a combined military operation which involved British troops landing successfully near the canal. Under international pressure, mainly from the United States, the troops were withdrawn and replaced by a UN force. Egypt gained ownership and sovereignty of the Suez Canal. It was an ignominious episode for Britain and reinforced Britain's declining status as a world power.

After the Federation of South Arabia had been granted independence, the British Government maintained a permanent garrison in the port of **Aden,** a former crown colony, because of its strategic importance. Between 1963 and 1967, the National Liberation Front and the Front for the Liberation of South Yemen continued a series of attacks, bombings and urban terrorism on the British personnel, civilian and military in Aden. By June 1967, British forces had lost control and the last troops left Aden in November 1967. At the same time, from 1963 - 1976 British troops were aiding the Oman Government put down the **Dhofar Rebellion.** The rebels aim was the creation of an independent state of Dhofar, but also the broader objectives of Arab nationalism and the ending of British influence in the Persian Gulf. The rebels were defeated in 1976.

Nearer home the British Army were involved in **Northern Ireland** from the late 1960s. The British Army was deployed after clashes in Northern Ireland over civil rights, mainly in policing sectarian conflict and counter insurgency roles against the IRA. The incident which became known as Bloody Sunday increased Republican hostility to the British Army which became the target for terrorist attacks which spilled over into mainland Britain. There were two ceasefires in 1994 and 1996 and eventually the Good Friday Agreement mainly marked the end of the '*Troubles*'. The British Army was stood down from Northern Ireland on 1st September 2007. It was the longest deployment in the British army's history, lasting over 37 years. Our contributor Mike Spence gives an illuminating account of service in Northern Ireland during the '*Troubles*'.

The **Falklands War** of 1982, where the British Task Force sailed thousands of miles to the South Atlantic to recapture the islands from Argentine invaders as covered in more depth elsewhere. While not large in scale or duration, it was a staggering logistical feat, and proved that where political will with military expertise is in place, success can be achieved and a nation's pride restored. A separate section with articles on the Falklands War is included in this book.

From August 1990 to February 1991 British forces were involved in the **Gulf War**, codenamed **Operation Shield** in its military build-up phase and **Operation Desert Storm** in its combat phase. Coalition forces from 35 nations responded to Iraq's invasion of Kuwait. The force was led by the US with Britain taking a major role. A campaign of air and sea bombardment was followed by a successful land campaign which liberated Kuwait. This was probably the first major war played out in the full glare of international media and live reporting on a day-to-day basis.

The volatile situation in the former **Yugoslavia** involved Britain as part of NATO and WEA taking part in the conflicts there from 1992 to 1999. The breakup of Yugoslavia resulted in conflict between the Serbs who wanted a centralisation of Yugoslavia and other nationalities and ethnic groupings who wanted their own sovereign states. The situation was particularly tense in Bosnia where the population were a mixture of Muslim Bosnians, Serbs and Croats The **Bosnian War** 1992-1995 involved the United Nations Protection Force. British forces in Operation Grapple protected the humanitarian aid convoys. British forces served for nearly 15 years in Bosnia, suffering 50 fatal casualties and many more injured. The Royal Navy were engaged in Operation Sharp Guard which enforced the arms embargo and blockade of the former Yugoslavian countries.

In **Kosovo** in the late 1990s, conflict had been taking place between Serbian forces and the Kosovo Liberation army. NATO deployed peace keeping force KFOR to which Britain committed 4,000 troops. British troops entered Kosovo on 12th June 1999 after a NATO bombing campaign and the Serbian withdrawal from Kosovo was completed. There are still a small number of KFOR troops in Kosovo including British troops.

British troops deployed to **Afghanistan** with US troops and other allies in the wake of the 9/11 attack on the twin towers in pursuit of *Al Qaeda* and the *Taliban*. From 2002-2004, British troops worked with NATO as peacekeepers and in organising reconstruction. From 2004, Taliban insurgency increased and by 2006 the British forces were operating in Helmand province in Operation Herrick which had several phases. In 2009 Operation Panther's Claw was the British attempt to provide security for the elections, which resulted in 109 British deaths. In 2010, the British troops were involved in the 'surge' joint offensive in Helmand. 2001-2012 British troops were being withdrawn and all combat British combat missions were ended by December 2014. British forces remain in a training an advisory role based in Kabul.

Operation Telic was the name given to the British military involvement in a coalition invasion of Iraq from March 2003 until troops were withdrawn in May 2011. British troops were involved in occupying the ground around Basra and suffered heavy casualties but secured Basra by April 2003. The invasion was effectively over by May, but British troops were deployed in Iraq for another six years in a counter insurgency war, providing humanitarian aid and helping with reconstruction.

In 2020 British troops are currently involved in **Operation Shader,** intervention in Iraq and Syria, and ongoing naval operations in the Persian Gulf.

Career in the RAF - Malayan Emergency

I joined the RAF as a 15 year old boy entrant in 1947. After my training I was posted to RAF Boscombe Down, a very interesting station. It was the Aircraft and Armoury Experimental Establishment (A&AEE). Whilst there I guarded the new Canberra bomber and saw the Brabazon fly over the station.

At 18, I was posted to Malaya in the Far-East. I was posted up country to 65 Squadron which was a squadron of five flights, all in various locations in Malaya. It was the time of the Malayan Emergency when the Chinese Communists were trying to overthrow the government.

My flight was 1914 Flight and we were based in the jungle at a place called Temerloh. We shared a camp with the Gordon Highlanders. Our airstrip was five miles away between a river and a swamp. We had five Auster Mk5 aircraft. My job was an airframe fitter and I had to do the DIs on the planes every morning and service them where they needed it! All the pilots were Royal Artillery officers or glider pilot sergeants.

When the monsoons were on, we had to travel to work in DKWS (amphibious vehicles) as the roads were really flooded.

In 1951, we moved to a much nicer place, Seremban in the state of Negri Sembilan. Here the airstrip was on the camp, which we shared with 5th Gurkha, who were wonderful fellows.

Whilst there I met my best ever friend Denis (Ginger) Adams. He was also an airframe fitter and we shared all the work. There were also engine fitters, instrument fitters, electrical fitters, a photo mechanic, and in charge was an airframe sergeant. The flight CO was Captain Wheeler – a very decent sort.

Denis and I had a Matchless 350 motor bike and would go into the local town which was quite nice. There was a dance hall called *Yam Yam* and lots of good restaurants and a cinema, which showed mostly Egyptian films.

After a year we changed stations again and moved to Taiping (No 4 camp) in North Malaya. It had a proper airfield there with Malayan Airways doing daily flights to Kuala Lumpar, Singapore and Butterworth. We had a corner of the airfield with a compound surrounded by barbed wire.

Most of our work was spotting bandit camps and informing the army and the RAF so they could attack them. As I had to go up spotting, I got flying pay of one shilling and sixpence (1s. 6d.) a day... 7 1/2p in today's money!

Whilst there I met Sir Gerald Templar, the Commander in Chief, who gave us a run down on the new methods we were using against the commies.

In May 1953, I had done my tour of duty and returned home just in time for the Coronation!

****

American historian Ned Forney, based in South Korea, recounts the remarkable story of CSM Bennie Adkins in March 1966 serving with US Special Forces during the Vietnam War.

A Green Beret Legend - Bennie G. Adkins

'During the 38-hour battle and 48-hours of escape and evasion, Adkins fought with mortars, machine guns, recoilless rifles, small arms, and hand grenades, killing an estimated 135-175 of the enemy and sustaining 18 different wounds.' Medal of Honor citation for Command Sergeant Major Bennie G. Adkins

Drafted into the Army in 1956 at the age of 22, Bennie G. Adkins, a native of Waurika, Oklahoma, went to Airborne School, volunteered for Special Forces, and by 1963 was serving in Vietnam. Over the next seven years, he would serve three tours in Vietnam as a Green Beret, receive three Purple Hearts, and be awarded the Medal of Honor for actions at the Battle of A Shau.

During his time in Vietnam, Adkins and his men became experts at jungle warfare. *'You just do. Quitting isn't an option,'* Adkins remembered. *'That's what you train for. In the jungle environment, we became better than some of the North Vietnamese soldiers.'*

Nothing, however, would prepare him for 9th March, 1966.

While on his second tour of Vietnam, Sergeant First Class Adkins and the men of Detachment A-102, 5th Special Forces Group (Airborne), 1st Special Forces, were hit by an overwhelming North Vietnamese attack.

In a barrage of mortar rounds and rocket-propelled grenades, hundreds of communist soldiers infiltrated the American camp. During the ensuing bloody, 38-hour battle, Adkins used *'mortars, machine guns, recoilless rifles, small arms, and hand grenades'* to kill between 135 and 175 enemy soldiers. Repeatedly rushing through *'intense enemy fire,'* the seemingly fearless sergeant first class also rescued countless wounded Americans, dragging them to safety and whenever possible putting them on waiting helicopters.

At some point in the harrowing engagement, a South Vietnamese soldier who had changed sides and was now firing against the Americans, jumped into a US helicopter. When Adkins appeared at the chopper door to load an injured Green Beret, the former South Vietnamese man pointed his rifle at Adkins' face and prepared to fire. Before the soldier could pull the trigger, however, a stray bullet - fired from somewhere outside the helo – struck him in the chest, killing him instantly.

'It was not my day to go,' Adkins said during a televised news conference in 2015.

On the final day of the battle, with most Americans and South Vietnamese at A Shau base evacuated by helicopter, Adkins and a small group of survivors disappeared into the bush.

With Adkins as their leader, the men spent the next two days in the steamy, mud-filled jungle, with little water or food, hiding from North Vietnamese patrols until finally rescued by a helicopter. *'We were not going to be prisoners of war, whatever we had to do,'* Adkins told Stars and Stripes in 2015.

For his heroic actions from 9th to 12th March, 1966, Adkins was awarded the Distinguished Service Cross. Nearly fifty years later, however, after a Congressional review of DSC recipients, his award was upgraded to the Medal of Honor.

'The medal doesn't really belong to me. I'm just a keeper of it for those other 16 in the battle, especially the five who didn't make it,' he told reporters, friends, and fans.

Postscript:
After more than twenty years of service to his country and fellow soldiers, Adkins retired from the US Army in 1978 as a Command Sergeant Major and moved to Opelika, Alabama, with his wife.

In March 2020, he was diagnosed with COVID-19 and spent more than three weeks fighting for his life in the intensive care unit of East Alabama Medical Center. He succumbed to the disease on 17th April, 2020. He was 86.

'Command Sergeant Major Bennie G. Adkins departed this life today, with beloved family at his bedside,' the Bennie Adkins Foundation, an organisation created by Adkins in 2017 to provide educational scholarships to Special Forces soldiers transitioning from military to civilian life, reported.

His burial at Arlington National Cemetery is pending due to the pandemic.

****

Group Captain Christopher Finn shares his experiences as a navigator in the Fleet Air Arm on Buccaneers in the 1970s. Chris gives a fascinating insight to his training, navigating at night without radar using Dead Reckoning, weapons testing and launching from and landing on aircraft carriers.

The Buccaneer - A Navigator's View
Carrier Flying

Christopher Finn grew up in Cheshire and went to William Hulme's Grammar School in Manchester. His interest in flying was sparked by a flight from Blackpool in a Cessna Skylane when he was just twelve years old. He joined 1196 Bredbury, Romiley and Marple Squadron of the Air Training Corps in 1966, thus beginning an association with the RAF which lasts through to today. A couple of weeks after his 16th birthday, he gained the Gliding A and B Certificates on the open-cockpit Slingsby Cadet at RAF Spitalgate. Then, in the summer of 1971, he undertook a flying scholarship at Perth which gave him 30 hours flying on the single-engine Cessna 150. Chris takes up his story:

In September 1972, I joined the RAF as a Direct Entrant Navigator on a Permanent Commission, my eyesight now precluding me from pilot training. At the Air Navigation School (which I later went on to command) at RAF Finningley, I discovered that I had a penchant for low-level visual navigation. Fortunately, the RAF agreed and having gained my Navigator's Brevet was posted to the Buccaneer force, via a 20-hour low-level lead-in course on the Jet Provost T.4a along with 25-hours in the Hastings T.5 'Flying Classroom', learning the art of low-level overland radar navigation.

The best of the best

The Buccaneer Force, and 237 Operational Conversion Unit (OCU) in particular, had a reputation as very demanding and professional organisations where only the best was acceptable – this was both right and proper, and true. The Buccaneer jet aircraft could 'bite' if mis-handled, particularly in the circuit, and both cockpits were often described as ergonomic slums. However, the S.2 Buccaneer, with its Rolls-Royce Spey engines was, at its operating speeds of 420 knots or higher a superb, stable but manoeuvrable low-level platform, with a good weapon carrying capacity and, after the F-111, the longest-ranged twin-engine bomber of its day in NATO service. The Buccaneer has the pilot's seat offset to the left with the navigator offset to the right, providing the navigator with a clear view forward. It was also extremely capable at high-level and could cruise at 30,000-feet plus at 0.8 Mach, burning only 10lbs of fuel for every nautical mile (nm) flown. However, by the early 1970s, its navigation system was already showing its age.

About two thirds of the way through the OCU course I found out there was a posting available on 809 Naval Air Squadron (NAS) and duly volunteered for it. At the conclusion of the OCU course I was duly posted to 208 Squadron! However, this oversight was quickly sorted out and I was then crewed-up with Brian Mahaffey for the Number Eight Post-graduate Pre-carrier Course. By this stage, I had 90 hours experience on the Buccaneer and the 30 hour course was designed to introduce us to some of the additional roles and weapons that we would come across on the carrier. The other objective was to introduce the pilot -

in particular - to landing the Buccaneer on an aircraft carrier flight deck. A dummy flight deck was painted on the left-hand side of the runway at RAF Honington and a mirror landing site, identical to that on the carrier, was just off to the left hand side of that. The process was known as Mirror Assisted Dummy Deck Landings, or MADDLS. A number of the RN pilots on the OCU staff were qualified Landing Safety Officers (LSOs) and they assessed each landing as to whether you would have got back on board safely or not.

One of the highlights of course was the two shots off the static catapult at RAE Bedford. This could only be done when there was enough wind and from the right direction – RAE Bedford could not steam at 20 knots into wind and there was only about a 20-feet drop off the Bedford catapult - as opposed to just over 60-feet from the deck of HMS *Ark Royal*. Our first launches were with an experienced RN pilot or observer in the other seat and then we launched off together for a low-level photographic reconnaissance sortie into Wales, recovering to RAF Honington for even more MADDLs. We were also introduced to the 2-inch rocket projectile and to live forward air control (FAC) on the Sennybridge Range in Wales. 809 NAS returned from sea at the end of July and I was crewed-up with Lieutenant Julian Bond RN, who was returning for his third tour on the squadron having just completed a tour as a QFI on Bulldogs.

Over the next 18 months I was to gain another 350 hours on the Buccaneer, complete more than 120 catapult launches and deck landings (cats and traps) and fly over 80 per cent of those sorties with Julian. Our first deck landing together was on the 22nd September 1975, when we joined HMS *Ark Royal* in the Channel for 'wire pulling'. This was primarily to work-up the flight-deck crews but also to give us some deck landing practice before we deployed as a full squadron. Julian and I worked well together as a crew and after a few months one of us had only to 'click' the microphone for the other to answer the question before it was even asked.

Anti-shipping role

One of the great things about carrier flying was its variety. 809 NAS with its Buccaneer S.2 aircraft had three different roles. Its primary role was that of anti-shipping, which is what the Buccaneer was originally designed to do. The weapons and attacks we could use in this role ranged from a single aircraft tossing a WE177 nuclear weapon against a Soviet capital ship, to formation attacks using bombs and rockets against fast patrol boats, at night, by the light of Lepus flares. However, the standard conventional (i.e. non-nuclear) attack profiles involved four-aircraft formations, always referred to as a four-ships, using various combinations of the Martel anti-radiation and TV guided missile, as well as 1,000-pound bombs tossed at the target from three nautical miles. These were practised by flying the attack profiles (without releasing any weapons) against naval or unsuspecting merchant shipping. Weapons deliveries were practised on most sorties, using small practice bombs, often against a 'splash target' towed behind the carrier or another warship. The splash target was a large raft, towed up to 2,000-yards behind the ship, and with metal scoops to throw up plumes of water to aim at.

Non-stick coating

But the squadron also had an overland role and my first squadron deployment afloat was in the late autumn of 1975 to the north Norwegian Sea for Exercise *Northern Wedding*. The Royal Navy very proudly told us that the ship now had a new non-slip coating to the flight deck. This was so until it was coated with salt water and aviation fuel, when it resembled a well-oiled frying pan! On one day, when the sea-state was particularly high, only one aircraft at a time was going to be released from the lashings holding it down to the deck and towed by heavy flight-deck tractors to the catapult. The first Buccaneer was unlashed and we all watched fascinated as the whole combo started slipping across the deck as the ship rolled from one side to the other. Fortunately, the engineers got the lashings back on it and the whole launch was - much to everyone's relief - scrubbed. From then on the exercise was known as *Northern Deck-slide*! A lot of the sorties were flown as four-ships against land targets in Norway, including FAC in support of the Royal Marines in the Narvik area.

The final role of the Squadron was that of air-to-air refuelling. This was to extend the range of the Buccaneers (which did not have the bomb-bay door fuel tank that the RAF aircraft later had) and of the Phantom aircraft of 892 NAS, whose primary role was to defend the carrier.

Carrier flying excitement

But carrier-flying had its own unique excitements. The launch got you from zero to about 150 knots in less than two seconds but, provided the Flight Deck Officer launched you when the bow was pitching up, was generally

410

uneventful. The next bit was - for the navigator - the most challenging. In the maritime role you often didn't know where the target was – but when flying from a carrier (particularly in those days) you often didn't know where you were starting from either. It was not uncommon to climb up to transit to an overland entry-point, take a radar fix and find yourself 30nm or more from where you should have been. You then had to be careful to correct the ship's position on your chart for when you recovered. This was particularly important on exercises when you were not allowed to use your radar within 100nm of the carrier to avoid giving its position away. In bad weather, or at night, you then had to navigate yourself by old-fashioned DR (dead reckoning) to a pre-briefed bearing and distance from where the ship would be at your designated recovery time, known as Charlie Time.

For the landing you were in the hands of your pilot and, to a lesser extent, the LSO. If the stern was pitching down as you landed it would be a relatively gentle arrival; if it was pitching up however, the landing gear was stressed to 6g in the vertical plane, and you felt it. I also had my first night sortie from the carrier with the Squadron QFI, who proceeded to demonstrate to me how not to do a night recovery and what a night 'Bolter' (missing the wires) was like!

On the 18th October 1975 I was flying with Julian in XV361, on my 14th sortie from HMS *Ark Royal*. It was a post-engine change test flight and, after shutting the new starboard engine down, at Fl200 or so, it wouldn't re-light. Eventually, Julian got it re-lit by diving to a much lower altitude. As we turned finals FLYCO called *'022 you have a lot of smoke coming from your starboard engine'*, at this point we had just rolled out on the final approach and in unison we both said 'LAND'. This was uneventful but as the cable pulled us back FLYCO then said *'022, shut down and abandon AT THE RUSH'*. This we did, remembering to disconnect the lanyard on your life-jacket from the dinghy pack you sat on – otherwise it would have pulled you up short as you slid down the flaps. The aircraft was towed into Fly 1 (the deck-park in front of the island) and we followed it. The engineers dropped the starboard engine cowling and a few gallons of fuel spilled onto the deck. There was a pinhole leak downstream of the Proportioner (fuel pump) and the black smoke was leaking fuel cleaning the muck off the outside skin and the jet-pipe!

TV Stars!

In February of 1976 we reembarked for a deployment, via Gibraltar and Puerto Rico, to the Eastern Seaboard of the US. This cruise was the subject of the BBC TV documentary *Sailor* and some of the most interesting flying, including bombing with live 1,000lb bombs on the Vieques Range (off Puerto Rico), featured on it. The maritime flying was much the same as in home waters, but in generally better weather. Julian and I qualified as a Night and Strike (nuclear weapons) crew at this time.

For most of its operational life the Buccaneer had no artificial horizon in the back cockpit – and you couldn't see the one in the front. It was often very hazy off the Eastern Seaboard in the spring and summer, which led to a phenomenon known as the 'goldfish bowl' – flying in a uniformly grey sphere of sea and sky with no visible horizon. At night it was worse! As you were fired down the catapult the fluids and sensors in your inner-ear spun around and, without a horizon to correct the sensations, you felt you had been rolled over to the right – a condition known as the 'leans'. I spent a few trips metaphorically curled up in the left side of the cockpit trying to get myself back to level flight, something that happened the moment you saw the ship and your brain was able to correct the mis-perceptions. We also spent some time ashore at the US Naval Air Stations at Oceana (Virginia Beach) and Cecil Field (near Jacksonville, FL) and flew low-level navexs along the coastal states and down into Florida.

The Everglades might have looked nice from 500-feet but were not somewhere you wanted to eject into! We returned home after a final 'run ashore' in Fort Lauderdale on the 4th July 1976.

Last Deck Landing

One of the least popular tasks was to be the Alert-5 tanker on deck during night and non-Diversion (when there was no ashore diversion airfield) flying. This was in case a pilot '*bolted*' (missed the wires) repeatedly and, rather than sending him ashore (if you could), the tanker would be launched. This would give him a breathing space, not that night-tanking was easy, and fuel for a few more goes at the deck. You briefed, kitted-up, crewed-in and then sometimes didn't fly. In order to be airborne in just five minutes the tanker was '*spotted*' in Fly 2, a wedge-shaped piece of the deck between the Island and the starboard wing-tip-safety line, close to the waist catapult and pointing about 11 o'clock to the ships bow. Once the launch and recovery cycle started you were fully strapped in, all pins out and the canopy closed. But you were also under the aft 965 radar, a huge rotating bedstead, and you couldn't eject from this position. Added to the recovering aircraft slamming into the wires right in front of you this made it a very uncomfortable place to be.

The 20th September 1976 marked my last deck landing, with my pilot of 14 months Julian Bond. The squadron QFI, it was his 485th deck landing and my 124th. We were the Alert-5 tanker, at night, non-Diversion and were launched to refuel and play target for an F4 at the end of Exercise TEAMWORK, off Bodo in Norway. It was a horrible windless night with no visible horizon – classic '*goldfish bowl*' conditions. This meant that the only wind over the deck was generated by the ship's speed and was therefore a crosswind from the right as the flight deck was angled by 8.5 degrees to port. Consequently, the pilot had to fly a constantly '*crabbing*' approach to stay on the centre-line. At 100ft we ran into funnel smoke and Julian called '*voice*' to get the LSO to increase his commentary. We emerged from the smoke as we came over the '*round-down*' to find ourselves aiming directly at the aircraft parked in Fly 1, at the bows of the ship. We couldn't safely '*bolt*' so Julian chopped the throttles, something one would never normally do because of the chance of missing the wires (known as a '*Whispering Bolter*'). We slammed into the deck, caught a wire and bounced a couple of times, during which I caught the Alert-5 tanker flashing past the corner of my eye, before coming to a stop much closer to the Island than was normal. There was a moment's silence and a '*phew*' from both cockpits as the hook and wings came up and we taxied forward into Fly 1. We only realised what a close call we had just had when walking into the Island from the screen door we met Lieutenant Tom Lloyd USN, the observer from the Alert-5 tanker that had replaced us when we were launched (his pilot was our other USN officer, Lieutenant Doug Hiatt). He was white as a sheet and I recall his words to this day: '*shit you guys, you nearly fucking killed us*'. We had finished up with our starboard main wheel close to the starboard wing-tip safety line which the wing tip (16ft right of the main wheel) should not have crossed. Tom later claimed that our starboard wing-tip had passed under their nose as we bounced!

Buccaneer Launch on HMS *Ark Royal*.
Chris Finn family archive

A Belfast tour in 1974

The long period of the *'Troubles'* in Northern Ireland, which started in the late 1960s resulted in the so-called Sunningdale Agreement after about five years of cross-border negotiations. At this stage the protesting Ulster Workers Council called for a strike which started on 15th May 1974 and the Province was almost brought to a standstill overnight. 2,000 soldiers and police were needed to keep the five main roads into Belfast open, electricity supplies were disrupted, fuel distribution became critical, civil telecommunications were intermittent, Catholic workers in major industries were threatened and intimidated, food distribution was disrupted and in places there was sewage in the streets.

Everyone held their breath, pun not intended. Work stoppages affected shops and services and paramilitary roadblocks sprung up across the Province. With hindsight, the Secretary of State for Northern Ireland wrote *'The Northern Ireland Office and the Executive in Stormont seemed powerless and speechless whilst the lack of planning revealed inadequate co-ordination between the Royal Ulster Constabulary, the Army, the Executive and service providers such as the NI Electricity Service. Lack of Government information made the BBC seem to be supporting the strike'.*

The man with the job of sorting this out was the new Secretary of State, Merlyn Rees, who had just been

416

appointed in early March 1974 following the Labour party's success in the General Election held at the beginning of that month. He had a sound background, having been the Shadow Secretary of State beforehand but he was picking up the problems arising from the Sunningdale Agreement which had yet to be agreed. All the negotiating powers, Westminster, Dublin, and the NI Executive were for it and all recognised that there would be no change in status until a majority of the NI population wanted it.

The issue that arose was the proposed Council of Ireland. This Council would comprise seven members each from the North and South for acting together on *'a harmonising and consultative role in the fields of natural resources, agriculture, trade and industry, tourism, roads and transport, public health, and culture and arts'*. There was also to be a second-tier Consultative Assembly made up of thirty members each from the NI Assembly and the Dail. It is easy to see now that the loyalist community saw this Council as the Trojan horse. The UWC's executive cell comprised active trade unionists from the main industries of NI with a policy to recruit key workers capable of promoting strike action. The committee set up to run this strike saw a need for both political and paramilitary action and armed heavies attended their meetings with the new Secretary of State. The strike brought down the NI Executive and this brought it to an end, leaving the Secretary of State to pick up the pieces and plan a future system of government for the Province.

After this strike the politicians got on with attempts at power-sharing and working for peace but we saw little of this on the ground. The *'Troubles'* continued with bombings, shootings, marches, murder and mayhem with security forces under continuous threat for twenty four more long and bloody years before the Belfast or Good Friday Agreement was signed. And that has not proved so satisfactory either.

My tour in Northern Ireland started in February 1974 and I had been on a steep learning curve by the time the UWC strike started. The appointment was for two years commanding 39th Infantry Brigade Headquarters and Signal Squadron. This squadron had up to 140 all ranks including the brigade staff in addition to the main Royal Signals element. We provided the headquarters with operational support in conjunction with Garrison administrative support. The signallers had a significant communications role whilst other key elements included Royal Corps of Transport drivers and Royal Pioneers who provided vehicle escorts. We were based in Thiepval Barracks in Lisburn which also included Headquarters NI and several other units.

Before the '*Troubles*' started 39th Infantry Brigade had been an air-portable brigade with a world-wide role. Its usual order of battle would have comprised an armoured regiment, an artillery regiment, three infantry battalions and support arms and services. It now had five battalions, two Ulster Defence Regiments, a Royal Military Police Regiment, an armoured car squadron and a Sapper squadron. Four of the battalions, sometimes a Gunner regiment in an infantry role, were on 4-month 'roulemont' tours and based in large requisitioned buildings such as the Grand Central Hotel, a number of mills, and a prefabricated camp in the city. They were all deployed on relentless

Internal Security duties whilst living a restricted life in ad hoc accommodation. At critical times the brigade was reinforced with more battalions up to the strength of a division. Reserve accommodation included HMS *Maidstone* which could take 2,000 men. At one stage it was used as a prison for high profile prisoners including Gerry Adams and others.

My squadron's role was to provide communications for these units in Belfast and the brigade's tactical area of responsibility which included Belfast and large parts of Antrim and County Down. This communications task was bigger than usual for an independent squadron as the normal VHF Larkspur range of combat radios, essentially designed for field operations in BAOR and world-wide, were unsuitable in the heavily built-up city of Belfast. The field radios relied on clear radio paths which in cities were blocked by the buildings so the solution was to use commercial radio which worked through relay stations, known as talk-throughs, using towers, masts and other high points covering the battalion areas in Belfast. There were 5 nets per major unit and Pye UHF pocket phone sets worked down to each 4-man patrol or *'brick'* as they were called. These nets were not secure so voice-procedure had to be good as we knew the opposition was monitoring our radios. We maintained all these sets in the squadron and the technical troop was kept very busy. In addition to the deployed radios, we held sufficient reserves to equip additional battalions joining the brigade for major operations and emergencies.

The squadron also ran the brigade's command net which was a secure VHF net working through a re-broadcast station on Divis Mountain overlooking Belfast. We shared the mountain with the BBC and others as it could provide radio cover of almost the whole province. We also shared the Army's site with other NI Royal Signals units providing communications to the other two brigades in Lurgan and Londonderry. A small team from the squadron lived up there and looked after our equipment and masts which would be covered in layers of ice during the winter months. The secure radios emitted a regular *'bleep'* at the rate of about 45 to the minute. Operators and watchkeepers in the operations room (captains on tours of 4-6 months) had to put up with this constant noise. In the long small hours at night they calculated how many bleeps they had to listen to for the rest of their tours. These bleeps also changed the Army's nickname for signallers from *'Scalybacks'* to *'Bleeps'*.

Other elements of the squadron provided the Brigade Commander's Rover Group which was out every day visiting units over a very large area. The commander would always be out on the ground for every major operational event, near the centre of the action and leading from the front. There are between 1,500 and 3,000 authorised Loyalist and Nationalist parades every year across the Province with the majority in Belfast and Londonderry between April and August. There were also a few unauthorised parades and any of them, including funeral parades, could and often did erupt into violence. Other incidents at any time of day or night could require the commander's presence out on the ground so this Group had to be fully prepared at all times and on the ball. The major marches such as the Orange Order's march on 12th July required small teams in addition reporting back to a base in the RUC's headquarters in Belfast.

Other parts of the squadron included the Communications Centre under its Yeoman of Signals. It provided an extensive teleprinter network linking all the units under Brigade command. These machines chattered away day and night with printed tape feeding messages over civil lines to the recipient where they would be printed out. Some of the operators were so skilled they could read the holes in the punched tape's code. A regular Signals Despatch Service also operated delivering packages and classified documents to military locations in Belfast. A small team of cypher clerks led a secret life in a large secret broom cupboard dealing with encrypted traffic from the MOD and other agencies. There was also a line team who laid field cable when required on some operations and another team with mobile relay equipment to extend the brigade's command net outside Belfast. On one occasion, when I deployed it on a test exercise with a new subaltern in charge it lost contact. The evening passed and I became more concerned but they came back on air about midnight and returned to camp. In the de-briefing it transpired they had a map reading problem - they admitted crossing the border and being firmly directed back by a friendly farmer.

One of the Squadron's busiest sections was the Technical Troop run by a Technical Officer and a Foreman of Signals. Their workshop repaired and serviced the vast number of radios and talk-through equipment we had deployed and held in reserve. A great novelty appeared when heli-telly was trialled and proved to provide immense value to operations. The technicians would fit the helicopter with a large camera and transmitter when it was to be deployed and remain on standby during its operations. A control room was established in a battalion headquarters from where the helicopter was directed for observation of events on the ground. This was monitored in the Brigade Operations Room and the Squadron.

I was lucky to have an excellent team with some first-class soldiers. Morale remained high and this was down to the Warrant Officers and NCOs who, as ever, form the Army's backbone. Due to its size and role, the squadron had a Warrant Officer Class 1 Regimental Sergeant Major rather than the usual WO2 Squadron Sergeant Major. My RSM turned out to be the best I knew after meeting many in previous and subsequent years. We still keep in touch. He accompanied me on all visits to battalions, meetings in Belfast and other frequent events. During these visits he kept a close eye on our isolated detachments, making sure they had all they needed and were looking after themselves. In camp he ran an excellent WOs and Sergeants Mess for all units in the garrison which held regular functions. These included a Saturday morning lunch time air pistol match in which the officers were invited to compete. The range was constructed in a large broom cupboard. He oversaw the Squadron Club which provided relaxing facilities for those off-duty with a popular bar and regular evening functions, one highlight being a visit by Harry Secombe. The club's profits paid for new strips for our outstanding soccer team which won the Army Minor Units competition. Other sports included rugby and cricket at Garrison level and secret orienteering competitions across the Province in relatively safe areas. We also supported the local civil community with help for a nearby home for MS sufferers.

The wives were all very helpful and played their part supporting their husbands and the squadron under difficult restrictive circumstances. Many had young children and were raising them in NI's restrictive circumstances. Married quarters were provided as far as possible but as always there were never enough and some officers and married soldiers lived in houses rented in Lisburn. There was a larger NAAFI stores near the camp and Lisburn was a reasonably safe place for shopping. Some also shopped in Belfast but it was limited and the barricades heightened the inevitable tension so few took it up.

My wife and the RSM's wife earned their notional NI General Service Medals during one of their visits to a young soldier's wife who lived in a rather lonely area. There was a small crowd with a disturbance going on down the street as they arrived and they noticed the young wife had rather naively hung out her husband's freshly washed combat kit on her washing line. It was on display to the whole world. They grabbed the washing and decided they had best all leave immediately. They dashed for their car when the crowd started coming down the street. As the wives reached the car a troop of the Blues and Royals armoured cars came round the corner and formed a road block - the cavalry had come to their rescue. The soldier and his wife were moved out of that house straight afterwards.

Schooling for service children meant they went to local schools. My daughter attended Ballymacash Primary School which at that time was located in Orange Hall Lane,

Lisburn. The head teacher confirmed the school was not sectarian and Roman Catholic children could attend – the single RC child attending was the daughter of a service family. It was a good school and my daughter was helped to pass her entrance exam for an English boarding school. All went very well although we were a little nonplussed when she came home one day and asked what a *Fenian Bastard* was. Our eldest son was boarding at school in England but used to fly over for holidays. Travelling as an unaccompanied minor he always had a good seat and on a couple of flights he had been sat next to Enoch Powell and then Ian Paisley. He found them interesting and entertaining but we were pleased that we only found out after each flight.

Those of us on the long tours were able to get out a bit and visit places such as the Giant's Causeway or Strangford Lough and there was much entertaining. Several old friends appeared on their roulemont tours and we were often able to hold small dinner parties for them with other friends.

They were interesting times and it was good soldiering which most of us were pleased to have experienced. It was of course more comfortable for those of us on long tours than those on short tours who had the rough end of operations and lived in rough conditions.

****

Helicopter borne television being fitted.
Mike Spence collection

Brigade Commander's Rover group.
Mike Spence collection

Harry Secombe visits the Squadron at the Horsehoe Club.
Mike Spence collection

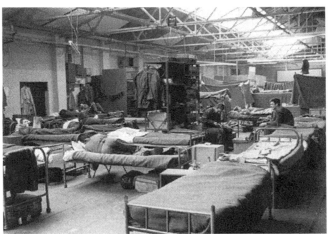

Roulemont battalion accommodation.
Mike Spence collection

Historian Dr. Matthias Strohn describes part of his earlier career serving with NATO forces in Afghanistan as part of the German Bundeswehr. IEDs were a constant danger to all who served in that theatre.

A German serving in Afghanistan

Serving with the German Bundeswehr in Afghanistan as part of the NATO forces.

It is an often-overlooked fact that the German Bundeswehr was the third largest contributor to NATO operations in Afghanistan. The Germans had their 'own' Regional Command in the North, with the HQ in the city of Mazar Sharif. This area was comparatively peaceful, but the Eastern part of the RC, the area around Kunduz, saw some heavy military action.

I deployed to RC North and first spent some time in the RC HQ. I then deployed to Kunduz. We flew by helicopter and the experience of flying over Afghanistan at low altitude, always expecting to be engaged by the enemy, was a first taste of what 'real' war is all about. Having arrived at Kunduz we prepared a convoy to supply an outpost station. The problem was that the convoy was road-bound due to the material we were carrying and that the road network dictated our movements. This was, of course, known to the enemy. We had to cross a ford at some point and this was the choke-point. Several convoys had been attacked, in particular with IEDs (the modern term for mines). During the days before we set out, attacks had been frequent and in the final brief we were told to expect '*dicke Luft*', or thick air, as the Germans call it.

The briefing took place in the early evening and we set out before dawn the next morning. During the night, we prepared the vehicles and our equipment and went to bed. Thoughts circulated around the possibility of an attack, our drills and how to react. A calm confidence in our training and equipment was evident, but so was the thought of potential losses. In the middle of the night, the camp was awoken by a large explosion. Nobody knew what it was or where it had come from. Was it a rocket attack? These were frequent and an unexploded rocket that had hit the camp's cook house was left in place (made safe, of course!) as a stark reminder of the realities of war.

Having checked the camp, it was concluded that this had not been a rocket attack and, after things had calmed down, I went back to bed. The next morning we set off with the grim determination to reach our '*Kameraden*' (the Germans use the term '*comrade*', it has a deep meaning for the German soldier and shows a general bond that cannot really be translated). When we approached the ford, we tightened the straps of our helmets and checked our weapons. We approached the ford slowly and then, one by one, the vehicles crossed the ford. When our vehicle crossed, I could see a huge crater next to the road. It was clear that this was new crater, but, at this stage, we did not know why it was there or what had caused it.

We reached the outpost and re-supplied the troops. Later in the day, some intelligence arrived: The crater had been caused by an IED, probably the largest one in the area so far. It seems that it had been 'reserved' for us and it would have done considerable damage to our convoy. The IED went off prematurely - this was the explosion that we had heard - for reasons unknown. In the German military, you wish each other '*Soldatenglück*' (literally: soldier's luck). This day we had been lucky.

****

The Falklands War

The war to regain possession of the Falkland Islands in 1982 has been for many both a source of national pride, grateful remembrance of sacrifice, but also of controversy.

The sovereignty of the Falklands Islands had been disputed since 1841, when the islands became a Crown Colony, but an aggressive stance on the matter was taken by General Galtieri encouraged, it is argued, by the Defence Spending Review of 1981 which recommended removing HMS *Endurance* suggesting a lack of interest by the British in defending the Islands. There had been repeated warnings from the men on the spot in the South Atlantic about the changing situation, but these had been ignored. This was also fuelled by pressure at home on the Galtieri Government to flex its muscles over *Las Malvinas* in order to restore some Argentinian pride and to deliver some good news to his people.

On 19th March 1982 the Royal Navy Ice patrol ship HMS *Endurance* was sent to investigate when a group of Argentinian scrap merchants landed on South Georgia. On the 2nd April the invasion of the Falklands Islands began. At the beginning of the conflict the odds were in Argentina's favour, as the military forces occupying the islands had 240 modern jets and eight French built *Exocet* missiles, against a force of 15,000 men with a hastily assembled armada of naval and requisitioned merchant ships that had sailed from another hemisphere.

A small detachment of Royal Marines had been posted to the Falklands since 1965. However, any reinforcements would take over three weeks to arrive. Mike Norman had spent a year on HMS *Endurance* in 1971 and was critical of what he saw as the complacency of the British Government in the years leading to the conflict.

The 69 members of the combined naval parties, under the command of Mike Norman prepared for the invasion which they were now told was imminent. They defended the invasion valiantly until told to surrender by the Governor Sir Rex Hunt. In a remarkable squaring of the circle, the men of Naval Party 8901 were present at the surrender of the Argentinian troops and run-up the flag on the reclaimed Governor's residence.

Prime Minister Margaret Thatcher, under her own political pressure at home on domestic issues, was not one to roll over easily to this challenge on British Sovereign territory. She demanded a military show of strength to persuade the Argentine government to withdraw their troops. The British Government hastily assembled and sent a task force towards the South Atlantic, 8,000 miles away, whilst also exploring diplomatic avenues to peace. A 200 mile exclusion zone around the island was declared. The Task Force included the aircraft carriers *Hermes* and *Invincible* and the nuclear powered submarine *Conqueror*. The liners *Canberra* and the *QE2* were requisitioned to carry 3 Commando Brigade and 5th Infantry Brigade respectively and the SS *Uganda* sailed as a hospital ship. The whole task force contained 127 ships. Fit-out of the civilian ships including full hospital facilities including operating theatres, and fitness programmes for the thousands of troops took place whilst sailing southwards. Few of the troops heading south really believed fighting would actually take place, expecting diplomatic and political pragmatism would find an acceptable solution before they arrived.

Under Operation Parquet, members of 42 Commando and the SAS and SBS retook South Georgia. The first attempt on 23rd April was hampered by terrible Antarctic weather and resulted in members of the SAS being stranded and subsequently rescued from the Fortuna glacier in a dangerous and remarkable helicopter operation. On 25th April, the men achieved success in a direct assault which provoked limited resistance.

Whilst the Task Force, under Admiral Sir John Fieldhouse, was on its way, stopping off at Ascension Island in mid Atlantic to re-stock and replenish, Operation Black Buck raids on Stanley airfield were accomplished by Vulcan bombers from RAF Waddington, requiring multiple mid-air refuelling operations en route. They inflicted direct hits on the runway which made the operation of Argentine fast jets very difficult from the airfield.

On arrival off the Falklands, the carrier force and its picket ships were immediately under attack from the Argentine air force and also from enemy submarines. The controversial sinking of the Argentine light cruiser General *Belgrano* by HMS *Conqueror* on the 2nd May resulted in the return of the Argentine navy to home ports. Two days later the British Navy suffered its first loss with the sinking of the HMS *Sheffield* by an *Exocet* missile. In the sea battle, HMS *Ardent, HMS Antelope,* MV *Atlantic Conveyor*, HMS *Coventry* were sunk and HMS *Argonaut* and HMS *Brilliant* badly damaged.

On 21st May, the men of 3 Commando, 2 Paras and 40 Commando were landed at San Carlos Bay, Port San Carlos and Ajax Bay. The initial battles of the land war took place at Darwin and Goose Green, and Mount Kent, a success which then enabled the British forces to break out of the San Carlos beachhead and begin the *'yomp'* towards Stanley. From the 27th May, the SAS and the Mountain and Arctic Warfare cadre fought Argentine special forces on Mount Kent securing a firm hold on the area allowing conventional forces to be brought in.

On the 8th May, RFA *Sir Tristram* and RFA *Sir Galahad* were attacked by the Argentine air force at Bluff Cove. On board were troops of the Welsh Guards who were planned to be part of the southern advance to Stanley. The decision not to disembark the guards resulted in catastrophic casualties when the Argentine A-4 Skyhawks attacked. 56 men were killed and 150 men were injured or badly burned.

On 11th June 3 Commando Brigade, with supportive gunfire from Royal Navy ships, attacked Mount Longdon, Mount Harriet and Two Sisters. HMS *Glamorgan* was badly damaged by a land based *Exocet* missile. After fierce fighting these objectives were captured and on the night of the 13th June Wireless Ridge fell to 2 Para supported by the Blues and Royals artillery, and the Scots Guards with bayonets drawn captured Mount Tumbledown. The Argentine garrison at Stanley surrendered on 14th June.

What were the military lessons learned? The conflict exposed the vulnerability of surface ships to anti-ship missiles as Argentine aircraft penetrated the Royal Navy's defensive measures repeatedly due to lack of anti-air capability. The importance of airpower in naval conflict resulted in the decision to maintain aircraft carriers for the Harrier short take-off and vertical landing aircraft and aspects of John Nott's defence review were cancelled. The war exposed the problems of maintaining logistical support over long distances. After the war, decisions were made to improve the logistical and amphibious capability of the navy. The utility of heavy lift helicopters in all aspects of the operation was emphasised for future conflicts.

The Falkland Islands remain a self-governing British overseas territory, and its people were given British citizenship in 1983.

The British force lost 255 men, 6 ships, 34 aircraft and the war cost £2.8 billion. The success of the war resulted in an increase of patriotic pride, with national rejoicing as the Task Force returned home in the following months. This success led to the increasing popularity of the Conservative government, with an increased majority for Margaret Thatcher in the next election.

The war was instrumental in the further recognition of Post-Traumatic Stress Disorder (PTSD), and for the first time in Britain's military history the repatriation of bodies was allowed.

Cedric Delves, Commander of SAS D Squadron, reckoned that it was a combination of moral toughness, discipline and the conviction that a terrible wrong was being put right that enabled the British forces to win against the odds. Helen Parr in her study of the men of the paratroopers that fought in the Falklands 'Our Boys: The 'Story of a Paratrooper' wrote *'This land was British land, reclaimed with British blood '.*

****

 *Major-General Dair Farrar-Hockley MC, OC A Coy 2 Para in 1982, describes the battle for Darwin during the Falklands War in February 1982, giving a vivid account of the tactics of the battle and the total determination of the men of 2 Para to overcome the odds to win the battle.*

The Battle for Darwin Thirty Years On

By an extraordinary set of circumstances, the company commanders of A, B & D Coys of 2 Para met at Darwin settlement on 3rd February 2012. It gave us an opportunity to look again at the Darwin and Goose Green battlefield and see what each company had experienced during those four critical days at the end of May 1982: a humbling encounter. Thus inspired, I determined to put on record A Coy's battle for Darwin Hill and the ridge to its west, as a tribute to our soldiers and their utter determination to win at all costs.

The lead up to the first land battle in the Falklands campaign had been one of marked contrast. For five days, exposed to the extremes of winter weather on Sussex mountain - before the days of goretex and other such comforts - we had watched while ships in the sound were attacked daily by Argentine aircraft; and notably the loss of both HMS *Ardent* and *Antelope*. Now at last it was our turn, and we were glad to get going with a view to inflicting our will upon the enemy.

The battalion, led by D Coy, moved south through the night of 26th May over broken terrain and after fourteen miles reached Camilla Creek House. In a bold move, the CO ordered us — all 450 men — into the house, conscious of the need for some rest and warmth before first light. Two hours' sleep, huddled together on shelves, in cupboards and the like were to prove invaluable. It would be a long time before we would sleep again. As we moved out of the house, the stunning news that the BBC had reported our advance towards Darwin & Goose Green on the World Service was met with incredulity and not a little anger. Adopting defensive positions in the open countryside, we hoped to find cover from enemy aircraft which we assumed wrongly were looking for us.

Later that day, 27th May, in a much delayed 'O Group', Colonel H had directed that *'2 Para is to capture the Darwin & Goose Green area'*: critically, taking the two settlements in daylight to avoid killing the civilians we had come to free after more than a month of captivity. Returning to my company, light was already fading as I prepared to give orders.

A Coy's initial attack in the early hours of 28th May was on Burntside House. Inaccurate intelligence *('the civilians in the house have left but it is now in enemy hands')* meant that we nearly killed the Morrison family. Happily, that was not so: but two Argentine soldiers just to the north of the house were killed while the remainder of their section

— we were never quite sure how many — disappeared into the night.

As B Coy followed by D marched south down the west of the isthmus to capture Goose Green, A Coy set off along the east side for what looked to be our most challenging task of the night: to destroy the enemy company on Coronation Point. So, 80 or 90 enemy, perhaps, holding a small feature on our direct path, hemmed in between the sea on our left and a track on our right – the boundary with B Coy. Not more than a kilometre of frontage and no room for an out-flanking attack. To our considerable surprise, the position was devoid of enemy.

Given that daylight was not much more than an hour away — and despite the fact that the orders required A Coy to be 'in reserve' for the next phase of the operation — we sought permission from Battalion HQ to move forward: on three occasions this was denied. *Wait for the CO to join you'*. As it was, he arrived more than an hour later — close to first light — and was insistent that we got going.

Placing 3 Platoon (Guy Wallis) on the edge of Coronation Point to give covering fire for our assault on Darwin Settlement (our third and final target) we were ambushed from the crest of Darwin ridge (some 100 feet above and to our right) as we made for the security of the gorse gully and the base of Darwin Hill — our start line for the assault on the settlement.

The immediate action of the leading sections was to take six or seven trenches at the base of the gully in short order. What followed as the light came up was not to be so easy.

Under cover of darkness, the advantage was in our favour: we could get amongst the enemy and overwhelm them with our aggression. With daylight, the advantage shifted as the Argentines could pick us off at range: thus, our rapid early success ground to a slog.

Of what did the enemy comprise, and where were they sited? Since orders for the battalion attack contained no plan to capture Darwin Hill nor the ridge to the west, it was a surprise to find it so heavily defended on the east of the Isthmus. Initially pressing 2 Platoon (Mark Coe) to try and outflank the enemy by heading up to the top of the gully, it became clear that sniper and fixed line machine guns would make that impossible. If we were to achieve a quick outcome (Colonel H's intent) it would be essential to get the enemy's head down with a bombardment of some description.

Our training had been in the all arms battle, but it was good that we had also trained for the unexpected. One by one, all the fire support which had been 'on call' was denied. Fog at sea prevented Harriers taking off; so too the attack helicopters of the day. The battalion's artillery support was woefully small given the loss of the *Atlantic Conveyor* a few days beforehand, in which ten out of eleven helicopters on board were sunk. We had knowingly gone into battle 'under-gunned.' With Special Company located to the NW of the isthmus, the rifle companies found themselves 'out-gunned' since none of Special Company's fire teams could engage the enemy — save the valiant efforts of a section of the mortars, despite high gusting winds.

The cold light of day brought a reality check. While B Coy was held up by the enemy at Boca House, A Coy too was on its own. Attrition, rather than manoeuvre in the all arms battle, was the order of the day. While I had no doubt that we would capture the hill, I had no idea of the time it would take; nor the cost in lives.

Battle is by nature chaotic and brutal and our experience was to be no different. Our strength lay in the qualities of the airborne soldier. Guts, an utter determination to succeed, professional fighting skills of the highest order, unstinting support for one another, ABI (or 'airborne initiative') — that indefinable sense of taking the initiative, whatever your rank — and a brand of infectious, dark humour: all of them were needed.

Such initiative led to a series of sporadic sorties from different parts of the gully to test the opportunities to close with the enemy. This culminated in Sergeant Ted Barrett (1 Platoon) creating a fire base and inspiring those around him. The now intertwined sections of 1 & 2 Platoons began in small groups to fight their way up the hill from the gorse gully: our firm base throughout the battle. It was a slow, demanding task. Our advance could not be affected by complete platoons, but by skirmishing in small groups. Control was crude, principally by NCOs shouting to those nearest to move or give covering fire. Literally, we clawed our way up the slope, with little more than tiny folds in the ground to give cover on the bare terrain: a billiard table as some have described it. The situation was not aided by enemy artillery fire — controlled as we discovered after the battle by an observation post on Mount Osborne to the north of the isthmus.

Unswerving efforts took place to recover wounded comrades. Small successes in one place contrasted with casualties and delay in another. Back in the gorse gully, still smouldering from artillery fire the night before, CSM Colin Price looked after the rising toll of wounded, including Argentine soldiers — casualties from the first trenches captured. Later, as ammunition ran low, he oversaw its critical redistribution. Suddenly enemy on foot could be seen entering the cemetery and attempting to turn our flank: the fire base dealt swiftly to silence this new threat.

Exceptional leadership from Cpls David Abols and Tom Camp was evident. But they were not alone: many others — not least those men we lost in battle — junior NCOs and private soldiers among them, made a major contribution to the success of the day against a determined enemy company well dug in with rudimentary overhead protection, supported by artillery and heavy machine guns. Meanwhile, 3 Platoon, still manning their fire base overlooking the settlement and with no cover from enemy view, were eventually driven off their position by .50mm machine guns; the GPMG in the light role no match for these. Reaching us in the gorse gully, they brought additional firepower to the assault. It was a day when all ranks bound together.

As we got closer — after something over three hours — the combination of hand held light anti-tank weapons and machine guns proved decisive. The enemy company surrendered. We had inflicted more than 60% casualties upon them: 18 dead and 39 wounded. Just over 200 men had fought against one another: 114 from A Coy and 92 Argentine soldiers, at a total cost of 74 casualties.

Lieutenant Esteves received the Argentine's highest award for valour.

Taking the surrender on this small corner of the battlefield, it was important not only to deal urgently with casualties but to prepare for counter-attack; for this, as daylight had revealed, was the 'vital ground' which dominated the isthmus in every direction.

And what of our CO's contribution both to the battle and to the campaign? His determined charge against the enemy, demonstrating physical courage of the highest order was seen only by his tactical headquarters. Not long afterwards, the enemy had surrendered. Significantly, Colonel 'H' had trained us to have a tremendous self-belief in our capability to overcome any enemy. In addition to his exceptional personal courage, his decision to set us to a difficult task, conscious of the strategic importance of an emphatic victory after nearly a week of relative inaction by the Task Force, spoke too of his moral courage. His example, will and leadership remained with us for the rest of the campaign to recapture the Islands.

An hour or so after 'H's' death, Chris Keeble (Bn 2IC), who had now taken command of the Battalion, came up onto Darwin Hill. Thankfully, he had brought with him the ammunition we had been requesting for a while. Ahead of his party had come by helicopter, the vital medical teams who would preserve the lives of our own and the enemy's wounded soldiers. I had also asked for the padre, David Cooper, to come forward: a welcome sight after our losses.

Chris Keeble's initial proposal was to send A Coy forward to join B & D Coys, and now C Coy, in the fight for Goose Green. My own appreciation was somewhat different. First, A Coy had suffered fifteen casualties and these were an immediate priority along with the need for resupply of ammunition. Darwin settlement was still not secure below us; and the hill provided a dominant position from which to influence the battle. Why give it up now? He readily accepted my counter-proposal to send forward 3 Platoon to join C Coy on their operation towards Goose Green.

It was a privilege to have commanded A Coy throughout this bitter, hard fought battle: their airborne spirit had won the day. And that was not to be the end of it. Only a few days after the Argentine surrender at Goose Green, 2 Para was on the move again, with A Coy securing the settlement at Bluff Cove by heli-borne assault, some 28 miles inside no man's land as part of a brigade plan to open a southern flank in the battle for Port Stanley.

With this accomplished, we were to fight again in the battalion's night/day battle for Wireless Ridge, and then lead the way into Port Stanley. Ordered by the CO to halt on the racecourse, it was with great pride that I watched these magnificent, but war weary, young men begin to gather in the simple wooden grandstand for a photograph; although efforts to raise the company flag on the flagpole were a little less convincing, and showed that more practice was required! It was a relief to us all to know that no more lives would be lost.

Major-General Dair Farrar-Hockley MC (OC A Coy 1982)

Goose Green/Darwin Map.
Dair Farrar-Hockley archive

Senior Nursing Officer Nicci Pugh of the Queen Alexandra's Royal Naval Nursing Service and Chief Petty Officer and BVUK member Terry Bullingham, Royal Navy, recount their memories of serving in the task force during the Falklands War in 1982. Nicci recalls the time when she was called up and the journey down to the Falklands on HMHS Uganda. She recalls how the medical team handled hundreds of wounded servicemen from both sides and what it was like to serve in a war zone. Terry was serving on HMS Antrim when it was attacked by Argentine bombers. He was seriously injured as a bomb exploded near him, and he lost his sight in both eyes. He describes the incident when the explosion happened, his treatment by Nicci and the medical team, and his subsequent treatment and life in the UK.

White Ship - Red Crosses

In April 1982, when Argentina invaded and occupied the Falkland Islands, I was working as a Senior Nursing Officer in the operating theatres at the Royal Naval Hospital Haslar in Hampshire. The P&O Educational Cruise Ship *Uganda* was quickly requisitioned by the UK Government to serve as a military hospital ship within the Total Exclusion Zone. The ship steamed north-west across the Mediterranean Sea from Alexandria to Naples, and thence to Gibraltar, where teams of Royal Naval medical and support teams were already converging with more than 90 tons of medical equipment and stores, to convert the vessel into a floating

444

hospital to serve in the South Atlantic conflict. Among the teams were forty female Queen Alexandra's Royal Naval Nursing Service personnel; officers, senior and junior ratings. As a qualified Trauma Operating Theatre Sister, my task was to help equip, commission and run one of three small surgical teams working in what turned out to be a makeshift 3-tabled Operating Theatre Unit located near the centre of the ship. A vital piece of equipment shipped out from UK was a steel helicopter landing pad, which was later to prove crucial in the embarkation of casualties as they arrived by helicopter from the battlefields and dressing stations ashore.

The rapid conversion from P&O's floating classrooms to Her Majesty's Hospital Ship *Uganda* took place in just three days in the Gibraltar Dockyard and we left for the uncertainties of the South Atlantic on 19th April 1982. By this stage the ship had been painted with the striking red crosses of the Geneva Convention and we would be bound by their restrictions for some months.

Work continued apace as the ship steamed south towards Ascension Island, the Task Force Forward Operating Base. By now we were fully operational with capacity for up to 600 beds, with a working Casualty Reception area, Intensive Care Unit, operating theatres, X-ray, laboratory etc and all the facilities that would have been available in both military and civilian hospitals ashore at that time. Our Royal Naval Nursing and Medical staff had been mainly selected with previous training & experience to run these specialised areas, but it was essential at this stage to train up our teams within their allocated units. We were fortunate to have Royal Marine bandsmen with us, whose traditional war-time role as stretcher-bearers proved invaluable as events unfolded.

Soon after leaving Ascension Island, we heard that HMS *Sheffield* had been attacked and sunk by the Argentinians; there were numerous casualties, including several survivors who had been badly burnt. It soon became obvious to us all that our hospital facilities were now urgently required within the Combat Zone.

Thus, between 12th May and 14th July 1982, a period of nine weeks, we continued to receive seriously wounded casualties by helicopters landing on the specially constructed helicopter landing pad at the stern of the ship. The hospital ship, HMHS *Uganda,* spent most of the hostilities at anchor in Grantham Sound, a sheltered bay just to the south west of San Carlos Water, where the Task Force amphibious landings had commenced on 21st May.

The wounds we treated were mainly from gunshot, mortar and shrapnel. We treated well over 100 burns cases and a significant amount of cold water immersion injuries. Nearly 40 British servicemen returned to the UK from the Falklands War as single or double-limbed amputees. We admitted over 700 servicemen from the conflict zone (of which over 100 were Argentinian), and carried out more than 500 surgical operations in our operating theatres. Sadly, three of our patients did not survive and we all felt their loss keenly.

As patients progressed through our carefully designed clinical areas, which, in the main were all located on the one '*Promenade*' deck, our recuperating 'walking wounded' patients could be transferred to the dormitory areas on a lower deck to prepare for their repatriation to UK. This was a cleverly planned three-stage voyage north, involving, initially, transfer at sea to one of our Ambulance Ships, (the converted-from-RN hydrographic vessels HMS *Hydra, Hecla* and *Herald,* a 4-6 day sea passage north west to Montevideo in neutral Uruguay, and thence by RAF VC10 to RAF Brize Norton in Oxfordshire. One of our more seriously injured patients on board the hospital ship at that time was Chief Petty Officer Terry Bullingham, Royal Navy, who reached us on 25th May. Terry describes this re-patriation process first-hand in some detail later in this account; his unique tale of courage, survival, return to the UK and his eventual rehabilitation make an inspiring read.

About a month after the Argentinian surrender on 14th June 1982, we de-commissioned as a hospital ship. *Uganda* returned to the UK as a troopship, carrying 1/7 Gurkha Rifles and 16 Field Ambulance RAMC, arriving at Southampton 9th August 1982, where we berthed 'starboard-side-to' berth 105 - just astern of P&O's SS *Canberra.*

There are several hardly known historical facts that returned to the UK with us, and it is my privilege to record them here, for the British Modern Military History Society's publication.

First: Although UK military Nursing Sisters had served with great courage & distinction on board previous hospital ships in many previous conflicts, this was the first time that Royal Navy female Junior Ratings had served at sea.

<u>Second</u>: In 1982, women in the Royal Navy did not serve at sea. The Queen Alexandra's Royal Naval Nursing Service personnel who served in the South Atlantic in the Falklands War were all serving under the Naval Discipline Act, and were the only British female military personnel to serve in the Falklands War.

<u>Third:</u> Her Majesty's Hospital Ship *Uganda* was the first British Hospital Ship to embark casualties by helicopter from the battlefields ashore, a process that undoubtedly saved many lives by reducing casualty evacuation times. Previous British hospital ships, (including the SS *Maine* which had served in the Korean War nearly sixty years before) had indeed treated thousands of equally severely injured servicemen, but their ships' role at that time was more to transport casualties to military hospitals ashore, as opposed to *Uganda's* role, which was very much a front-line, active and fully-equipped floating military hospital.

Like many of my colleagues who were all so suddenly caught up in a totally unforeseen series of challenging events in a battle being fought in the wild and notoriously windswept South Atlantic Ocean, my memories remain as clear today as they were when I walked ashore from the ship in Southampton nearly 40 years ago. That is the nature of war.

But I also see it all as a huge privilege, to have been able to help all those courageous men who were so badly injured at sea, on land and in the air, all those years ago.

Our hospital ship personnel still feel quietly proud of our achievements; clearly demonstrating how much can be achieved with strong motivation, adaptability & the will to overcome difficulties. We were working far from home, our families and our support hospitals, in difficult, demanding and dangerous conditions; inevitably, the bond between us all, even after nearly forty years, remains extremely strong.

Following the UK's national commemorations for the 25th anniversary year of the Falklands War, held across the country in 2007, I had the privilege of organising The Inaugural Hospital Ship *Uganda* Reunion. This was held in 2008 on board the P&O Cruise Ship *Aurora* in Southampton, the port to which both SS *Canberra* & SS *Uganda* had returned in August 1982. This would be the first time most of us had re-united or seen each other for 26 years. The event was unique as we wanted to include our former patients, as well as all levels of personnel who had served on board the hospital ship in 1982. In spite of many of us, myself included, admitting to a certain amount of trepidation at such an undertaking, the event was a huge, unique and memorable success. Several hundred of us attended, many colleagues travelling from other countries for the unprecedented event.

It was a day of strong emotions, as few of us had heard of or seen each other in the intervening 26 years. We had last seen our former patients in the wilds of the South Atlantic Ocean, as we bade them farewell for their long voyage home, from latitude 52 south to the UK latitude of 52 north! As a group, we realised what unique memories we were now all able to share, so we have subsequently formed a small but enthusiastic Falklands War veterans' group that we named The Hospital Ship *Uganda* Reunion Group, or, appropriately 'HUGS' for short; we have held 6 subsequent reunions in a variety of locations and, should any of us survive, plan to hold our eighth event back on board the P&O cruise ship *Aurora* to mark the fortieth anniversary of the Falklands War in 2022. The majority of our supporters are members of the tri-service association for veterans of the Falklands War, the South Atlantic Medal Association www.sama82.org.uk

One of the many former patients who attended our inaugural event was St Dunstaner Chief Petty Officer Terry Bullingham Royal Navy, who had lost all his sight on board HMS *Antrim* on 21st May 1982. (St Dunstan's being the original name of the Blind Veterans United Kingdom Charity, BVUK, as it is now called.).

So it is with great pleasure that we now have Terry's permission to record, for this publication, his account of his survival in 1982, followed by his early affiliation with St Dunstan's:

'Spring 1982 saw me in my second year as part of the Fleet Air Arm helicopter maintenance team of the RN County Class destroyer HMS *Antrim*. Our *'raison d'etre'* was to keep 'Humphrey', the nick-name for the ship's venerable Wessex HAS-3 helicopter serviceable. After playing a significant role in Operation Paraquet off South Georgia in April, *Antrim* was one of six warships protecting the SS *Canberra* as she started to disembark the troops in San Carlos Water on 21st May. A flight of four Argentine Skyhawk fighter-bombers passed over the ship, dropping a pattern of eight 1,000 lb bombs. One of the bombs came inboard through the Sea-Slug missile launcher and came to rest unexploded in the after heads.

Immediately above, on the flight deck, we were pre-occupied deploying the ship's fire hoses and failed to notice the follow-up attack by a pair of 'Dagger' (Argentine Mirage-3s) aircraft who strafed the upper deck with their 30mm cannon. I saw the splashes in the water coming towards me followed by a sickening impact. I found myself on the deck, but unable to see anything! The ship's Medical Officer reached me fairly quickly, and after a spell lying on the wardroom floor with other casualties we were transferred to the *Canberra* in an RN Sea King helicopter. This was a bit hairy as the aircraft only had room to perch one wheel on our somewhat precarious flight deck.

I passed a delightful spell in a stretcher on board *Canberra,* listening to the small-arms fire of the 1,000 or so soldiers still on board, as they repelled the air attacks. Apparently, I was the first patient the medical team on *Canberra* operated upon and I remember their teams discussing 'patella tap' (my right knee had also been injured). At this stage I was informed that I was to be transferred to the hospital ship *Uganda* when circumstances permitted.

I was transferred, after a night on HMS *Hydra*, by the ship's Wasp helicopter, to the Hospital Ship *Uganda* and was welcomed on board by the Royal Naval Chaplain Father Chris Bester. I joined other patients in what was called Sea View Ward – slightly ironic considering both my eyes were bandaged! I was situated next to a colour sergeant from the Royal Fleet Auxiliary vessel *Sir Lancelot* and with a P&O First Officer on board *Uganda;* these two gentlemen helped me a lot at this time, as I was still unable to see. *(Note from Nicci – yes. cigarettes are mentioned here!)* Terry continues, 'I recall two trips to the operating theatre on board *Uganda*. One was for the enucleation of my left eye and the other for skin grafts.'

From Nicci who was working in the hospital ship's operating theatres at that time: *'We all remember Terry very well on board* Uganda. *We were obviously aware that he had lost the sight of one eye, but all desperately hoped that Terry's right eye might regain some sight in the longer term. Terry was incredibly stoical at this stage and those who cared for him remember his sense of humour amongst all the trauma and difficulties we were experiencing.'*

Terry continues: After a week on board the Hospital Ship, HMS *Herald's* Wasp helicopter transferred a party of us to the ambulance ship for the 6-day passage to Montevideo and the subsequent 15-hour onward flight to Brize Norton eventually arriving in a ward in RAF Hospital Wroughton (latterly RAF Princess Alexandra's Hospital Wroughton) on the Falklands War Victory/Surrender Day (14th June). After an overnight stay, the naval casualties journeyed to the Royal Naval Hospital Haslar by road. I was later informed at Moorfields Hospital in London that what was left of the retina of my right eye was not worth putting back – at least I knew my bottom line. I then had another operation to remove some shrapnel from my left knee that was causing a problem and I was subsequently discharged from the Royal Naval medical system.

Autumn 1982 and winter 1983 were spent undergoing basic rehabilitation at St Dunstan's, Ovingdean, near Brighton. The training was intensive and thorough, comprising: learning to type, read and write Braille, in addition to mobility using the long-cane technique. Following this period at St Dunstan's, I became an information officer at the Fleet Air Arm Museum, Royal Naval Air Station Yeovilton in Somerset, where I was re-united with 'Humphrey', HMS *Antrim's* much loved and venerable Wessex helicopter, by now part of the current Falklands exhibition. Strange to say, feeling 'his' familiar components was quite reassuring. The museum environment was extremely useful as it allowed me to get used to dealing with the public in my new role, within the social life and support of shipmates I had known for many years. During winter 1983, I decided it was time to move on and I left the Royal Navy in February 1984.

Further training at St Dunstan's followed and I subsequently enrolled as a student Technical Officer for the Blind in Leeds, during the winter of 1984 and into spring 1985, subsequently taking a post with the Grampian Society for the Blind in Aberdeen. After a year's experience as a field-worker, I attended a two-year Social Work course in the City, returning to field-work on completion. Autumn 1990 saw me as a social-work lecturer at an RNIB college in Birmingham. In summer 1993, I took up my final position as a public speaker for St Dunstan's, finally retiring in 2005. During the 1980s and 1990s I used to race walk (a St Dunstan's tradition) and I have completed the 'Action Heart' London-Brighton run on my tandem. My main hobby is model engineering using 'Meccano' and I am pleased to be a member of several guilds. I am the proud possessor of a Myford 'Super-7' lathe that I have adapted for my use. At that time I used to assist my wife, Maria, on our allotment, by digging using a 6ft x 4ft wooden frame. High-fidelity audio and tape-recording using open-reel machines is another interest I have maintained since my teenage years. I don't really miss television since the pictures on the radio are so much better. The choice of radio programmes has increased dramatically in recent years and I find I can follow most sports relatively easily although this has been an acquired skill.

I look back to my time on the hospital ships with nostalgia, since it surrounded such life-changing events and exemplified the very best of comradeship and mutual support that is so much part of naval life. I have deliberately avoided mentioning the wonderful Queen Alexandra's Royal Naval Nurses and members of the various ships' companies individually, as the things they did for me are simply too numerous to mention. I would just like to take this opportunity to thank them all.

With the publication of this book in 2021 by the British Modern Military History Society, I would also like to take this opportunity to include my particular and personal thanks to all those professionals at the erstwhile St Dunstan's (now BVUK) at Ovingdean near Brighton. It was through their patience and understanding, that they restored my confidence and independence in the early days. Amongst so many other things they taught me were to regain independent mobility using the long cane technique, and typing; which in addition gave me back my literacy through use and familiarity with the Braille system. The St Dunstaners themselves also deserve a special mention and I thank all those whose camaraderie and friendship will stay with me over the years.

This collaborative contribution has been written by former Queen Alexandra's Royal Naval Nursing Service Senior Nursing Officer Nicci Pugh, working with BVUK member former Chief Petty Officer Terry Bullingham Royal Navy, one of the many former patients treated on board Her Majesty's Hospital Ship *Uganda* which served in the South Atlantic throughout the Falklands War fought between Britain and Argentina in 1982.

Nicci Pugh is the author of: White Ship – Red Crosses - A Nursing Memoir of The Falklands War.
Nicci is an experienced NHS and former military Operating Theatre Sister. In 1982, she served on board the P&O requisitioned hospital ship SS *Uganda* as a Royal Naval Nursing Sister, helping teams of trauma surgeons deal with countless wartime injuries to military personnel from land, sea and air battles.

Teams of Royal Naval Medics and QARNNS Operating Theatre personnel preparing equipment and training en route for the South Atlantic early May 1982.

Nicci Pugh archive

HMS *Uganda* leaving Gibraltar.
Nicci Pugh archive

A Brief History of Germ Warfare

Historian, Nick Brazil, outlines the history of germ and biological warfare, from ancient times to the modern day.

An Invisible Death

'When it comes to germ warfare there is nothing new under the sun'

The first recorded case of a biological attack was in 1500 BC when the Hitites drove diseased hostages into the lands of their enemies to lay them low with a nasty disease called tularemia. This is a highly infectious disease found in ticks and contaminated water causing skin lesions and high fever.

In 400 BC, the Scythians used arrows in another form of bacteriological attack. Their archers would dip their arrow tips in decomposing bodies or blood contaminated with manure. This would ensure that even a light flesh wound from one of these arrows would lead to a painful and unpleasant death.

In 190 BC, Hannibal, that remarkable Carthaginian general, used a novel form of biological warfare to win one of his many battles. In the naval Battle of Eurymedon he successfully defeated King Eumenes of Pergamon by catapulting clay jars of venomous snakes onto the decks of his opponent's ships.

Poisoning wells using dead animals or people has been a crude but effective form of biological attack by many ancient armies. In 1155 Barbarossa attempted to break the siege of Tortona by poisoning the city's water supply with the decomposing bodies of dead soldiers.

Probably the most destructive and far reaching biological attack was on the Crimean City of city of Kaffa in 1347. On that occasion, the besieging Mongols suffered an outbreak of the plague. Turning this setback to their advantage, they catapulted the bodies of their plague victims into Kaffa. It is a fair bet this action helped trigger the Black Death pandemic of 1348. Its ultimate death toll is estimated to have been 25 million fatalities throughout Europe and the Near East.

But sometimes elaborate biological attacks have been drawn up only to be aborted at the last minute. During the Venetian-Ottoman War in the mid-17th Century the Ottomans laid siege to Candia (modern day Heraklion). Lasting from 1648 to 1669 it would turn out be the second longest siege in history.

As the siege ground on year after year, both sides must have been very keen for an end to this expensive impasse. Out of this desperation, the Venetian Intelligence Service came up with an ingenious plan. They created a deadly liquid made from the spleens and buboes of plague victims. This would be used to infect the Ottoman soldiers with the plague thereby raising the siege. Historical records indicate that this audacious plan was cancelled at a very late stage. The reason why is lost in the mists of time.

In 1763, at the Battle of Fort Pitt in America when the British Army were fighting the local Indians, they gave items such as blankets infected with smallpox to Indian peace emissaries. Although a small number of local Indians succumbed to smallpox, this nasty trick had only a limited effect.

During the First World War, the Germans were particularly active in developing biological weapons including anthrax, glanders, and cholera. It is alleged they spread plague through the Russian city of St Petersburg. They also sparked an outbreak of glanders amongst mules in Mesopotamia, thus hoping to cripple the main method of transport at that time. As its name suggests, glanders attacks the glands and has a high mortality rate particularly amongst mules and horses but also humans. Russian army horses suffered similar attacks by the Germans on the Eastern Front. The Germans also tried to spread glanders amongst French cavalry horses.

The Geneva Protocol of 1925 prohibiting the use of chemical and biological weapons was piously signed by 108 countries. This did not stop their secret development. Both the US and the British weaponised such diseases as anthrax and bubonic plague in secret germ warfare establishments at Fort Detrick and Porton Down. In the case of both countries, they have never used them in war.

This was not the case with the Imperial Japanese Government. It set up the notorious biological warfare Unit 731 in Manchuria during the Sino - Japanese War in 1938 - 1945. Under the leadership of Surgeon General Shiro Ishii the unit not only conducted live vivisection experiments on Chinese prisoners with no anti pain medication, but majored in the nastiest forms of germ warfare.

One of the most notorious incidents was the bombing of the Chinese cities of Ningbo and Changde with thousands of fleas infected with the bubonic plague. Another operation spread typhoid throughout Nanking. The total death toll from these attacks is thought to be tens of thousands, mainly Chinese civilians.

At the very end of the Second World War, the Japanese planned a mass biological attack on San Diego, California. Codenamed *'Operation Cherry Blossoms at Night'* the plan was to release the plague bacillus into the city's population. Scheduled for 22nd September 1945, it would have undoubtedly caused many deaths. Fortunately, the Japanese surrendered on 15th August 1945 and San Diego had a lucky escape.

In 1945, twelve mainly senior Japanese officers involved in these atrocities were put on trial by the Soviet Authorities and were imprisoned in gulags for 2 to 25 years. But their wily leader Shiro Ishii never faced any retribution having traded Unit 731's many secrets with the US authorities in return for his freedom.

Since the Second World War, biological weapons have been replaced by deadlier chemical-based agents such as ricin, sarin, polonium and novichok. Whether it is in the case of murders of individuals such as the Bulgarian dissident Georgi Markov in London with ricin (1978) or Alexander Litvinenko with polonium in his tea (2006) or mass terrorist attacks such as the sarin attack on the Tokyo Metro (1995) these are silent killers that are near impossible to counteract.

It will probably be some years after the current virus has vanished that we will know the full truth of its origins. But even now the behaviour of Covid-19 has shown all the hallmarks of a man-made virus. The possibility it is a bacteriological weapon cannot be ruled out. If so, the coronavirus pandemic of 2020 could well go down as the world's first germ war. Let us hope it is the last.

****

List of Contributors

463

Glossary

A&AEE   Aircraft and Armoury Experimental
                 Establishment based at Porton Down

AIF   The Australian Imperial Force. Created on
                 15th August 1914 following Britain's
                 declaration of war on Germany

Al-Qaeda   Al-Qaeda is a militant Sunni Islamist
                 multi-national organization founded in
                 1988. It operates as a network of Islamic
                 extremists and Salafist jihadists and has
                 been designated as a terrorist group by the
                 United Nations Security Council, NATO,
                 the European Union, USA, China and
                 other organisations and countries

ATA   Air Transport Auxiliary – the civilian men
                 and women who transported allied military
                 aircraft from factories to airfields and other
                 places as required

BAOR   British Army Of The Rhine – the British
                 occupying forces in Germany after the
                 Second World War

Bletchley Park   The country mansion in Buckinghamshire,
                 England, where German Enigma codes
                 were decoded and decrypted. At its peak,
                 it employed about 8,000 men and women
                 'cracking the codes'

Blighty   Nickname given by British First World
                 War soldiers when referring to England

Blitz	Name adopted for the bombing of London and other cities in the Second World War
Blitzkrieg	*'Lighting war'*. Aggressive, fast paced attack by German land and air forces in the Second World War especially in Poland, the Low Countries and France
Blue Jacket Doppler Navigation System	A type of radar system installed on the Fleet Air Arm Blackburn Buccaneer aircraft to detect Russian warships. Often referred to as Blue Parrot
Chain Home	A predecessor of RADAR using static transmitters and receivers that were focused out to sea towards France and the Low Countries to give advanced warning of incoming aircraft. It would not detect low flying aircraft
CMRP	Continuous Mosaic Radar prediction
CWGC	Commonwealth War Graves Commission, responsible for British war cemeteries and memorials across the world
D-Day	The invasion of Europe on 6th June 1944 by allied forces creating the so-called second front. The landing on five Normandy beaches supported by airborne forces of hundreds of thousands of men and vehicles was the first step to the eventual liberation of occupied western Europe in May 1945

DUKW	DUKW (colloquially known as Duck) is a six-wheel-drive amphibious vehicle. It was used by the US military in the Second World War and Korean War
EAMNS	East African Military Nursing Service
Enigma	The Enigma machine is a cipher device developed and used to protect commercial, diplomatic, and military communication and was employed extensively by Nazi Germany during Second World War, in all branches of the military and was considered to be totally secure. Unknown to the Germans, the codes were broken at Bletchley Park giving the allies access to vital information
FANY	First Aid Nursing Yeomanry – Formed in 1907 and originally on horseback, these nurses provided medical care in casualty clearing stations in the Great War. In the Second World War, the roles varied from being motor mechanics to working as agents under cover in occupied Europe as well as forgers and signallers for the Special Operations Executive
Fleet Air Arm	(FAA) The airforce of the Royal Navy, usually planes flying off aircraft carriers
Grand Fleet	The Grand Fleet was the main fleet of the Royal Navy during the First World War
IFF	Identification Friend or Foe. An automatic timed transmission through an aircraft

	transmitter to identify it a friendly aircraft to plotting room personnel
Kamikaze	Literally means 'divine wind'. The suicide bombers of the Japanese airforce used against allied ships in the Pacific War
KFOR	The Kosovo Force is a NATO-led international peacekeeping force in Kosovo
Kindertransport	The rescue of young children, normally Jewish, from Germany and other countries in the mid/late 1930s from the Nazis. Over 10,000 children were saved mainly by train
KOYLI	King's Own Yorkshire Light Infantry
KPA	The Korean People's Army are the military forces of North Korea
KSLI	King's Shropshire Light Infantry
Legion d'Honneur	French military gallantry award
MADDLS	Mirror Assisted Dummy Deck Landing at RAF Honington. A dummy aircraft carrier deck used by the RAF for training pilots
Market Garden	The allied airborne operation to cross the three main bridges across the Rhine in late 1944 with the intention of shortening the Second World War

NAAFI	Navy, Army, Air Force Institute. The social centre for British forces on many military bases
Navigators Brevet	A single wing with an 'N' enclosed in a wreath worn on the right-hand side of an airman's tunic
Oboe	A form of wireless navigation and bombing using two transmitters based on the English coast to determine the exact position of an aircraft over Europe and a precise point when bombs could be released on the target
OCU	Operational Conversion Unit. An RAF unit that trained crews on new types of aircraft while they were still available to fly on operations
POW	Prisoner(s) of War
PPI	Plan Position Indicator. The display on a radar screen where the position of the viewer is at the centre of the screen and plots appear on concentric distances from that point
Pre Carrier Course	RAF pilots training course for landing on aircraft carriers
QARNNS	Queen Alexandra Royal Naval Nursing Service
QRA	Quick Reaction Alert – aircrews kept on high alert as part of NATO operations

QWI Course	Qualified Weapons Instructors Course
RADAR	'Radio Detection And Ranging' – system used extensively in the Second World War and since for detecting enemy planes and ships
RAE	Royal Aircraft Establishment in Bedfordshire, England
RAFVR	RAF Volunteer Reserve – created in 1936 in preparation in event of war
RFC	Royal Flying Corps. The forerunner to the Royal Air Force. The RAF was formed out of the RFC on 1st April 1918
RNVR	Royal Navy Volunteer Reserve
SAS, SBS	British Special Air Service 'The regiment' with highly trained elite forces formed by David Sterling in 1941 initially operating behind enemy lines in the north African desert. The SAS and its naval equivalent, the Special Boat Squadron, are still regarded as the pinnacle of military units in the world.
Sicherheitsdienst aka SD	The German intelligence service in the Second World War
SOE	Special Operations Executive. A department formed upon Churchill's orders to 'set Europe ablaze' by uncover operations in occupied Europe. The aim of the men and women agents was to destroy

communication, transport links and to cause general disruption to German occupying forces

Spandau	German machine guns used in both world wars
Sunningdale Agreement	Signed in December 1973, this was an attempt to create a power sharing agreement in Northern Ireland. It collapsed the following year
TACEVAL	Tactical Evaluation. Assessment of the ability of a force to meet an external threat, identifies any areas of concern and recommends appropriate action to remedy any failures
Taliban	Sunni Islamic fundamentalist political movement and military organisation in Afghanistan currently waging war (an insurgency, or jihad) within that country
TFNS	Territorial Forces Nursing Service
TOC H	An organisation that is derived from a social club set up behind the lines in World War 1 known as Talbot House and shortened in the then signallers parlance to Toc H. Later to become a world-wide Christian organisation with many branches. Its symbol, a Roman Oil Lamp, derived the saying 'As dim as a Toc H Lamp'

ULTRA	The top-secret information derived from German messages intercepted at Bletchley Park. Few had access to the information, and great care was taken to ensure the Germans did not find out their codes had been broken
USAAF	United States Army Air Force. In September 1947 it became the USAF; United States Air Force
VAD	Voluntary Aid Detachment – British voluntary nursing service in the Great War
VE Day	Victory in Europe Day – 8th May 1945. It marked the unconditional surrender of German forces across the globe. The surrender document was signed by General Jodl and Grand Admiral Karl Doenitz as representatives of the German armed forces and the German State
Versailles Treaty	The treaty signed in 1919 at Versailles where the allied armies detailed the terms of surrender over the German Imperial Army. It was signed in a railway carriage in Compiegne, just outside Paris
VJ Day	Victory over Japan Day – 15th August 1945. The day the fighting ceased. The actual surrender was signed on 2nd September 1945 on board USS Missouri in Tokyo Bay
V1	German flying bomb, often referred to as doodlebugs or buzz bombs. Over 9,500

	were launched and were aimed mainly at London and southern England in 1944/5, causing over 24,000 casualties, of which 6,000 people were killed
V2	The first inter ballistic missile used by Germany as *Vergeltungswaffe 2*, 'Retribution Weapon 2' were fired mainly at London and Antwerp from August 1944. They travelled at supersonic speeds and were inaudible. Over 4,000 British and Belgian civilians were killed and more than 11,000 injured
WAAC	Women's Auxilliary Army Corps
Waffen SS	The Waffen-SS was the military branch of the Nazi Party's SS organisation. Its formations included men from Nazi Germany, along with volunteers and conscripts from both occupied and unoccupied lands
WAS(B) aka *'Wasbies'*	These were the group of women recruited to support the British and allied armies in Burma by providing tea, biscuits and a friendly smile. They worked just behind the front line in the same difficult, humid jungle conditions as the soldiers
WRNS aka TheWrens	Womens Royal Naval Service. Women recruits of the Royal Navy. They did not fight in the front line in the Second World War, but have since become an integral part of ship's crews

WVS	Womens Voluntary Service. A civilian organisation during the Second World War that helped with a variety of roles such as running mobile canteens and Rest Centres for bombed out families, to knitting and salvage work

Acknowledgements

When we started on the formation of BMMHS back in June 2019, none of us could have conceived that only a year later the world would be so very different and that we have been through the rigours of multiple lockdowns and living with the anxiety of and in some cases the tragic consequences of COVID-19.

The idea for *Glimpses of War* was born out of giving something for our supporters, our friends, neighbours and families to help take their mind off COVID-19 during the first national lockdown. We felt that by giving them the opportunity to delve into the family archives, to maybe get some papers on a family member's military service out of a drawer or loft, this would help shift the focus away from the terrible COVID-19 virus. We felt it would also contribute at least in a small way to improving mental and overall wellbeing during these challenging times.

We also wanted to continue to raise funds for charity. After much consideration, we chose Blind Veterans UK (formerly St Dunstan's) as we wanted to select a charity which does fantastic work with all branches of the armed services and across the United Kingdom.

We had no idea as to how many or what type of articles we would receive. But as we explored further and broadened our approach to include historians, speakers and other members of the public we were amazed at the scale of the response. So far we have received in excess of 220 articles in the region of 330,000 words – sufficient for three volumes at least.

A big thank you goes to everyone who has taken the time to research and submit contributions to us, from our regular members, to overseas articles from as far afield as Tasmania, the USA and many European countries. There are too many names to mention but the thank you for embracing this project in aid of a wonderful charity.

Some of you may be disappointed not to see your article or contribution in volume one, but with so much superb and interesting content, we are having to split it between three volumes at this stage. These will be published over the coming couple of years.

Equally, if you or your family have a wartime experience you would like to be considered for future volumes, please drop us a line or send it to us at info@bmmhs.org

We also want to thank those of you who have helped get us across the finishing line. For the advice on publishers and publishing options from many people including Steve Richards, Robin Brodhurst, John Boyes and Philip Allan, Damien Lewis and others. To Geoff Simpson, our thanks for his insight and advice in marketing the book. A special thank you to local historian and researcher, Trevor Hancock, for his support in providing articles, making almost daily postings to our Facebook page and his all round support.

For the help with proof reading.... numerous people have assisted including Nick Brazil, Pauline Garrett, Trevor Hancock, Chris Leworthy, Tim Lowe, David Vassallo, David Drew, Phil McCarty and Steve Oliver. Alongside our proof readers behind the scenes, our very own '*Miss*

Moneypenny', Karen Wheeler, who has shown great patience and perseverance in working with us, making all the proof reading changes and giving expert advice on the finer points of 'Word' in our manuscript. We thank her most sincerely and hope she will be happy to help with future volumes.

Richard Macauley for his help and support with our Zoom talks and with the graphics for the fantastic *Glimpses of War* book cover, and for helping promote the book, through the Society of Friends of Fleet Air Arm Museum.

A special thank you goes to the very talented artist Simon Atak for kindly allowing us to use his superb, very moving and thought-provoking picture of the Lancaster bomber on our front cover. A hugely generous gesture.

The support from BVUK has been superb, embracing the whole *Glimpses of War* project with a fantastic piece by their Chief Executive Major General Nick Caplin, and great assistance to help promote and market the book through Jackie Harbor and her team.

With COVID-19 forcing us to cease face-to-face meetings and to move to the virtual world of Zoom for both our talks and for the editorial discussions, it will be a pleasure to return to meeting real people once more for our live meetings in Woodcote Village Hall, and to be able to meet friends and colleagues in person. It just reinforced that having real contact with friends in person is so important. When we can return and what the 'new normal' will look like remains to be seen, but at least as we go to print, there is genuine cause for some optimism as the vaccination programme rolls out apace.

That process of moving to the virtual environment of Zoom talks was itself challenging as BMMHS, our speakers and our supporters had to get to grips with this new medium. Our thanks for his encouragement must go to Chris Finn (Chris is still the only person we know who had used Zoom before lockdown) for his advice and guidance on running Zoom talks. Our thanks to our speakers too for adapting to this new world where feedback during talks is minimal and the sight of dozens of staring faces can be somewhat disconcerting. The positive response to these talks from the attendees has been overwhelming.

Also we want to thank all of you for making a financial contribution through donations to the costs of the Zoom talks. Without them we would not have been able to carry on and build for the future of the BMMHS, and they help us to secure the services of such high class speakers. Also, all of your messages of support and encouragement have been so good for morale and help us keep going. So please keep them coming. It is greatly appreciated.

We would also like to thank our partners for their patience in supporting us. Susan, Jerry's wife, has found her job extremely stressful (as have many others) and taxing over these last months, not least as Jerry has had the habit of pinching the broadband, which has at times ground her Zoom or equivalent meetings to a halt. To Jane, Andy's fiancé, for putting up with the hundreds of hours on his laptop working on *Glimpses of War*, and not least allowing publication of her father's wartime experiences. Two other largely unrecognised contributors are of the four-legged kind. Nigel and Linda have Buddy the beagle while Jerry and wife, Susan have black labrador, Gemma. Their support in dragging us away from the coal face of the *Glimpses of War* manuscript and hauling us out into the countryside in all weathers has been immeasurable.

We apologise to anyone we have forgotten to include in the long list of helpers and supporters. We, of course, take full responsibility for any errors, whether typographical or factual. They are entirely accidental or inadvertent and we will correct these at the earliest opportunity in further editions.

And finally, we thank all of you who have seen fit to purchase this book. You are contributing to a very special charity and your support is hugely appreciated by both BVUK and their beneficiaries. Please recommend *Glimpses of War* to your friends and family and continue this support by purchasing future volumes, which are already in the pipeline.

Andy, Jerry, Nigel and Linda

About the Editors

BMMHS Executive Committee and Editorial Team

Andy Cockeram is chairman and a founding member of BMMHS, having spent most of his career in corporate life, mainly in the motor industry. His love and interest in military history have been from a very young age, and probably started at the time of the death of Winston Churchill when a series in black and white called '*The Valiant Years*' about the Second World War was broadcast on television. Andy has travelled widely and has visited numerous battlefield sites and memorials across the globe. Working for 12 months in the Netherlands recently gave great opportunities to explore the battlefields of north-west Europe. His main areas of interest are the Second World War, especially life under occupation and resistance movements.

Andy still works as a motor industry consultant and has started a career as a writer of novels, very much with a military history flavour. He lives in South Oxfordshire.

Jerry Cockeram Thanks to the chance 'bumping into' Linda Parker back in 2019 at a Western Front Association meeting, the idea formed to set up BMMHS. Always passionate about military history, whether it be through books or films, he has been fortunate to travel to a fair number of Europe's battlefields to further his understanding of some of those key events in our more recent past. Having spent a career in IT working across a range of industries including aerospace and F1, and by virtue of his being 'the least *Luddite*' of the founding group, Jerry is responsible for the bmmhs.org website and IT support infrastructure.

Dr Linda Parker is a former history teacher, now researcher and author. Her research areas and publications include the histories of forces' chaplains in the 20th century, and polar history, although she is interested in most aspects of military history. She has published six books with Helion and Co, the most recent one being '*Nearer My God to Thee: Airborne chaplains of the Second World War*' (Helion 2020). She enjoys speaking at conferences and giving talks to various societies. In addition to her involvement with BMMHS, she is a member of the Western Front Association, The Society of Military History and the United States Commission for Military History. She enjoys travelling to cold places and musical activities. She is married to Nigel Parker.

Nigel Parker has followed a career in Engineering and for 23 years ran the Cryogenics Department at Oxford University. Having a lifelong interest in military aviation and being involved in the research and recovery of many crashed military aircraft, he was editor of the Bomber Command Association Newsletter for seven years. He chose to take early retirement and follow his passion; writing a twelve volume series on the German Air Force losses over Great Britain in World War 2; '*Luftwaffe Crash Archive*', followed by a three volume series entitled '*Gott Strafe England*'; the German air assault against Great Britain 1914 – 1918. He is now writing a book on the V1 and V2 campaign and also a revised history of the Battle of Britain.

Contributor sources

The First Mass Transport into Auschwitz

Albin, K., 2003.*Warrant Of Arrest.* Oświęcim: Auschwitz-Birkenau State Museum.

Antoniewicz, B., 1972. [Relacja] Państwowe Muzeum Auschwitz-Birkenau, Oświadczenia Tom 74, Oświęcim.

Lekcja.auschwitz.org. 2020. *Muzeum Auschwitz-Birkenau.* [online] Available at: <http://lekcja.auschwitz.org/en_15_ucieczki/> [Accessed 20th June 2020].

Bałut, T., 1945. *Testimony From Judicial/Criminal Proceedings.* [Testimony] IPN GK 196/85, IPN, Gdańsk.

Białaś, S., n.d. [Relacja] Państwowe Muzeum Auschwitz-Birkenau, Wspomienia, Tom 199. Oświęcim.

Bicz, B., 1946. *Supreme National Tribunal.* [Testimony from judicial/criminal proceedings] IPN GK 196/84, IPN, Gdańsk.

Borkowski, W., 1986. [Relacja] Państwowe Muzeum Auschwitz-Birkenau, Oświadczenia Tom 115. Oświęcim.

Chlebowski, J., 1947. *Volume IV Of The Transcript Of The Trial Against The Former Members Of The Auschwitz Concentration Camp Crew.* [Court Transcript], IPN GK 196/164, IPN, Gdańsk.

Cyba, B., 1973. [Relacja] Państwowe Muzeum Auschwitz-Birkenau, Wspomnienia Tom 98. Oświęcim.

Cywiński, P., Lachendro, J., Setkiewicz, P., Mensfelt, J., Pinderska-Lech, J. and Brand, W., 2017. *Auschwitz From A To Z.* Oświęcim: Auschwitz-Birkenau State Museum.

Czech, D., 1989. *Auschwitz Chronicle, 1939-1945.* New York: H. Holt.

Drecki, Z. and Drecki, J., 1992. *Freedom And Justice.* Z. Drecki.

Fingerchut, M., 1954. [Relacja] Państwowe Muzeum Auschwitz-Birkenau, Wspomnienia Tom 40. Oświęcim.

Garliński, J., Foot, M. and Polonsky, A., 2018. *Fighting Auschwitz.* Los Angeles: Aquila Polonica Publishing.

Hordyński, J., 1998. [Relacja] Państwowe Muzeum Auschwitz-Birkenau, Oświadczenia Tom 140. Oświęcim.

Höß, R., 2001. *Commandant Of Auschwitz.* London: Phoenix Press.

Kielar, W. and Flatauer, S., 2017. *Anus Mundi.* Oświęcim: Auschwitz Birkenau State Museum.

Konieczny, A., 1995. *Hefte Von Auschwitz, , 'Bemerkungen Über Die Anfänge Des KL Auschwitz'* Oswięcim: Wydaw. Panstwego Muzeum w Oszięcismiu.

Langbein, H. and Zohn, H., 2017. *People In Auschwitz*. Oświęcim: Auschwitz-Birkenau State Museum.

Malcherczyk, J., 1947. *Testimony From Judicial/Criminal Proceedings*. [Testimony from judicial/criminal proceedings] IPN GK 196/171, IPN, Gdańsk.

Moorhouse, R., 2019. *First To Fight, The Polish War 1939*. London: Penguin.

Piper, F., 2000. The Origins of the Camp. In: F. Piper and W. Długoborski, ed., *Auschwitz 1940-1945, Volume 1*. Oświęcim: Auschwitz-Birkenau State Museum.

Stojakowski, J., 1970. [Relacja] Państwowe Muzeum Auschwitz-Birkenau, Oświadczenia Tom 68. Oświęcim.

Strzelecka, I., 2002. *Księga Pamięci: Transporty Polaków Do KL Auschwitz Z Krakowa I Innych Miejscowóśći Polski Południowej, 1940-1944*. Oświęcim: Państwowy Muzeum Auschwitz-Birkenau.

Wachsmann, N., 2016. *KL*. London: Little, Brown.

A Preview of Future Volumes

BMMHS in collaboration with Blind Veterans UK will be issuing further volumes of *Glimpses of War*.

We have received some fantastic stories and historical articles already. Here is a taster of what to expect:

- The Wooden World – Life in Nelson's Navy
- Emily Cameron -Widowhood in Wandsworth in 1915
- Zeppelin Raids on England in 1917
- Landing at Gallipoli
- Letters from 'The Few'
- The Little Ships at Dunkirk
- Fighting with the Black Tarantula Division in Burma.
- The female SOE agents in France
- A POW under the Japanese
- Memories of the Women's Land Army
- V1 Bombing of Weald House
- Life in Soviet Poland and Beyond
- A Lanky Yankee in the Battle of the Bulge
- HMS *Active* chasing the German Battleships
- Last month of the war in the Netherlands
- Fix Bayonets in Northern Ireland
- Submarine Life in the 1970s
- A doctor in the Falklands War

And many, many more articles too.

We are very happy to accept new articles or personal accounts for future volumes of *Glimpses of War*. If you have a personal or family story to tell, or have an interesting article you would like to submit for consideration, get in touch.

Contributions can be any length but no more than 2000 words ideally. Diary extracts, copies of personal letters, some photographs and images can be included too, but you must have ownership/copyright to them. And remember, they do not have to be tales of great heroics or valour. Ordinary people's experiences in war time - any war, any role, civilian or military - are just as much interest to us. Articles from writers and historians are welcome too.

Do contact us on info@bmmhs.org if you have something you would like us to consider and include.

About the Cover

November 1942

A newly-formed bomber aircrew's operational flying career has to start with its first 'Op'. Puffing nervously on cigarettes, they check and recheck that their flying kit, harnesses and straps are correctly webbed up, nothing too slack that would snag on anything and trap them in the event of a bale-out emergency as the pilot is taken through the Form 700 with the 'Chiefy', a fatherly man to the new crews he's seen coming and going on the unit. His groundcrew have been busy since morning preparing the aircraft for this night's 'Op' oiled, fuelled and bombed-up, the engine mechanics work with a flashlight as they connect the starter and ground earth cable to the port inner Merlin for start-up.

These seven airmen have been training with their Lancaster B.I for perhaps two weeks since forming together after leaving their Training units for life on an operational front-line Bomber Squadron.

They have already seen the empty tables at breakfast after the previous night's operation from their Station. They didn't know the men who were lost. But they know it will be their turn on a 'trip' soon enough. So for these young lads, it has been night flying tests and working-up training flights by daylight to knit them all together as a crew.

Tonight, they will be doing it for real. And will see them tested over a target deep inside Hitler's Ruhr valley steel and munitions industries. And finding their way home to their airfield in the dark, if they survive this night, will not be so easy. As with many Bomber Command aircrews, they are not, by any means, an all-British crew. The Navigator wears a CANADA flash on his upper-arm sleeve. The Wireless-Operator is also a trained air gunner and comes from Australia.

The Pilot signs the Form700 and the Lancaster becomes 'his'. And so begins the first Operation to Hitler's Europe. As the moon slips into clouds that will cover their RAF Bomber-Stream in pitch black darkness... and no moon tonight.

Copyright Image and Text Simon W. Atack

Images on the back cover

Top Row - From Left to Right
- Buccaneer launch on HMS Ark Royal
- Hurricane pilot Geoffrey Gledhill
- Brigade Commander's Rover Group in Belfast
- Vi Molinari: Wartime memories as a teenager in London
- Falklands conflict HM Hospital Ship Uganda
- David Dill 2nd SAS - Executed under Hitler's Commando Order

Centre Row – From Left to Right
- Captain Mervyn Wingfield RN Submarine Commander
- A Japanese flag acquired by Allan Jenkins at the Japanese surrender in Singapore in 1945

488

- Dorothy Volkert, US Army Nurse aboard a hospital ship
- The U-boat Surrender Type XX1 U2505
- Herbert Mockford served on the Somme in July 1916
- Geoff Botting flying with Canadians in 1941/42

Bottom Row – From Left to Right

- Witold *"Lanny"* Lanowski Polish fighter pilot
- Major-General Dair Farrar-Hockley MC, Officer Commanding A Company 2 Para Battle for Darwin
- The arrival of the M.V. Derbyshire - the first troopship in Singapore after the surrender of Japan
- George Johnson, D Day diary, Normandy 1944
- WASBIES in Burma
- Wing Commander Jim Wright DFC, navigator with Bomber Command Pathfinder Force

Printed in Great Britain
by Amazon